To dad
with love
Fiona
x.

SCOT FREE

SCOT FREE

A journey from the Arctic to New Mexico

Alastair Scott

JOHN MURRAY

To my parents

© Alastair Scott, 1986

First published 1986
by John Murray (Publishers) Ltd
50 Albemarle Street, London w1x 4BD

Lines by Robert Service quoted on
pages 170 and 178 by permission of the
Estate of Robert Service:
© Dodd, Mead & Co. 1907

Typeset by Inforum Ltd, Portsmouth
Printed and bound in Great Britain
by The Bath Press, Avon

British Library CIP data
Scott, Alastair
Scot free : a journey from the Arctic to New
Mexico.
1. America—Description and travel—1981–
2. Arctic regions—Description and travel
I. Title
917'.04538   E27.5
ISBN 0–7195–4253–7

Contents

Illustrations

Maps

Photographs in colour

BETWEEN PAGES 72 AND 73

Hills near Eysturoy, Faroes

Disko Bay, Greenland, in the glow of the midnight sun

An old Inuit going to fetch water; Qeqertat, North-West Greenland

An Inuit practises throwing a harpoon

The author sets up camp near Umanak, West Greenland

Houses in Jakobshavn, West Greenland

Space Needle, Seattle

BETWEEN PAGES 152 AND 153

The Grand Canyon before a storm

The lights of Las Vegas

A Rainbow man

Fijian warrior at the Calgary Stampede, Alberta

North Falls on Silver Creek, near Salem, Oregon

The author by his camp-fire in Alaska

Cowboys near Carrizozo, New Mexico

For my part, I travel not to go anywhere, but to go. I travel for travel's sake. The great affair is to move; to feel the needs and hitches of our life more nearly; to come down off this feather-bed of civilisation, and find the globe granite underfoot and strewn with cutting flints . . . And when the present is so exacting, who can annoy himself about the future?

ROBERT LOUIS STEVENSON, *Travels with a Donkey in the Cevennes*

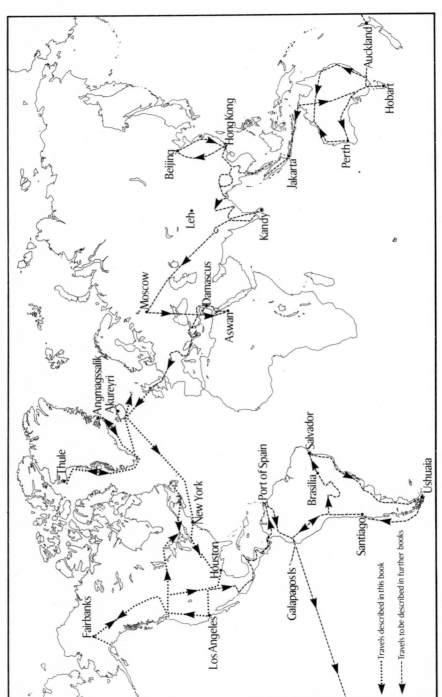

Five years and 194,000 miles

Prologue

In the eyes of an eight-year-old, she was terrifying. She was quick to chastise, constantly threatening and hungry for youth. Nevertheless each year I was taken to pay perfunctory homage to this ogre – for great-aunts must be respected if not through understanding then on account of their great age. It was in her house that my fascination for the world began, when I discovered a large, brightly coloured globe in a room full of ghostly shapes under dust sheets. My fascination ended that same day when the globe crashed to the ground after achieving a pleasing number of revolutions per second and the resulting skelp I received from the practised late-Victorian hand of my great-aunt, intending to knock some sense into my head, brought about the opposite effect. It dislodged most of my knowledge up to that period as well as my early childhood memories, and caused me to regard the world with acrimony for many years thereafter. If my great-aunt had not happened to come along at the precise moment of the accident, my relationship with the globe might have been different; indeed, I might have inherited it in the same way that my sister was to acquire the baby grand piano which she used to thump mercilessly to relieve her own boredom, delighting the few remaining senses of our ancient deaf relative. But such an easy inheritance of the Earth might have reduced me to meek apathy and possibly that initial skelp was needed to inspire my later wanderings, for Fate works in mysterious ways – certainly if my great-aunt was anything to go by.

We lived in Edinburgh at the time, and my family had deep roots in that part of Scotland. There had been lawyers, farmers, doctors, a minister, a rugby international, a rebel against Henry IV and an ogre all mixed up in my Lowland lineage, which offered me a reasonable scope of pursuits that could be classed as traditional. Later my father's work in the whisky trade took us north to the Spey Valley where my childhood turned to adolescence, and ended in a Yorkshire boarding-school. The common features were hills, open countryside and the kilt (which I wore on Sundays, along with a few other displaced Scots). The physical challenge of sport and the outdoors appealed to me more than academic studies, and provided temporary relief from my incompetence at algebra. I trudged a middle course between the rebel and the divine, and was content to leave school with the possibilities for my future still as multifarious as my ancestors.

So the urge to travel did not stem from childhood ambition. It had to overcome the prejudice of the past and then it grew gradually amongst the Yorkshire Dales and during wanderings in the Highlands with my father. By the time I was twenty-one and had left university with a joint degree shared between a subject that was still incomprehensible (economics) and another that was simply dull (German), the urge to travel was firmly established. It had become something I wanted to do, and something that had to be done. Two years in a photographic studio reinforced my determination to go and see the world but were more important in that they taught me how to use a camera and to develop the photographer's interest in recognising, simplifying and isolating the essential features of character, contrast and background. I held no pretensions of being aesthetically or spiritually tuned, but my awareness was sharpened. I merely felt receptive and prepared to search. My camera was to provide the justification for travelling, adding a sense of purpose to the extensive journey that I had in mind.

I wanted to wander freely, without pressure of time, to see a world I had been deprived of spinning.

Over the next five years I wore out four pairs of climbing boots and eight pairs of shoes. I faced the emotional hardships of walking and hitch-hiking in severe climates and of being constantly exposed to the dangers that confront a stranger in a foreign land. I felt the loneliness of having no friends, just brief acquaintances; the alienation due to my language, colour and clothes; the frustrations of countries where communications, timetables and logic failed to work; the discomforts of trying to write my diary around the soggy blotches on the paper caused by sweat dripping incessantly from my face in the humid tropics, of the desert dust that permeated every pore of my burnt skin and of sleepless nights when the cold seemed to siphon out every drop of heat from my shivering body. Sometimes the world just passed before me and left me feeling as neglected as is the tenth lamppost by a dog with a capacity for only eight.

But when courage failed, an inexhaustible supply of kindness and hospitality from those around me in every country would lift up my spirits and carry me on to experience more of the world's spectacular scenery, the joys of new discoveries – as well as less pleasant ones which evoked internal conflicts of feelings and moral obligations; the ugly bruises, as if caused by the fall many years earlier when the globe had crashed to the ground.

My job with the studio was followed by nine months of labouring on an oil platform in the North Sea and when this came to an end, it was a shock to realise that the time had come. It was either then, or probably never. I had the inclination, time and opportunity for starting my travels and no commitments to use as an excuse for procrastination. I also had the security of my oil platform savings which, together with my earnings along the way, were enough to complete the trip. Within a month I had left home with £250 in my pocket.

Right from the start my plans were deliberately vague so that they would be flexible. My route was to start with the Arctic and then follow the shortest distance between continents that was consistent with some means of transport connecting them. I tried to read up about each country before entering it to discover the places of interest and the conditions to expect, but in practice I was often to cross meaningless borders and have to discover these things by experience. In many ways it was the best method, for I arrived without expectations and therefore without prejudice. In other respects it was less satisfying and more open to abuse – an admission of ignorance, an invitation to be led and misled. My luggage, which included a less practical burden of twenty-eight pounds of camera equipment, provided a basic level of self-sufficiency in clothing, warmth and food by containing a tent, sleeping bag, adequate clothing, porridge oats and a small cooker. Otherwise my preparations were kept to the minimum necessary to satisfy the immigration requirements of each frontier and to ensure their entry stamp on my ninety-page passport. Time meant little to me. I would glance at the clock every so often and note the seasons. Apart from that we had scant respect for each other.

In this way my journey passed through fifty-three countries and crossed six continents, ranging from near the North Pole to Tierra del Fuego in the south, from Australia to China and then maintaining its zig–zag course overland back to Europe.

But before setting off I went to a certain plot of land where once I had dreamt of dancing and planting nettles. I couldn't be sure that my great-aunt had really inspired my travels but I gave her the benefit of the doubt and offered some belated gratitude at her final resting place. Neither could I be entirely sure that one so ancient had really passed on and it seemed prudent to placate an ill-humoured spirit before a journey that was in itself a risky undertaking.

Then I did what a self-respecting Scotsman might be expected to do, and after placing the order for my special requirements, a week later I made my way along worn cobblestones, past buildings blackened with age and reeking of history, to a dingy shop in the backstreets of Edinburgh.

1 · An optimist in Iceland

A cluster of bells jangled as the door opened, interrupting the hard tatatatack of an antique sewing machine and causing the hoary face of its operator to look up and peer at me through cataracts and bifocals. He was a kilt-maker. His father had been one as had his grandfather, and all his relatives as far back as memory and tradition could recall. Some men claim a diversity of ancestors ranging from almost-kings to hanged sheep-stealers, but not this old man. He was content that his family had preserved the modesty of near-royalty and thieves alike with a cloth of gay colours that came from the sheep-stealer's booty. His line of kilt-maker forefathers seemed to be as long as the thread which he had just worked into a piece of Scott tartan – this kilt was now finished and so was tradition as the elderly bachelor snipped the thread with a pair of oversized scissors. He gave the kilt a final shake and eyed it for a moment as if it were a prized heirloom he were about to give away.

'Do you know much about a kilt?' he asked. I shook my head.

He fell silent. The shadows of the surrounding gloom advanced from dusty shelves where rolls of tartan were stacked in disorder, their ends hanging down like shreds from a torn fleece, and heightened the atmosphere of suspicion. He seemed to be assessing my worthiness to wear the result of his labour and experience.

'It takes eight yards of cloth to make a kilt and eighteen continuous hours to cut it, shape it and sew in over nine thousand stitches,' he said with a tired but proud sigh. My eyebrows rose in genuine awe, admiration and also some apprehension that this was the build-up to a price that would, appropriately, send me reeling – as that, after all, is a little bit closer to a Scotsman's heart than the number of stitches on the top of his kilt. Little did I realise at the time what a bargain it was. A uniform that attracted carte blanche credit, high interest and spontaneous mischief, though never in a predictable order. I departed with a tartan passport to the unknown.

J. Munro, *Kilt and Skirt-maker* (the difference later caused me some confusion but is important, especially to the man inside) withdrew

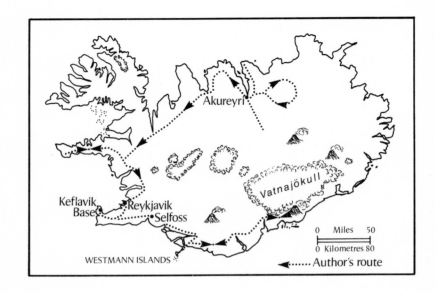

My travels in Iceland and the Faroes

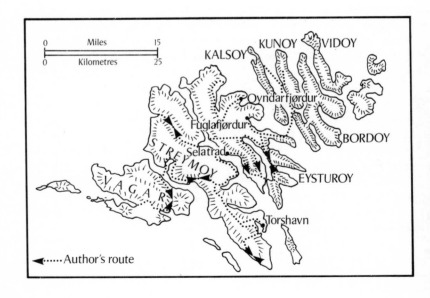

an old ledger where biros never dared enter. As the doorbell's ringing faded he turned over the marbled inner leaf, much stained with thumbmarks, and flicked through the pages until he had located the last order. '£45 PAID', he scrawled in permanent royal blue, and thought about the stranger who had just left.

He was in his mid-twenties, a few inches short of six feet and with the lean build of a runner, the long-distance kind. His hair was fair and inclined to curl in all the wrong directions and his ginger beard had an unusual white streak on one side. His cheeks glowed with excessive health and he professed to come from the north, but his rounded accent was distinctly Sassenach. He wore a tie as uncomfortably as a foreigner's attempt at swearing in English, and you could see at once that he would be happiest on a mountain in a blizzard. Funny, but there are people like that.

A chill wind was changing the seasons, ripping autumn off the trees with spiteful glee when a strange sounding Fokker Friendship took me away. September was a good time of the year to be going abroad and my thoughts, along with swallows and the dreams of many others, turned to warmth and the south. But I was heading north. And in Highland dress. (Nine thousand and fifty-seven stitches. I'd caught it on a nail at the airport and been forced to add some more thread myself, leaving visible evidence that my own ancestors had been more interested in stealing the sheep than in sewing them up into sartorial works of art.) My sudden embarrassment over the kilt was picked up by my neighbour for she was tuned in to these sorts of things, a nun swathed in voluminous black, although she was probably quite small inside.

Smoked salmon arrived. She refused hers. My inclination to ask for an extra helping was stifled by a glance that said 'Biafra'. Her eyes rested for a moment on my kilt. She blushed, florid cheeks framed in black, bordered in white. The colours of an Icelandic landscape, black lava in the land of fire and ice. There augured nothing optimistic in starting a long journey beside such sanctimonious abstinence. All that came to me was the excuse that a little sin is necessary to keep everything in perspective and I attacked my smoked salmon with new relish.

A hostess came along with newspapers. She motioned to offer me one and then saw my kilt. She smiled slightly and withdrew the paper. I still felt sensitive and raised my eyebrows sharply to indicate that I too might want to read it, whatever I was wearing. She gave it to me, reluctantly. I realised my mistake at once but for the next ten minutes I tried to conceal my misunderstanding, and my self-consciousness, by avidly scanning columns of Icelandic. The wimple suddenly turned to me and revealed a face that was intrigued, almost impressed.

'*Talar thu Islensku?*' she asked.

'No. Not a word,' I replied, sounding repentant. Bedlamite, said the eyes. Again they lingered on my kilt and then left me for good. But my first lesson of the journey had already been learnt. I would have to accept myself in a kilt before anyone else would.

'Fasten your seatbelts, please . . .' Commercial flying is the worst means of transport. It offers no appreciation of distance, change of climate or culture, and neither does it offer a choice of travelling companion. The ferry service from Scotland, however, had stopped for its winter hibernation a month earlier and so there had been no alternative but to fly. The check-in clerk at Icelandair had been unable to conceal his amusement when I arrived. ('So you're the one-man-expedition, are you?' he smirked.) I had declined to respond, nodding as I paused to tighten the straps holding a box of bagpipes to the bottom of my pack and lashing an umbrella to the top. He could laugh if he wanted. By being granted expedition status I was exempt from paying for excess baggage weight, which would have been considerable on a load of eight-four pounds. And so, within two hours I had left the security of my homeland and been instantly deposited as an alien.

I took a connecting flight from Reykjavik to Akureyri. The hostesses wore thick overcoats during the entire journey for reasons that were all too apparent when we landed at one o'clock in the morning. The shock of minus 10°C hit me like a hammer in parts least designed to withstand it, which explained at once why Iceland had never invented the kilt. The other passengers were amazed that Scotsmen in startling outfits did actually exist outside whisky bottle labels ('100 Pipers') and even more so to find one up here in the remote north at the beginning of winter. All gathered around the luggage-return office to watch as two officials wrestled my pack up onto the counter. Anxious to escape the rows of eyes that lit up in the dismal twenty-watt atmosphere with the whiteness of their scrutiny, I slipped quickly into the straps and stepped away without noticing a vital buckle was missing. The sudden shift of weight threw me off balance and left me lying on the floor, half-buried under my load, my kilt rucked up dangerously high above my knees. There was a muted whisper in English about a Highland Fling and then Cimmerian laughter, while I turned red and wondered how often my tenuous connection with sheep would destine me to feel like one. They had to search the plane before finding the missing buckle, and then I fled out into the night.

Twenty-three creased pleats scuffed along the snow towards the town lights, a mile further on, where winter was fiercely illuminated. Deep holes ending in impressions of Commando tread marked my progress as I tramped through drifts looking for a place to camp. It was a depressing prospect. I thought how little I knew about this country, and how harsh was the reality that lay between the lines of cosy armchair travel reading. A leaflet had told me that Iceland was a misnomer, that Greenland and Iceland should really swap names because here the winters could be hard but were not as severe as the island's latitude might suggest. Bananas were even grown here, in greenhouses heated free by geothermal power, hot springs that emerged from the ground at 97°C. 'Bananas!' the leaflet had repeated with an exclamation mark, winter being passed over for other statistics. My socks fell to my ankles, the snow became packed inside against my skin, and I felt annoyed for being naïve.

Iceland was the only country in the world, the leaflet said, where the annual number of seats sold on domestic flights equalled the country's population. Apart from their love of flying, 220,000 Icelanders were fanatical chess-players, bought proportionately more books per head than any other nation, and generally spoke good English. They were fervently proud of their culture and resented being taken for a bunch of Eskimos, which, incidently, they were not. Of course not, I thought, Eskimos don't grow bananas.

Then I came across a spot for my tent on the sheltered side of a stone barn and felt little compunction about scattering a group of sheep, my inescapable associates, which had also been attracted to the light covering of snow. Once the tent was up and my gear stowed away inside, it was a relief to find there was still some room left for me. I brewed some soup despite the late hour and my

An optimist in Iceland

enthusiasm returned with the comforting roar of the primus and the cloud of steam that smelt of broth.

It was one of those wonderful Arctic nights, the air so fresh you felt the purity as you breathed, the heavens so clear they assumed a new dimension. Across this immense vista stretched three parallel bands like rainbows of neon green light. Vertical shafts of energy pulsed along the length of each one like the hypnotic ripple of centipede legs in motion and then the bands turned to twirls and loops, always shimmering, always vibrant; Aurora Borealis, the 'heavenly dancers', the mysterious Northern Lights. They lasted for over an hour and were still there when I went to bed.

Despite my tiredness, sleep would not come. My mind was a hive of excitement, questions, hopes and ambitions. It is one of my regrets that I am unable to cure insomnia by counting sheep jumping over a fence. All goes well until the sixth, then the seventh trips and falls, eight, nine and ten jump over together and this, aided by a few refusals, makes a mockery of the whole thing. And as I probe the elliptical corners of my mind trying to see what is holding the remainder up and on the other side, where the hell they are now off to, I am wider awake than ever. I sank more deeply into my sleeping bag until eventually the sleep that had eluded the imaginary shepherd claimed my consciousness. I was content. My journey had started, perhaps not quite in the way I had intended – but at last it had started. The first steps of a 194,000-mile trek around the world.

'Akureyri welcomes you,' continued the leaflet, 'and expects you to enjoy your visit to the friendly town by the Arctic Ocean and its virginity.' A smile crossed my face at the kind invitation. 'The Sheriff has resided here since 1853 and the Doctor since 1861 . . .' The land around me seemed to reflect the same agelessness that must possess the Sheriff and the Doctor; a range of black herring-bone hills lay on either side of the fjord and hemmed in the narrow valley with their shoulders that fell abruptly down, ending in truncated spurs. They held their snub noses high in the air as if they too found the eternal wind of the fjord distasteful. Akureyri, the second largest centre of habitation in Iceland, was spread out along the sea, boasting twelve thousand citizens, colourful roofs, a youth hostel, two fish factories and a shipyard with an unpronounceable name that sounded like Slipshod. It made a pleasant view from my tent the next morning.

There was a wee nip in the air (and in a kilt that is considerable), which caused the dilemma of whether to put my loyalty into Scottish woollen underwear or tradition, but the nip made a fairly strong case. After a warming bowl of porridge, I set off at a brisk pace and soon found that Icelandic sheepdogs are remarkable in that they will run half a mile just to bark at a passer-by. It does not matter if the snow is so deep that they have to leap vertically out of one hole to gain a yard before disappearing down into the next – their dedicated sense of duty to show face, especially towards one-man expeditions, is restrained only by a drift that proves taller then their bounce. My walk was accompanied by an assortment of these barking jack-in-the-boxes as I lent forwards against the weight of my pack and pushed myself through air that was heavy with the oppressive smell of thousands of fish hanging on racks to dry.

The youth hostel was run by a German woman of formidable proportions and the manner of an irate Viking, but she had moments of great humanity and a congenial friendliness that appeared, for example, when you came to pay your rent. However, unlike most battleaxes of the period, hers was only one-edged and she ran a warm establishment that was to become my home for the next three months. Her husband's paintings were festooned to the walls like limpets but they were all unfinished; smoke was missing from some, others had no waves and one had a crowd of featureless faces which resembled the one at the airport the previous night. She explained that he was a beginner and had not learnt certain techniques yet.

'And why haf you kom hier?' she asked with a Teutonic lack of tact.

It was a good question and as I gazed at the icicle frozen onto the base of a window, defying her attempts to remove it and thus preventing the window from closing, I too began to wonder.

My aim was to go around the world, hitch-hiking and working to pay my way, to see life at grass-roots level and to live with its different cultures and peoples. By wearing the kilt I would be unusual, not just another run-of-the-mill traveller but a curiosity who would hopefully attract the curious, encourage local contact and help break down the ethnic barriers and silent stares that surround a stranger. And the bagpipes? They were to complement my image and because they would be expected of me. I also hoped they would earn me my supper on occasion as a wandering minstrel.

I wanted to find the offbeat places, to visit the more common ones but in the wrong season, to go around the back of the world's Taj Mahals and to run my finger through the dust that no one else saw – to throw myself into situations where the outcome was uncertain, to have experiences that would be different. These I would record on film – the journey was to be my apprenticeship as a freelance photographer. In my mind was the nurtured hope that a portfolio of photographs would establish my career in this field.

Idealised goals seem readily attainable when ambition is fresh. Ahead of me lay the times when my kilt was to achieve all my expectations, and each of these strengthened my resolve, allowing discomfort and problems to be discarded as trivial inconveniences. But ahead of me also lay the other times when the kilt was to create the obstacles I sought to remove, and even to incite the outright hostility I feared. Under these circumstances, and those when I failed to distinguish between the degree of risk that would safely provide a novel experience and that which would senselessly endanger my life, my lofty goals were forgotten and I wanted no more than to survive.

North seemed to be the least common direction for leaving Britain, and Iceland in winter had a unique ring about it. So I had set off north with kilt, camera and a sporranful of dreams. 'And why haf you kom hier?' It was hard to explain it all. I said it was because I was cold.

'Ach, you vant to vork at Slippstödin,' said Mrs Viking, attaching another unfinished limpet to the wall.

'Slippstödin?' Oh! Slipshod – now, there was an idea.

Slippstödin's canteen was full of welders, carpenters, electricians and all the others who somehow stopped smoking their pipes for long enough to put a ship together. Pipe-smoking was common here and for some it was debatable whether their pipe was an accessory of life or one of its vital organs. Pipes seemed to be intrinsic extensions of the Icelandic breathing apparatus. We were eating a tough red stew which I found pleasant to the taste until they told me the meat was horse. Soup came as a second course. Pepper emerged in a stream from the cellar with a single hole on top and salt was to be found in the pepper pot, a discovery that came too late, so the soup failed to save the meal. The manager had offered me a job at once and it began after lunch. Palli, the foreman, led me away to the dry-dock and gave me five gallons of red paint and a small roller brush. His English was quite clear.

'You see ship over there?'

I nodded.

'Good. Paint it.'

Before me rested a steel hull with the area of two tennis courts. I began optimistically in the middle as the full expanse of unpainted trawler seemed daunting from either end. The paint went on easily and a large cluster of barnacles disappeared under a generous layer of red before I had even noticed that they were there. Palli returned just as it was going rather well and gave a choked gasp. He pointed angrily at a little plaque that was now at one with the acre of red around it, and ran off to get a can of solvent. As he set about removing the paint, my face blended in with the colour that echo-sounder windows should never be.

The days went past and filled my life with horizons of rust and hues that were measured by the gallon. Grey paint, grey days. Red paint, grey days. The work was monotonous but I felt lucky to have it. I grew to love the savage beauty of this country, which claims to have the oldest parliament in Europe and whose language has been almost unchanged in one thousand years. The famous sagas, re-counting the fantastic exploits of warriors fighting on after losing the odd arm or leg, can still be read in their original texts. Iceland's principal unit of exchange is the cod, divisible into lesser denominations of woollen sweaters. Cod is traded for wheat and cod for computers. This is a nation of fishermen to the extent that shops never even try to sell fish. The government zealously guards her waters and yet allows more of her own trawlers to deplete the fishing grounds, following the same policy of too much chasing too few as the sixty per cent annual inflation accepted as normal. The only way to beat the continually changing price tags, Icelanders joke, is to run to the shops. Houses are seldom completed but left with exteriors of raw concrete. Rates are cheaper that way, it is said, but I suspected that with so many volcanoes around, people feel it is pointless taking too much trouble over the finishing touches. (The last major erup-tion was in 1973 when over five and a half thousand villagers were evacuated from the Westmann Islands.) Perhaps inflation and vol-canoes also account for the devil-may-care attitude of the people.

They work hard and long during the week and then drink and spend recklessly at weekends. There is an aura of complacency about them, understandable in an insular people who can grow bananas in the Arctic. They feel as indestructible as their sagas and put their trust in cod.

But I found them to be friendly and generous. Work is a catalyst, cold is a hardener and together they develop a strong bond of cameraderie. Iceland's winter and her endless ships in need of repair combined to form the basis of many friendships. The men at Slippstödin quickly accepted me, and my failings, as part of their team. 'Skot of the Arctic' they called me, and my smile tried to conceal that I felt the cold more than my heroic namesake of the south.

In the shipyard there was a wall of many colours. It was similar to the Biblical coat only not so static as it changed to the colour of the last brush to shed a stripe of excess paint over its surface at the end of each day. On passing one evening, I had the idea that the changing-rooms behind this abstract free-for-all would be a good place to practise my bagpipes. The manager had no objection and so I was there the next evening only to find that no one had warned the night-watchman, who spoke very little English. He stared at the strange contraption as if it were some surprise from an Al Capone violin-case and looked me hard in the eye. When my pipes were rigged up, there was a glint of recognition in his features and he seemed more at ease. It did not last long. Unaware that the pipes are incompatible with any peaceful form of human activity, he returned to his television at the far end of the room.

The art of playing the pipes has not come easily to me – indeed, some might say it has not come at all – but that evening the room was soon reverberating with the full range of skirls that an unhappy set of pipes can produce. A cacophony in nine tortured notes. The watch-man turned his television off and tolerantly endured the process of a Scotsman's revitalisation. He came over twice; once to peer down a tenor drone and once to prod the bag. As I was putting them away he became more cheerful.

'Very loud,' he said.

The next evening was, I felt, a marked improvement.

'Bravo,' he said.

The third evening I was back in form with lilting marches and laughing jigs.

'Drainpipes?' he asked, holding a small dictionary.

The big annual event, Slippstödin's Christmas party, gradually drew nearer. 'You'll play your bag for us?' Palli asked. Feeling flattered, I accepted. Over the next few days my doubts began to grow, however, when I was constantly asked if I knew the songs of Abba and when I explained that it was a different kind of music, they asked just as eagerly for the Beatles. While I nervously brushed up my grace notes on the chanter, other party preparations were also in full swing. In little outhouses elementary science apparatus bubbled away as they distilled something that was procured from chemists in brown bottles, but only in single purchases, in exchange for a wad of worthless kronur and a signature. They added hydrochloric acid which was said to remove the bad smell and then used it to 'spike' Brennivin, Icelandic firewater, which never needed any antagonising even in its most mellow moments.

The great day came and work stopped after another lunch of fish. If only God had blessed Iceland with a surfeit of horse, or at least had made the shoals boneless. The canteen was covered with colourful cobwebs of paper and there was even a tinsel octopus squatting on the clocking-in machine. The silvery tentacles did little to conceal the business-like gape of its open mouth and nothing to alter its morose 'click' into something more festive. Someone handed me a bun which he said had cassowary seeds on it – but I was more interested in what was on the seeds. He explained that it was a speciality of shark which had been buried in sand for three months and allowed to 'mature' (rot); it smelt revolting, but the taste was worse. While I was contemplating this someone else came along to discuss the Cod War. It appeared to be all a joke now and he held no grudge against me, just as long as I kept my damn trawler out of Icelandic waters in future.

On the dance floor you didn't dance where or even with whom you wanted, but where the crowd deposited you on the occasional free patch of floor space and with whoever else came to land on the same spot. Luckily it was a casual affair, and a relief to be wearing my climbing boots. I tried to calm my nerves by saturating them with the nameless extract from brown bottles which, in comparison to the deceased shark, smelt and tasted pleasantly indifferent. A disco version of the Seven Dwarfs singing *Hi-ho, Hi-ho* . . . had just started when Palli thumped me on the back, and said I was on next. My God! I thought. How on earth was I to follow a jazzed-up Snow White on a synthesiser with *The Piobaireachd of Donald Dhu* when my drunk audience was expecting the hits of the Beatles?

I went outside to tune up my pipes with the problem unresolved and only the notes of funeral marches and retreats coming to mind. But the great thing about the pipes is that the sheer volume alone is enough to impress those who have never heard them before and such power at his fingertips is reassuring to the piper. So I marched in with a lively reel that instantly had them all clapping with such enthusiasm that I had finished my second Slow Air before anyone realised the tempo had changed. Just as I reached a particularly hard and fast part of a hornpipe a huge cheer broke out for some latecomers which was fortunate as a series of bad mistakes were lost in the uproar. My face was dripping with sweat and my cheeks were as red as the nose of a paper reindeer that was suspended from the ceiling, waving two limp antlers in the turbulent air.

By then the workers were revelling in festive abandon and even more spiked Brennivin; the welders in one corner were shouting for more *Scotland the Brave*, the carpenters opposite them clammered for more *Amazing Grace*, the painters seemed to be inert under tables and the scattered electricians looked as if they wanted the dwarfs back. So I walked from side to side pleasing the welders whilst trying to placate the carpenters and stepping over the painters whilst trying to avoid the electricians. Then it became just a hazy recollection of playing on until my balance began to fail, a middle course of *Amazing the Brave* was not working and my drones were lost in a tangle of streamers.

Iceland has thirteen Santa Clauses. Each one has a day leading up to Christmas and leaves a gift inside the largest shoe that Icelandic children can find to put on a windowsill at night. By the time the last Santa has been, each child will have also received a new article of clothing for there is a large cat that prowls around and eats those who have been missed out. My own boots were always empty and my clothes were old, but I walked unmolested down the road that led south from Akureyri, ending forty miles later where the uninhabited interior began. Slippstödin was closed for a short holiday.

It was Christmas Day. Not the best time for anyone to be on his own and far from home.

The bold curve of a whale's jawbone formed the lintel over a wicker gate that was set in a broken fence. The path through it was well-trodden and led up to a little wooden church whose turf roof, all but hidden except for a few stalwart stalks of grass poking through the crust of snow, was ringed with icicles like teeth in the jaws of a glacier. The sound of music and singing seeped out of the walls and even the old pine tree growing by the door, its branches covered in lights, seemed touched by the soothing refrain of *Silent Night*. The heads of the congregation turned as the door was pushed gently open, swinging on finely wrought hinges that announced the arrival of each latecomer with an uncharitable groan. I took my place quietly at the back.

The Lutheran minister gave a powerful sermon which seemed to express anything but peace and good-will, making me wonder if volcanoes, like dogs, can impress their characteristics on their owners. The words were as meaningless to me as to the occupant of a frilled lace bonnet who was propped up near the font and seemed to be waiting for the christening with gurgles and innocent chuckles. It was an enchanting atmosphere as the organist pedalled away on the footpumps and played more carols. The final piece was marred slightly when there was a disagreement as to just how high the top note should be and it was not resolved by the last chorus when there were four simultaneous soloists in the choir of six. A blessing followed, whose sentiments could easily be imagined, and then we all shook hands – after all, Christmas is Christmas and People are People, whatever the language, wherever the place.

After the service I resumed my walk towards the end of the road. A car later pulled up beside me. Iceland was full of the rough country vehicles; Land Rovers, Land Cruisers, Broncos and a host of other four-wheel drive marvels, which were usually fairly new. But this one was home-made, a skeleton of an igloo on wheels with its rear half stuffed full of manure. A broody hen sat on the dashboard and ogled at me with staccato head movements. The driver invited me to wriggle aboard but warned he was not going far. He was as good as his word and he let me out two hundred yards later at the turning to his farm.

I scanned the bleak landscape and wondered how a farm could exist here in what appeared to be snow, mountains and jagged lava. Only one per cent of Iceland is cultivated, twenty per cent is rough grazing and seventy-nine per cent is useless (although the Americans found it good for testing a moon buggy). This area seemed to be a part of the seventy-nine per cent. Great clumps of black rock formed a deep trough, letting steep mantles of scree sweep down from their serrated edges. The glacial bulldozers that had gouged out this valley had left piles of morraine scattered along its floor, and amongst them lay strewn the odd boulder of lava like a dark solidified sponge, displaced from more distant hills by an old eruption. The scene was one of utter granulation. The land had been shattered and was now mortared together with snow.

My kilt still smelt strongly of farmyard when I paused beside a small waterfall which was frozen and stood posing as a baroque extravaganza in ice. My camera shutter jammed as I tried to take a photograph of the formation, making me curse that I had over-looked having my equipment specially 'winter-lubricated' in the rush of departure. Sub-zero conditions create special problems for the photographer; mechanical movements freeze, batteries work less efficiently and film becomes brittle. The cold air tingles, stings and then numbs your fingers as you fumble for the exposure settings which will compensate for the background bias of bright snow, and photography becomes a test of willpower. You soon become dis-criminating and the visual appeal of a situation is weighed against the physical discomfort of recording it. I had to hold the camera under my clothes for five minutes before my body heat had thawed it sufficiently to allow a quick photograph to be made. Then I walked briskly to the end of the road where a vague sheep track led me deeper into this black and white wilderness, coloured only by brown tufts of tussock-grass and a milky-green river.

A friend in Reykjavik had invited me to spend Christmas with his family but I had declined his kind invitation. Instead I sought the peace of lonely places and the solitude of mountains, where the annual festivals stop and the calendars of millennia begin. Mountains and sea – there is something calming and reassuring about their stubborn existence and their disregard for all other forces. What is it exactly, the fascination that they hold for us? It is much more than their vastness, their emptiness and simply because they are there. It is something stronger than purely the desire to dominate them, for their magnetism outlasts the victories of those who make conquests and even extends with equal force to those of us who will never row an Atlantic or scale an Eiger. Is it a longing to be a part of their resistance to a changing world? An admiration for the way they defy our attempts to move and control them? Or is it because they are now amongst the last wilderness areas on this planet, playgrounds of the unpredictable where we can test our strength and courage, fight our weakness and fear and, in doing so, discover a part of our enigmatic Self?

Having shunned hospitality and tables of food for a bleak landscape and my frugal packets of broth, I walked and walked and sat and thought, trying to find that part of me which was missing. Something was missing and as the miles went by and the rocks where I rested became more numerous, gradually I realised what it was.

Iceland was a beautiful country with all the sea and mountains a searching spirit could ask for, but it was all too similar to home. I wanted to find a different way of life, a different culture, and a place where adventure was not created but where it just happened. I took out my pocket-sized map of the world and amongst the wrinkles and creases, the word 'Greenland' was faintly legible – the name flashed like a beacon and instantly made a clear impression on my mind.

The route that eventually took me there proved to be a devious one, but that was not important. As of that moment I was fixed on a destination, not a direction.

A week later, painter 257 put a final stripe on that multicoloured wall and hung up his paintbrush for the last time, doubtless to the relief of many barnacles which were spared a clatter of bright red paint. The post office accepted a large parcel of belongings which had lost their status as 'essentials', and amongst them was a sizeable box of drainpipes. It was a reluctant decision but I had found that one-man bands don't mix with one-man expeditions and the pipes had become a liability. My kilt, however, remained. Mrs Viking at the youth hostel smiled benevolently as I paid my outstanding dues.

When the exact amount lay before her, she wished me well.

I left Akureyri early in the New Year. A young boy stood at his garden gate and emptied his entire English vocabulary over me as a greeting.

'Hallodogcat.'

It was a brave gesture and needed encouragement rather than correction.

'Halloandgoodbyedogcat,' I replied, and he beamed with delight at the power of elementary communication. My knowledge of his language had not progressed much beyond the word *kannske*, but this was usually sufficient. *Kannske* was used so often that simply to know it meant you were all but fluent in Icelandic. It meant 'maybe'.

This time the sheepdogs did not run down from their distant farms to bark at me. Maybe the snowdrifts were now too deep. Maybe I had become accepted as a local. *Kannske*. They called this the 'land of maybe'.

A Frenchman staying at the hostel had commented on my intention of hitch-hiking to Reykjavik at this time of year, saying it was *très courageux*. It was minus 16°C. The snow was falling gently on the three hundred miles of gravel road that lay between me and the problem of finding a way to Greenland. If anything, it was a case of being *un idiot optimiste*.

2 · Fall in the Faroes

Reykjavik. The name means 'Smoking Bay' and refers to plumes of steam that early sailors saw rising from nearby geysers. It is a pleasant, clean and spacious city of eighty thousand, one third of Iceland's population. The modern cathedral stands tall like a rocket and its wings fall away sharply, taking on the appearance of organ pipes set in high-pitched crescendos of concrete. It is guarded by a larger than life statue of Leif Ericsson, the discoverer of America in 1000 AD, showing determination in his stance, defiance in his swollen chest. He holds a battleaxe in his right hand and gazes menacingly towards the unpopular NATO base at Keflavik.

A truck took me in silence for nine hours through a sporadic blizzard. The Icelandic scenery was framed by the windscreen and could have been captioned 'This is a temporary fault. Do not adjust your set.' The driver let me out in a street of the capital where traffic was mimicking droves of morris dancers, and the sound of their clinking wheel-chains filled the air – cold air that rasped my throat with purging freshness. A man employed by the government to knock icicles off buildings as a public service was at work under the eaves of a shop. A glassy dagger over one yard in length shattered at my feet, causing me to skip nimbly around a corner – as nimbly as is possible with sixty pounds on your back. And there before me, peacefully humming, lay an electric cemetery. At this time of year it was customary to put fairy lights along the outline of each graveside cross. The crosses burned brightly and covered the hillside in ranks of yellow, floodlighting plastic flowers in the snow and making this graveyard as daringly cheerful as an octogenarian's birthday cake.

I hurried on down to the harbour where they told me that boats seldom went from here to Greenland. Maybe there was more chance of finding one in the Faroe Islands, said a crusty seaman, where boats had quotas to fish Greenland waters. I looked at my map, wanting to leave this land of *kannske* and Arctic bananas. But the Faroes lay halfway back home? He nudged me. Quick, a Faroese boat was about to leave. I rushed over and shouted to a figure in the wheelhouse. The skipper was evasive. He was going to the Faroes but not directly as he would be fishing for a week, and then followed excuses. I pleaded, promised to work hard, offered to pay . . . Did I have money? A passport? Was I a good sailor? Yes, yes, yes – and then I was aboard. Perhaps it had been my enthusiasm that had won him over or maybe it had been the kilt, but at 2300 hours the lights of Reykjavik slowly merged into the stars and another dotted line began on my journey.

The *Kronberg* weighed 862 tons. We steamed 180° due South at fourteen knots, making for the mackerel grounds north-west of the Butt of Lewis. I was heading for Scotland and on my way to Greenland.

Extract from my diary

3rd January. The boat see-saws up-and-down along its length and also with a slow roll from side to side. You run forward four steps downhill and then have to change your lean and struggle one step uphill. Just when you get used to this the left wall suddenly comes rushing in and you have to find something to grab as the room seems to turn upside-down. By then you've forgotten the floor is now pointing downhill and off you trot four paces forwards again. Murderous. Feel like a ball in a maze game.

The cook is amazing – I had to hold fast to the kitchen walls while he stood in the centre as if his feet were stuck to the spot, leaning out at 45° and defying all of gravity. He held a frying-pan in one hand, a bowl of mix in the other, swirling fat, adding the mix and tossing pancakes while the room turned circles around him. What a waste of talent – although it turned out to be more spectacular than edible. Had a small lunch. The table is covered in a non-slip mesh of the same squelchy rubber as joke spiders. Ten minutes later I felt sick. Doesn't help when everyone else is eating heartily and in such bloody good humour. Made a casual exit and promptly lost my lunch overboard. Feed the fish, catch the fish – ugh, wish we'd just leave them alone and go back to land. Am a lousy sailor and hate boats more than I've ever hated anything. What the hell am I in for?

4th January. The bridge is so full of electronic gadgetry it resembles an amusement arcade of space invaders. A satellite navigator gives a constant digital read-out of our exact location and is linked to a computer. Feed in the coordinates of any point in the world, say Rio in Brazil, and it instantly gives the correct bearing, our actual heading, the drift, the distance, our current speed and the time it will take to reach Rio at this speed – but not our horoscope. Two sets of radar with colours that distinguish between ship, land and iceberg and whose scales can be changed to fill the screen with half a mile to 48 miles of coverage. A depth meter that disgorges yards of paper, four radios and, best of all, two ASDIC fish-finding sonors (like the one I painted red). One emits a constant 'klack' sound which changes when it finds fish and then it draws the shoals on a paper print-out. From the shoal formation and its depth the skipper knows at once what type of fish they are. The other has a screen which has a picture of our boat on it with the line of our course behind us (showing every turn we've made) and a projected straight line in front of us. The shoal is portrayed in the same way showing both the way it has come and its projected route, and is lit up in flashes by arrows that fire out from the side of our boat. We just steer to intercept it on the diagram, drop the net, loop around the back and the screen shows our circular route and, if successful, the surrounded fish in the middle. Incredible! But I feel sorry for the fish.

On reaching EEC waters we sent a telex to Brussels advising them of our entry, and when we leave we shall have to notify them again with details of our catch. We fish at night as mackerel go deeper during the day. Sat drinking coffee, waiting. By midnight we were still waiting. There had been three false alerts which sent us scurrying up on deck but either the shoals went too fast or they went too deep. Despite all our scientific aids we still need the predator's patience and luck.

Our boat motors steadily along at quarter speed. Its rigging bristles with antennae, electronic ears tuned to the inaudible words of the air. Radar scanners turn tireless circles as they search the night, and below us, endless streams of insidious waves are penetrating the depths. On the bridge the atmosphere of expectancy is so oppressive I hardly dare to breathe. The skipper's concentration is intense. The room is in darkness except for the glow of moving neon dots, a patchy mosaic of red bulbs and a modest light illuminating the entrails of paper that issue from a machine. There are advisory bleeps, warning pings, the abrasive shuffle of paper print-out and the heavy klack of the ASDIC, as regular as heartbeat.

The klack suddenly changes. It becomes high-pitched and faster. A screen glows more brightly. The skipper doesn't move but his eyes swing from screen to paper and back again. He increases our speed, turns the wheel, his eyes never leave the screen. Two lines intersect. He waits and watches.

'*ALT I LAGI.*'

The shout is echoed by every loudspeaker around the boat and suddenly pandemonium is let loose. Men are throwing on oilskins, stamping on waders and within seconds luminous yellow figures are on deck untying safety ropes, pulling on levers, attaching cables and then, just as suddenly, the action stops. We are trailing the end of the net behind us and the white light on the marker buoy dances in our wake. We wait . . .

'*NUNA.*'

. . . and already the winch drum is freewheeling as 500 yards of nylon net, weights and floats pour out into the sea. We complete our circle, pull in the marker buoy, locate the vital cable and soon the winches hum as they haul it in, closing the net in around the shoal.

I feel the thrill of the hunt as the tone of the winches changes to a groaning, gnawing whine with the increase in weight. The circle of buoys gets smaller and inside it a seething mass of motion makes the sea begin to boil. When the net becomes too heavy, we lower a large tube in amongst the tightly packed fish and pump them up, water and all. I feel like a phosphorescent penguin hobbling around in waders borrowed from an absent giant, three thick jerseys and oilskins that are invaluable. Without a sou'wester, the run-off, spray and shredded fish soon find their way down your back.

Over the next two hours 250 tons of fish pour continuously into the hold – down a tube they flow, tens of thousands of silvery shapes, flexing, thrashing, leaping, slithering, twitching, dying. Each new flood of vibrating bodies triggers off fresh spasms of nervous energy in the ones already there. We wade up to our thighs in fish, adding slats to raise the height of each compartment as the hold fills up. The water around our feet turns red and the bloody extract is pumped out over the side to fall amongst the captive fish awaiting the same fate.

When we are finished, the nets are made ready again and we have an hour's rest before the shout to action rings out once more. The sea has built up and driving rain sweeps the deck. By the time dawn comes we have brought in our third catch and turned about. Now we are heading for a fertiliser factory in Fuglafjørdur.

5th January. Days merge into nights and both hours and dates are meaningless. Feel exhausted but elated. Skipper is also happy. We aren't full but have 450 tons – almost one and a half million fish. How do such shoals find enough to eat? Skipper says mackerel have been known to form a single shoal ten miles square!

Still have fits of unbearable queasiness. Slept in the mess-room my first night, and have lost track of the others. Now am shown to a spare bunk. Two men in each room and the man indicates the sleeping figure in the bunk above mine and says, 'Don't worry, he's a bit . . .' and as he doesn't know the word he imitates a boxer or someone drowning. So don't know if my room-mate has nightmares or psychopathic tendencies. The weather is wild. The boat treats me as if I were on a pastryboard, rolling me about, sliding me from end to end along the sheet until the skin on my back is stretched taut. Then it bucks around, lifting me up and dumping me down on another part of the bed until head, feet or arms hit the sides. Give up trying to sleep and join the skipper on the bridge. It's Gale Force 9 and he enjoys my concern.

'Very fine weather for sailing,' he beams. We are now low in the water with the weight of fish. I watch in horror as our bow crashes down into a trough and the next wave is already upon us. It swells up to a towering crest and bursts over our deck, covering it in a foaming turmoil of surf. And still we roll, leaning over until my eyes are wide with alarm, freezing momentarily when we reach our limit and then suddenly dropping that little bit further, before swinging back to right ourselves and to repeat it on the other side. A wall of spray smashes against the windows and this time I think it has gone too far, this time the bow will not reappear. But when the window clears water is rushing down the deck and our bow is faithfully rearing up to meet the next one.

'Very fine weather for sailing,' he repeats. His humour is comforting, but land will always be something precious to me and never more so than right now. *Kronberg* must think so too and she battles on into the storm with her compass set for home.

They call them 'The Islands of Sheep'. Eighteen islands consisting of steep grassy slopes watered by a thousand streams, where eighty thousand sheep outnumber man at the ratio of two to one. The age-old struggle against the forbidding Atlantic has left the coast-lines with a natural fortification of cliff walls as immense and sheer as in any fantasy. With a breathless sigh we humbly gaze up at their rugged majesty and learn the difference between the mortal and the everlasting. Fulmars and a host of other seabirds ride the breezes with effortless arrogance, seldom bothering with a wingbeat except to turn an inevitable collision into a piece of acrobatic showmanship – below them the sea toils away at its endless task of pounding these rock walls, and after each blow it withdraws for a few moments to observe its progress, tugging at the matted strands of kelp like an inspired hairdresser, before pounding once more at these obstacles to its motion. Eighteen outposts of resistance that appear to have hurt the pride of the North Atlantic and that must now face its resentment forever. The Faroe Islands.

Fuglafjørdur is the chief town of Eysturoy, the second largest of the islands. We arrived early in the morning as the sun broke out over another treeless land, but it was solid land and I placed two feet squarely on it and savoured the stability of *terra firma*. It was going to take twelve hours to unload the boat and no labour was needed as the entire process was automated. I watched for a while as the fish were transported along a conveyor belt into the factory. There is some-thing fascinating about a conveyor belt's infinite capacity for work. That is, of course, assuming it has not just deprived you of a job.

I walked down the road of a country whose name meant little more to me than storm warnings on shipping broadcasts, as the sun disappeared and sleet began to fall. The skipper had warned me about the weather, saying that they had six months of bad weather and six months of rain. I mentally tried to conjure up his idea of bad weather when Gale Force 9 was 'very fine'.

The town was small by most standards and, accordingly, quite large for these sparsely inhabited islands. Sheep were eating seaweed on the shore, others were being chased out of gardens and brazenly walked the streets as if bovine and sacred. A gaggle of sleeping geese lay huddled against the door of the post office and obviously considered themselves, at the very least, untouchable.

The houses were all taller than they were broad with a stone basement that once sheltered the owner's livestock but now housed the modern equivalent, his central heating system (and a few cod heads hanging up to dry). The upper half was of wood or corrugated iron painted in undiluted red, blue or yellow and some of the houses had turf roofs with skylight windows straining to see out. The street as a whole resembled a stack of refills for a child's paintbox. There were no street names or house numbers as everyone knew where everyone else lived, and what their ambitions were.

Children were skating down the streets, making use of the natural slopes and the covering of hard-packed snow and ice, creating a paradise of Cresta runs for all but the occasional motorist and those irrepressible sheep. At the far end of the main street I saw a boy on skates grab hold of the bumper of a passing car to be towed along behind. The driver stopped, waved the child away and continued. Undaunted by his rebuke the skater caught the car up and hitched a ride once more. Again the driver stopped and angrily sent him away. When it happened a third time the car suddenly accelerated, its winter stud tyres biting in and finding a grip, with the boy clinging on for all he was worth. This didn't appear to be much in the eyes of the driver who just as suddenly turned off into an empty carpark, while the boy, whiplashed into a final burst of speed, let go and carried on down the street. He passed me at about thirty miles an hour, his eyes bulging like tennis balls, arms flailing the air in an effort to maintain his balance as he rapidly bore down on a sheep that stood in the middle of the road with its back to him. It was nonchalantly chewing on a plundered rosebush when it happened to glance up and see the human missile coming hurtling along. Four legs became a blur of motion as they scrabbled for a hold on the ice, finding one as the boy brushed past its tail. He managed to lift a skate in time to avoid tripping over the hastily discarded rose and his arms renewed their frantic gyrations as he sped off into the distance. I lost sight of him disappearing over the brow of the hill that led to the factory, where 1,463,000 other poor souls were also bumping involuntarily along towards their fate.

As the sleet turned to a sandblaster of a hailstorm I became more conscious of my own fortunes, and retreated to the warmth of a café.

The woman serving said she came from the nearby island of Kalsoy.

'There's a nine-mile road and two tunnels,' she proudly informed me and then added as an equally proud afterthought, '. . . and three cars.'

The price of the coffee seemed to include a raffle ticket with a colour television as first prize. She smiled as I handed over the money and then came another afterthought.

'Of course it won't be much good to you if you win, will it?' I looked at my full pack and nodded – but that was evidently not her meaning. 'Because there is no television reception in the Faroes', and she closed the lid of the cash-box with an unnecessary bang that added a solemn finality to the masterstroke of her salesmanship. Feeling like a premature April Fool I clutched my apparently worthless ticket and set off for Torshavn, the capital of the Faroes.

A woman stopped to give me a lift but conversation was hard as her English was broken and her constant remarks about delivering people left me wondering if she were a taxidriver, a missionary or a midwife. She let me out near Oyndarfjørdur where there were said to be two mysterious boulders that moved of their own accord.

Legend has it that Viking ships used to attack and plunder the village here. After many years one of their ships sank near this spot and a witch cursed them saying that their fate was to rock these boulders unto eternity. As long as the boulders moved, the Viking ships would not return – and they never did. Scientific examinations have not revealed the cause of these 'Rolling Stones', and they remain an inexplicable phenomenon. There is no visible movement but it is indisputable that they do actually move, and there is a rope fixed to the top of the larger one so that those who doubt can hold the other end and feel the tug that comes every few seconds. They stand two yards off the rocky coastline and are big enough for about ten people to sit on. They gently rock to and fro at a constant speed regardless of whether the sea is calm or raging.

With my grasp on reality slightly shaken by these moving boulders it was disconcerting to find a mobile haystack approaching. Only when it stopped to talk to me did it turn out to be a farmer buried under bales of hay going on a moped to feed his sheep. We chatted and I explained my hope of finding a boat to Greenland, but he said it was too early and the season wouldn't start for another month. The Honda haystack drove off, straw streaming out behind as it hit top gear and then swerved to avoid an oystercatcher, the national bird, which had been fooled by the camouflage. A month? Greenland took one step back. And yet I knew the waiting would not be tedious in a land so full of surprises. I would try to work here while looking for my elusive lift to the far north.

The next car to stop was driven by an old man in the traditional Faroese hat, a collapsed tea-cosy in crimson with delicate black stripes. The road snaked up hills, disappeared into the darkness of a long tunnel, snaked down to sea-level again, ran along the high-tide mark, bumped over blind summits, teetered on the edge of cliffs, and then snaked upwards into the next set of hills. Man seemed to have made very little impression on the scenery, rearranging some rocks into walls and shelters but otherwise letting his life be interrupted by nature's obstacles. My driver pointed to a bay where, the previous day, pilot whales had been hunted. Whenever a school of *grind* was sighted, houses, factories, entire villages suddenly became empty and the placid Faroese went berserk, grabbing any kind of boat, driving the whales into shallow water and then stabbing, harpooning and butchering the creatures in a messy bloodbath. This practice was excused on the grounds that it was as old as my driver's hat. It seemed to be the only grudge the people bore against nature.

Torshavn, with twelve thousand inhabitants, made no pretence of being anything other than a small town despite having the title and functions of a capital. The Faroes exercise a degree of autonomous rule but are still largely under the wing of Denmark, their foster-mother. They have their own flag and also their own language which, as a testimony to the islanders' national pride, survived a hundred and fifty years of Danish administration without having any written form. All alcohol must be ordered from Denmark but even then, only on production of a card that proves your taxes have been paid up to date.

Work was hard to find and eventually I found myself baiting longline hooks. Two hundred and fifty hooks at one-yard intervals on a length of thick cord that came up in tangles and had a magnetic attraction for my clothes. The bait was frozen squid, mackerel and frequently my fingers as they soon became so cold it was impossible to feel the difference. The locals were sympathetic but found it difficult to believe that not everyone in the world is born with a longline in one hand and a filleting knife in the other. Ten hours later

I had baited one mile of hooks and left with punctured fingers, eighteen pounds in wages and roughly the equivalent value of damage to my clothes in terms of holes and tears.

A week later I was back in Fuglafjørdur as the fish factory needed workers. The problem was that there was nowhere to stay and so I went to see the woman with two tunnels, nine miles, three cars and many afterthoughts. I hadn't won the television but she was grateful for the donation to the cause, funds for an Old Folk's Home. I explained my lack of accommodation and suggested they start a new raffle for a Young Folk's Home. 'You could make the first prize a television transmitter and that would keep last week's winner happy too,' I added.

She suddenly understood my confusion and explained that although no one had television now, broadcasts were due to start for the first time in the summer and everyone was now buying a set. She turned out to be one of those wonderful surrogate mothers for wandering sons and phoned everyone she knew (which was everyone) to see if there was a room to rent. When the town had been asked, a room was found with an elderly couple.

It was a cosy house, cluttered up with objects that smacked more of sentimentality than of good taste and with the homely atmosphere that I missed. My room was economically designed to fit around a short bed, and a cracked china vase stood on the windowsill as a decoration. One solitary rose lent out horizontally and turned the tattered silk petals of its eternal bloom towards the woodworm holes in the floor. It was perfect for my needs. The old man showed me the loo that was concealed in a tiny room and explained with a wry grin and a wink, 'Ha! No bulb. A *piece* in the dark, yes?' His wife wrung her hands in the background and blushed slightly in her role as reluctant and long-suffering companion to his unvarnished wit.

My job began the next day, unloading the trawler catches; haddock, ling, plaice, whiting and the occasional halibut so large it had to be dragged into the factory by two men. The most abundant fish was still the humble cod with its large eyes, thick lips and delightfully gloomy face which expressed regret at supporting the main industry of Iceland and the Faroes. Under its chin it had a barbel like the one on the masks of Egyptian pharaohs, but the connection is doubtless as fanciful as the names are coincidental. Some cod were opened out flat and stacked into huge piles with bold handfuls of salt scattered between each layer. The salt rubbed into the open cuts on my fingers and the pain was proverbial but the work had to be done because Greece and Spain were partial to salted gloomy cod.

The ugliest fish was the monk fish. An evil grin came naturally to what was basically a set of jaws attached to a tail, and it was flat, covered in lumps and dangled a luminous lure over its mouth while trying to conceal an array of teeth as long and sharp as gramophone needles. It was so ugly only the tail was used, being frozen and then sold euphemistically as Rock Salmon. One day I was loading tails into the freezers which were kept at minus 23°C, and as I emerged with my beard crusted in ice, a young man with a halo of flaming red frizzy hair came up to me.

'Training for Greenland, are you?' He introduced himself as Bill Knudsen. He worked on a prawn-fishing boat that was due to leave for Godthåb in six weeks time, and word had got around that I was looking for a lift. Bill said he would ask the captain if I could come. He returned the next day, smiled and nodded. The answer was yes. It was my ticket to a faded name on a wrinkled map.

I was beginning to believe more and more in my luck and that if I put myself in a position where help was needed, it would usually come. Desperation, or even a simple indication of enthusiasm, has a facility for attracting success. At that particular moment I felt so happy that a smile just wasn't big enough to show it.

But the next day I was not smiling and the realisation of how delicate is the balance of fortune was brought home to me with brutal impact.

The sun rose as a red fireball, the way it does on any clear morning. It was a beautiful Saturday morning and I decided to go for a walk around the coast at Selatrad.

A farmer warned me that the path was only a muddy sheep-track and patches of snow made it dangerous. Saying that I would be careful, I thanked him and carried on. The sky promptly clouded over and it began to rain, so I put on a full set of oilskins and felt glad of my rubber boots. Soon high cliffs rose up on my right and the path traversed a slope of closely-cropped grass that fell away steeply from the base of these rock walls for fifty yards and then suddenly disappeared, plummeting vertically down to the sea.

One moment I was standing there admiring the view, and the next my feet had gone from under me and I was sliding down the slope on my back, very fast and out of control. I could do nothing – the oilskins and the smooth, sodden incline were perfectly matched for sliding. Panic-stricken, I turned onto my stomach. I remember feeling that my hands were incredibly strong, and my fingers spread out and became like iron claws – I desperately tried to dig them into the ground but they just raked the surface and cut into the turf without finding any hold. My terror mounted as my helplessness became more apparent. I turned over onto my back, tried to dig my heels in, tried to rip off my jacket and then, as I shot over a slight depression that might have slowed me down, my last hope had gone. I had fallen about twenty yards and was almost on a patch of snow that covered the final thirty yards, ending abruptly in a sheer drop of fifty feet to the rocks below. The edge was rushing ever closer and the snow would accelerate me over it in an instant.

Then a strange feeling came over me; I no longer felt afraid and my mind was suddenly filled with calmness, complacency and total acceptance of the inevitable. My life was finished, but death was coming without fear, without pain. Death was providing its own anaesthetic, numbing emotion and yet allowing thought to remain lucid. Events seemed to slow down as past, present and future merged into a confusion of images flashing through my mind, removing me from reality, detaching me from this frail superfluous body, still falling . . . The newspapers, how would they report this accident? . . . Peace . . . The echo of a farmer's warning . . . A Scotsman, 25, working in the Faroes. . . Snow . . . They say the idiot was wearing oilskins when they found him . . . Floating, weightless. . . Was I found dead, or dying? . . . They say he was just out for a walk . . . Closer . . . My parents, what'll my parents think? . . . Born Edinburgh, 9/3/54, a brother for J . . . Not far now . . . They? Who's they? . . . By letter, or telegram? . . . At Selatrad . . . Tears . . . Must have slipped . . . Why *him*? . . . Oh, shit, I've really messed it up . . .

Had there been a recent frost then the snow would have proved lethal, but it was thawing, wet and heavy – and my saving grace. The snow piled up under my legs and brought me to a halt just ten yards from the edge. In disbelief I let my head relax and sink back, closing my eyes and letting out a long sigh that released some of the tension in my body, thanking an unknown God that I was still alive. Several minutes passed and then adrenalin surged up and seized my body in the uncontrollable shakes of delayed shock. My forty-yard fall had only lasted about twelve seconds, although it had felt like minutes, but it was hard to believe that my body could change so quickly from a relaxed, peaceful state to one where the muscles were knotted with tension and shaking wildly.

After recovering sufficiently to get to my feet, I carefully made my way back up the slope to the deep scars, three yards long, which my locked fingers had torn in the turf, and slowly began retracing my steps along the path, not daring to look down to the sea that had fascinated me moments earlier. Then it happened once more. This time it was a shorter slide but again I felt the same panic, acquiescence and shock.

To have come so close to death twice within five minutes was as much as my nerves could stand. When I reached the safety of the road, my energy was gone and I felt exhausted. Tears suddenly welled up in my eyes. I couldn't hold them back, and I began to cry. Tears ran down my cheeks, silent tears of which I was not ashamed. They were the tears which others had been spared in sorrow, the tears of relief and of reawakened joy. I looked around me and for the second time in my existence, I experienced the gift of life.

A school bus gave me a lift home and I told the driver about my fall. He recalled that two years previously a Dutchman had gone missing and after a massive search, his partially decomposed body was found at the bottom of cliffs in another part of Eysturoy. He had been dead for two or three months but nobody knew if he had died instantly or had suffered a lingering death from his injuries. I returned home feeling very vulnerable, very humble and extremely grateful that my route had not ended with a small cross on the cliffs of Selatrad.

A month later, Bill showed me our boat for Greenland. *Westaland* was one quarter of the size of the mackerel boat and was a toy in comparison. Twelve of us were going amongst icebergs and across one of the world's roughest seas to Greenland, in *that*? Bill saw my dismay.

'She's a good boat,' he chortled. But his words seemed to have the same ring about them as 'fine weather'. A good boat, yes, but they said that about the *Titanic* as well. My thoughts went unspoken. A weak smile forced some enthusiasm from a mind that held a vision of rampant nausea.

Delay after delay followed with our departure always imminent but never taking place and I began to suspect that *Westaland* was welded to the jetty. After ten days she proved me wrong and three long mournful blasts of her horn sounded as we cast off, leaving a huddle of figures waving goodbye at our deserted mooring. Soon our wake trailed behind us like a streamer holding loved ones together. It broke, and Torshavn slipped slowly away into the distance.

Goodbyes are an intrinsic part of travelling and the saddest part of a wanderer's lot. He learns to accept the constant string of severed friendships and incomplete acquaintances as well as to suffer the emptiness of departure and the uncertainty of ever meeting again. And yet goodbyes never become any easier. Each one takes a part of him with it, until he wonders if there will soon be anything left to give. This goodbye was no exception.

We passed along under those immense cliff walls and again I meekly gazed up at their rugged majesty, knowing that the charm and beauty of these Islands of Sheep were a part of that same everlasting that had shown how I myself, in comparison, was so pitifully insignificant, so horribly mortal.

3 · Sea-eagles off Greenland

Seagulls followed us, skimming low over the water, weaving in and out of the wave crests, occasionally trailing a lazy wing tip in the surf and appearing to fly from the sheer love of it all. *Westaland* chased the waves as they ran away from us, catching them up one by one, and tearful spray burst out beneath our bow. At eight and a half knots the bursts of spray seemed to tick off the paces of our 1,100 mile journey to Cape Farewell, the southernmost point of Greenland. It was a fine feeling.

Eric the Red, the father of Leif Ericsson whose statue stands in Reykjavik, is said to have given Greenland its name in the tenth century. He was expelled from Iceland for three years as a murderer and went to live in a land to the north-west. After his exile he returned to Iceland with the intention of bringing people back to start a settlement in this new land. He knew that if he described the ice and the harsh winter then no one would come, so he called it a 'green land' and evidently interested enough people! He was, in effect, an early estate agent.

For the first four days Eric was as far from my thoughts as the nearest piece of solid ground was from my feet, being the seabed at over five thousand feet below me. I had decided not to take any sea-sickness pills as they merely postponed what was inevitable and it seemed best to get the discomfort over with as soon as possible. The days were spent below deck preparing the nets and splicing heavily greased cables. I helped where it was possible and tried not to get in the way where it wasn't, while struggling in waves of dizziness and vomiting. My misery was exacerbated by the pungent stench of desiccated fish scraps that was vented with each movement of the old net, until the atmosphere became suffocating. It was grim trying to be brave when I just wanted to surrender – but my sea legs gradually developed, the sickness slowly passed and my pallid cheeks reverted to their ruddy glow. Then I felt well enough to sit at the table and watch my cornflakes slop from side to side in the bowl and my potatoes and peas roll off the plate to join everyone else's in a mixed-vegetable bagatelle. It was as good a way as any of getting to know the rest of the crew.

Otmer, the skipper, had the calm efficient manner that is the mark of a true professional, coping with the rough as easily as the amateur copes with the smooth. Nothing was beyond him and he was always ready to supply a solution, and a joke to help it along. Eysen was the first mate. His roar of laughter came straight from his pot-belly, and this was its primary function. The second mate, Kal, who reminded me of Mole in *The Wind in the Willows* with his snub nose and short strong arms, could turn his hand to anything. He put his weight to best advantage behind a spanner and kept the others enthralled with his stories which he acted out at the same time, once kicking his feet in the air to illustrate a point over the breakfast table. The first engineer, Samson (a risky name but fortunately he was well built), spoke no English but smiled and so was multi-lingual. The cook did a good job on the whole (and on the whale, which we ate occasion-ally) despite his feelings of sea sickness; these may have been caused by his cakes which were a weak point. Bill called them 'a cook's Achilles cakes' as he enjoyed tongue-twisters, which the cakes certainly were.

Bill was a deckhand, incorporating the best of all the others, and he remains the most dynamic character of all my travels. Darning wool came as easily to him as welding metal, the cold left him untouched and his friendship was as generous as his sense of humour was rich. He had sailed the world in merchant ships and he had caught penguins in the Falklands to take back to a British circus. He understood the sing-song lilt of Swedish, the throaty warble of Danish and could get by in Icelandic, which falls somewhere in-between. His English was almost flawless, and he also spoke a little of the Greenland language which is verbal shrapnel with every second letter being a *t*, *d*, *k* or *q*.

'There are not so many words in Greenland,' he explained, and then he spread his hands as wide apart as an unsuccessful angler, 'but they are all this long.'

And there was Gunnor, the most notable of the three other deckhands. A born survivor who had escaped unhurt from at least two ships that had been abandoned at sea, and, with slight injuries, from a plane crash that had killed seven people. He was a virtuoso in sign-language, and had a remarkable collection of tattoos on his arms. Amongst them was the name 'Kristina' which he was going to get made inconspicuous as a rose. In classic tradition, that romance had ended and he was engaged to another girl. He ate vegetable soup with three large spoonfuls of sugar. Perhaps Kristina did not.

It was indeed a good ship and a good crew. But soon there would be goodbyes as it had been arranged that I would be dropped off at Godthåb when *Westaland* took on final supplies for her long fishing trip. Greenland would still be deep in winter. The icebergs were becoming more numerous by the day and the nets had been secured off the ground to prevent them from freezing to the deck. Otmer looked out of the window.

'I certainly hate to have to put you out at Godthåb in this,' he said, as hail lashed our deck with violent percussion.

'Och! I'll be all right,' I said, thinking how much I was going to hate *having* to be put out in this. Would Greenland prove to be just too ambitious for a one-man expedition at this time of year? I was about to find out.

A week after leaving the Faroes my name was called out over the loudspeaker. The crew regarded me as a bit of an eccentric as I was always photographing fish and things which to them seemed very ordinary. I used the empty prawn cooker as a temporary aquarium to keep some of the stranger fish that came up in the trial run of our net. One of these was the lumpsucker which was a small round ball of spikes that clamped itself to any object with a disc on its side and frequently floated up to the surface to blow miniature fountains into the air. Skates were also much more entertaining than goldfish and I collected thirty-nine of them before Otmer decided he wanted the aquarium back as a cooker. When frightened they would first curl up into a ball like a hedgehog and then suddenly swim off, gliding gracefully through the water by oscillating their wings in ripples of perfect symmetry. There was the Irish Lord whose mottled colours were dazzling, and catfish with jaws like gintraps which I was told could remove a man's finger. It was quite a kettle of fish.

So I was always called whenever anything of unusual interest appeared. This time I rushed up on deck to see a black shape swimming on the surface and frolicking in the waves as only fifteen tons of whale can frolic in such icy waters; rolling over to let a flipper gently smack the surface, and lifting its tail up into the air to spread the flukes wide like a fan as it performed a series of shallow dives. With a final snort of condensation it sounded, and left me wondering how anyone could bring himself to aim an explosive-headed harpoon at such playful innocence.

Suddenly I noticed land on the horizon that had been empty for so long, and ahead of me lay the world's largest island, comprising an area that was almost the size of Europe, and five-sixths permanent ice – the land of the Greenlander, Kalaallit Nunaat.

There was an endless chain of mountains that time and ice had flattened, sharpened, truncated, squashed and finally quarried to rubble. Each bore its own hallmark; of scree, ravines, cliffs, the pockmarks of corries or an array of needles to quicken the blood of a climber. It was as if the panorama had been simplified into sharply delineated forms, being either snow, black rock or sea for as far as the eye could see until the distant shades of hazy blue. There were no houses and no signs of life to say that man had ever set foot on those formidable mountains. Their primordial wildness sparkled in the clarity of the cold air and I shuddered involuntarily, for there was something harsh and unforgiving about their beauty. It was my first view of Greenland, and there wasn't a hint of green anywhere.

The next day we reached Færingehavn, an Arctic filling station for ships, dominated by ugly tanks of diesel marked 'Polaroil', an abandoned fish factory and the names of hundreds of ships painted on the rocks as multi-coloured crosswords.

The policeman was drunk, drunk as an Irish Lord. His duties had largely deserted him since the closure of the factory two years earlier, but he was also the harbour-master and it was to exercise this capacity that he came out to greet us, as he had greeted every ship for the last twenty-five years. He stopped, tried to pull his trousers up over his bulging stomach and finally had to let them find their own level as he bent his small frame into the wind that blew off the sea carrying horizontal showers of snow and sleet. He struggled on towards us, all the time puffing out his cheeks and noisily releasing his trapped breath as sudden schnapps of steam.

The thought of this factory as it had once been, with the activity of machines, people and boats, enhanced the impression of loneliness as I gazed at its neglect. The only movement came from bits of net and sacks flapping in the wind – and that old man had spent twenty-five years in this place . . . No wonder he drank.

There was a small shop, here in the middle of nowhere, with a quaint doorchime in case some ocean freighter should drop in unnoticed. We unloaded supplies for the base and then decided to stay the night. The policeman invited us over to his house that evening to watch a film, a far-fetched adventure that was a welcome change from my own. The hero, a dog, had just routed an entire cavalry on his own and in the final scene he stopped to lift his leg on a cactus before wandering off into a desert sunset. It seemed a strange contrast to this land and I wondered how he would fare here amongst the snow and ice, where there was no vegetation for the relief of a hero.

The following day we made for Godthåb, and I was preparing to leave when events took another turn and changed my plans again. Kal, the second mate, fell on a sharp piece of metal and cut his arm so badly that most of the tendons and muscles were severed. Otmer radioed a doctor who gave advice on what to do and the ambulance was waiting for us on arrival. We went to visit him in hospital later the same afternoon and heard that he was to be flown to Denmark for special treatment. He accepted the blow with cheerful resignation. The skipper was deep in thought and, for once, his face was serious. He turned to me.

'We're a man short now – will you stay on and work for us?'

I looked at Kal, embarrassed at the thought of taking advantage of his misfortune.

'Come on, one man dead is another man's bread,' said Bill, and Kal roared with laughter. I slowly nodded my agreement.

'But I'm afraid I won't be much of a replacement for your second mate.'

A smile returned to Otmer's face as he looked me in the eye.

'Och! You'll be all right,' he mimicked.

Godthåb was the same size as Torshavn and played the same role. The following day, Queen Margrethe of Denmark was officially giving Greenland its semi-independence. (They called her 'Dronning Margrethe' which I had assumed was a reference to her speeches but Bill pointed out that *dronning* means 'queen.') No one seemed particularly taken with the event except a group of children who were rolling around on the red carpet outside the Hotel Grønlands. The Danish, who constitute about one-sixth of the population of fifty thousand, perform certain skilled and professional services. While working here they avoid Danish income tax. They are not popular amongst the locals. 'FREE GREENLAND . . .' protested some graffiti on a wall (and a less politically-minded hand had added, '. . . take away the pack ice.').

Greenland's house-building philosophy is bewildering. If some awkward-shaped boulders cannot be found to build the house against, between or (ideally) on top of, then it must reluctantly be placed on flat ground. The country is fortunately well endowed with asymmetrical boulders and so the little one- or two-roomed houses crown the tops of rocks everywhere with their nice garish colours. Godthåb contained a cinema, a post office with no sign, bars, supermarkets selling fresh fruit and Dundee marmalade, motorbikes and a surprising number of cars. The harbour was packed with boats of all sizes and descriptions. For a country whose towns are spaced out at roughly two-hundred-mile intervals without a single connecting road or track, boats are as much an essential means of transport as they are a hobby and a way of life. Alternative ways of getting about are the expensive helicopter service or, in winter, dog-sleds.

There wasn't time to learn more as we left Godthåb to head for the fishing grounds. Our net was ready; fifty yards of nylon that came in orange, bright green, dark green, faded green and cowpat brown. In many respects it was a marine version of a see-through kilt and it needed the same kilt-maker's tradition and skill to put it together and to keep it that way.

Evening found us in the icefields of the Holsteinsborg Banks, lying sixty miles off the coast. We steamed slowly through narrow channels of water between thick crusts of ice that covered a vast area and slowly turned pink in the setting sun. The sea was deep blue even at that late hour and flat calm, sheltered by the natural breakwaters. Later it began to freeze and our boat cut a path through the thin ice, leaving a trail that was visible for a long way behind us – and amongst these pinks and blues of the Arctic lustre, we lowered our net eight hundred feet to hunt for prawns.

A prawn fisherman! I didn't even know what a live prawn looked like.

I soon learnt. The process was relatively simple. We trawled our net along the bottom for two or three hours, hauled it up, emptied the catch and put it straight down again. This would go on day and night for two months. The laden pouch end of the net was hoisted above our stern and a special knot was undone to release the catch into a tank of water. Here it was sorted and anything that was not prawn was scooped out, usually to be eaten by hundreds of gulls which appeared at this time with uncanny precision. Red Fish (also called Soldier Fish) were the most common and the change in pressure caused these deep-sea redcoats to come up with eyes bulging, tongues bloated and mouths extended wide open as if in a silent scream.

Below deck the prawns passed over vibrating bars, the smaller ones falling through to be thrown out while the large ones were collected in trays and moved along to my former aquarium. Prawns must be alive when they are cooked so the pull of a lever sent ninety pounds of them to a sudden death and four minutes boiling, where they changed from translucent red to milky pink. Then they were rinsed, dried, quick-frozen, weighed, boxed and stacked up in the freezer-hold.

From a prawn fisherman's diary

We have been split up into two shifts, six hours on and six off. The cook wakes me at 6 a.m. Go to wash – miss the first basin as it has no plug, miss the second as the tap is stiff and use the third one, but gently as it has a powerful jet that knocks your toothpaste off the brush. Throw some water into my face but it's so cold I let most of it slip through my fingers. A good breakfast as they eat well here. Porridge. I'm the only one to put salt on and the cook always stares at me. Salami, spreads, fruit and jam, but we have to eat well as our heat loss must be enormous. It's a good excuse anyway.

On with my waders and I meet Bill coming off work. 'Morning,' he says healthily, 'how are you? Fresh as a sea-eagle, eh?' It's a lovely image but personally I feel closer to the dodo. The net is coming up so I go on deck to help out. It's the best job as the cold wakes me and the icefields are fascinating. I pull on ropes and the freezing water runs through my woollen mittens. Rubber gloves are useless and wool is the only answer, keeping your hands warm even when soaked.

Soon I have to go down to the small room in the bow for my normal job of freezing, weighing, packing and storing. This boat used to be a salmon-netter but was converted for prawns and as such is very cramped with all the extra machinery. Most prawn boats have 32 mm. of metal to keep the water out but we only have 9 mm. and as the ice scrapes past, the noise is unnerving.

The bands that go around the boxes have to be stapled shut with a manual tool that has a strong spring but I'm getting used to it and must be developing a vicious handshake. Soon my mind wanders as I work like an automaton. It's better that way and when you stop to concentrate you usually just mess it up. I come across a white prawn. Do you get albino crustaceans? Maybe this one is just a bit off-colour. We all have our off-days, and this batch of prawns certainly aren't having a good one.

Thorgjald comes down to help. He is second engineer and loads the staples in upside-down which possibly explains his rank. He's the odd one out on board as he is always sneaking off to avoid work – not easy on a small boat but he has it down to a fine art. Maybe if I'd spent thirty years at sea I'd do the same. His English is patchy and he tells me a story about a girl he once met and how he was going to take her out to the pictures but ended up on a bowling-green. There is a joke in it somewhere but he always misses out vital bits of information and I'm presented with an incomplete jigsaw of phrases. I go through all the possible meanings, puns and innuendos but still fail to decipher it. And yet I laugh when he laughs as I appreciate his effort and don't want to hurt his feelings.

We go up in turns for a quick coffee. There is a box of 'Carr's Table Water English Crackers' on a shelf and the word 'Crackers' looks ridiculous on such a de luxe box. Hasn't anyone thought up a euphemism for it yet? My gaze, trying to find something new in a claustrophobic world, settles on my hands. They are so cut and cracked they look like an aerial photograph of parched earth in a drought. The cook has optimistically left out a plate of cakes. They too are drought-stricken and under a false name. I'm tired but it's back to work. The hours go by so slowly when we work and so fast when we have to sleep.

Then they shout for me to stand in at the cooker for a while. I feel slightly criminal killing all those prawns but you get used to it. I open the lid, forgetting to switch on the overhead fan, and everything disappears in steam. The buzzer goes to tell me to give the prawns a stir, a gentle stir, they say. How is it possible to be gentle with a standard roadmender's shovel for a spoon? Then the cook puts on taped music. We have no control over the loudspeakers so have to suffer his choice, which is like his cakes. All he ever plays is *Country Favourites*, and *Clementine* has worn my endurance to breaking-point.

My relief comes at last. A quick bite to eat. Funny – am not even tempted by the prawns now whereas my first few days I was eating them all the time. Straight to bed and leave my clothes in a heap where they fall. The net is coming up. The engine changes pitch, the winches moan and minutes later all the hardware of the net is clanking along the deck. It's an infernal noise, as if we are passing under a waterfall of nuts, bolts and scrap metal. Peace. Then it all happens again as the net goes back out. How the hell am I expected to get to sleep? I'll be up in four and a half hours . . . but then my mind goes blank and I sleep the sleep of the grateful dead.

'Wake up, Sea-Eagle!' Again? So soon? Sometimes I feel inadequate. I go up for breakfast and find it's supper, and another half-day begins . . .

It was hard work but with many rewarding experiences. Sometimes I used to sacrifice my sleeping time just to watch the midnight sun – when the sun set and rose without disappearing and the sea reflected the black clouds in their ever-changing kaleidoscope of patterns as they moved across the blazing sky. Or else I would stay up to photograph a strange fish, converting the tackle-room into a studio, and infuriating the cook once when I borrowed a glass shelf from the fridge. It was ideal for a squid to sit on and while I was focusing on its brilliant emerald-green eye, it became bashful and gradually turned itself inside-out.

One day a small bird landed on the boat and Gunnor took it down to the warmth of the kitchen. It was exhausted but refused any food and stood on a piece of sacking, tucked its head in and tried to sleep –

just a weightless ball of fluff that expanded and contracted with each breath. An hour later it fell over, dead. Gunnor threw it overboard and a seagull gulped it down before it had even hit the water.

The crew always tried to include me in conversations and Bill taught me some Faroese. Once he appeared with a hermit crab. 'It's called a *krabbakjogga*,' he explained, 'and you're one too. It has its house on its back and we use the same word for a backpacker.' His explanation was interrupted by the news on the radio. He listened for a moment, lowered the *krabbakjogga* and turned to me.

'Did you understand that?'

'No – was it something to do with the elections in Britain?'

'Yes. The Conservatives won. Margaret Thatcher is to become the first man in Britain.'

It was not all plain sailing and we ran into a week of problems. Our net came up empty or only with weed or sponge, and once, so full of red fish that we couldn't get the net on board and Otmer had to slash a hole to spill the unwanted catch. The prawns had vanished. He smiled bravely and every day said, 'maybe tomorrow . . .' We moved to a new area where things got worse. We brought up rocks that tore the net – we changed to the spare, repaired the damage and then up came the spare net torn. Every cast produced a torn net that meant endless changes and endless repairs. Then a cable broke, straining the remaining one until it too gave way and seven thousand pounds' worth of net was lost. We trawled the area for several hours with a hook but never found it.

And the cold – the air temperature was well below zero and the chill factor reduced it still further. During one bad period, when we had all worked four consecutive shifts without sleep, mostly on deck mending the nets in fingerless gloves, we experienced the coldest spell. Repairs were meticulous and every torn square was accounted for and replaced with special knots. Holes were sometimes enlarged to make a more convenient shape, knots were carefully cut to sever only one strand, and nylon cord of various strengths was used in fourteen different combinations, each having its own proper place.

The net froze on the winch and ice formed on it the moment it left the water. Every so often one of us would drop his work and leap up and down, swinging his arms in circles to slap his back violently and although it looked absurd, it was very effective but only if done vigorously. We worked hard and as a team, driven by the common urge to fill the hold. There was always someone to crack a joke and each one seemed to raise the temperature and ease the strain. But no one smiled as our faces were so cold that the muscles of expression refused to work. Our beards were frozen over and the cold chilled us to the marrow, until at last we went down below for coffee. We had to feel for our mouth to know where to tilt our mug and no one said anything for ten minutes until our faces regained some colour and some control in a fever of pins and needles. I understood then why prawn cocktails are always an expensive *à la carte*.

Tomorrow finally came, the jinx departed and soon we were back amongst the prawns. They flooded our decks and work became frantic to keep up with the heavy catches. Tempers became frayed and stress set in, until, suddenly, it was all over. The packing room had been filled as well as the hold and then the last box was being stamped in under the trapdoor. After two months at sea we returned to land at Holsteinsborg.

Greenland girls are pretty. Brown eyes, jet-black silky hair and their skin has a healthy dark tan. Like their landscape there is a wild beauty about them that excites the hunter. There was, however, no need for *Westaland* or her crew to do any more hunting and the girls were waiting for our arrival on the pier. Not professionals, but just girls out to find free drink, a good time and a different crew. They were soon all over our boat and the inevitable party began.

There was one girl who, they said, had been around for as long as *Westaland* and she could reel off the vital statistics of every crew member for the last nine years. I was warned to be on my guard for she had evidently left many an early-morning bed empty, as empty as the owner's wallet. She made a pathetic figure as she did the rounds of men but her flattery won no admirers. She overacted her theatrical manner in a way that failed to conceal her insincerity. Her laughter did not disguise the true colours of her character, her pleasantries were simply flags of convenience and her intimate gestures were the semaphore of artifice. She was past her best years and knew what that meant in a harsh climate where the aging process starts early and accelerates quickly. But drink, the great postponer, was flowing freely and soon she had temporarily forgotten her worries in an alcoholic haze, and a corner, of her own.

The revelry continued all night and I thought back to the small bird that had been eaten by the gull. Here in the frozen North it seemed that love, like life, had no sentimental meaning but merely a calorific value. But for those that had been cold, it was some party.

The next day *Westaland* sailed for home and again she was one man short. A pensive figure with a backpack at his feet stood alone on the pier. Through his mind passed vivid pictures; emerald-green eyes, endless trays of prawns, silhouettes against the midnight sun, ice and bitter cold, steaming hot mugs, determined faces and a savaged Clementine . . .

One *krabbakjogga* waved out to sea and somewhere out there on the thin line separating voids of ocean and space, ten sea-eagles waved back. Then I turned to face the mountains, and the challenge of how to travel eight hundred miles north of the Arctic Circle to try to find the real Greenland, the real Greenlander.

4 · The Land of the Greenlander

Alone again – and yet it was not an unpleasant feeling. The world around me appeared enormous after the confines of a boat so I set off up the road to explore it with a naïve enthusiasm that made my steps light and belittled the weight of the 'house' on my back. It was still heavy at forty-eight pounds, of which over half was photographic equipment.

The road was unsurfaced and as corrugated as a washboard but this did not deter the taxi-drivers in the least. It was expensive to import a car here and because they could only be used as a runabout within each isolated town, every car in Greenland was a taxi. One of these was an old Mercedes and it came kangarooing along, achieving short bursts of weary flight until a loud crunch of metal fatigue brought it to a sudden halt and caused a cloud of dust to envelop me. When it had cleared, a group of adults and a young child emerged and without even looking at the damage, all eight-and-one-quarter hailed a second car that was approaching. The driver was last to emerge and he glanced down at his broken rear-axle, aggressively kicked the bumper, twice, and then he too crammed himself into the other car. It set off slowly, working itself up with a series of cautious bounces and bronchial wheezes until its speed and confidence grew and it developed the bold mechanical hops that had just deserted the wreck beside me.

Holsteinsborg, the second in size, was the southerly limit of the 'dog towns'. Sledge dogs were only allowed here and in the towns to the north where they were used for the winter hunts of seals, birds and caribou which migrated closer to the coast at this time. Dogs were not considered essential in the south where there was little hunting, and had latterly been banned altogether because strays were a constant menace. A team consisted of between eight and twelve dogs and as both father and son usually had a team of their own, it was common to see over twenty dogs outside every house. They were tethered to a long length of chain and sat out the inactive summer months amongst a quagmire of mess. Further north some

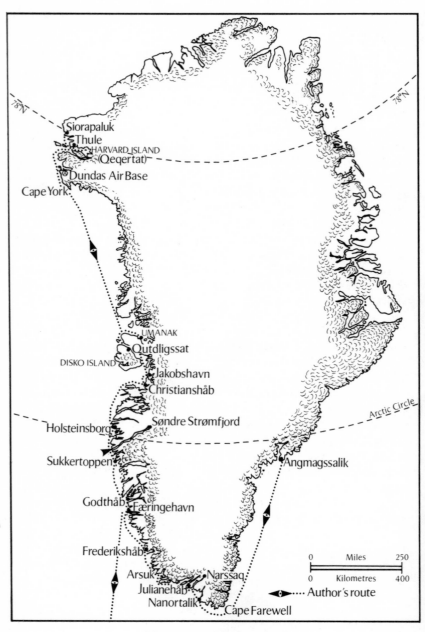

My route round Greenland

families each had their own small rocky island where they marooned their dogs every summer, visiting them periodically to throw them raw meat or fish. I passed a group lying on bare rock, all except a small flossy puppy that was curled up on top of the only clump of grass. Obviously it took time to harden up to the rigours of Greenland life.

Outside a store three old men sat posing as no-evil monkeys. See-no-evil had a wizened face that only just protruded above a high collar before disappearing into a cap that was too big, and was mostly hidden behind the huge dark glasses of a bygone vogue. His turned-down mouth suggested he had already seen too much evil and added to his aura of ill-fitting gloom. Speak-no-evil had a lovely smile and he eagerly posed his bent frame for a photograph. I used a wide-angle lens at a short distance, perhaps unfairly, as the distortion bent him just that little bit more. After I had thanked him with a '*guanakssuaq*' he hobbled off, sweeping each leg out in small semicircles as if the traditional thigh-length boot, the *kamik*, had done to him what the horse and saddle sore had done to the cowboy. Hear-no-evil appeared to be deaf and whistled loudly through broken teeth.

Inside the store everyone was buying fresh flowers which had newly arrived from Denmark and had been impassively dumped between off-the-peg sealskin jackets at £450 and a gift-wrapped accordion. A young shop assistant chatted to me, speaking fluent English in a country where it ranked a poor third behind their own distinct language, Eskimo, and Danish. He invited me to accompany him back to his flat for lunch.

The flats were rectangular wooden blocks on four levels and the architect responsible had either lacked imagination or a free hand but he clearly had not broken sweat over their design. Inside they were warm and comfortable and my friend, Epling, had hi-fi and every mod con. He spoke openly about Greenland.

They had the world's highest per capita consumption of alcohol. The average person over the age of fourteen drank two hundred bottles of beer each month. The Greenlander worked for a few days, mainly on boats or in fish factories, went off to drink his wages and returned when the money ran out. In a few weeks drink rationing was to be introduced, allocating each adult seventy-two points per month; a bottle of beer would be one point, spirits would be twelve.

(His laugh became a sigh. 'They say we will soon know who our neighbours are because we will all be at home, and for once we will be sober.')

Denmark had tried. Within twenty years of making Greenland a welfare state she had changed it from being a country with endemic tuberculosis, abysmal housing conditions, poor education and in-adequate or non-existent systems of transport and communications. Now they even had cable television. (He switched it on. A list of 670 names in alphabetical order moved up and out of the screen and continued for ten minutes. This was an attempt to embarrass those who had fallen behind on their rental payments. Judging from the numbers it seemed more embarrassing to have been omitted.)

But Epling saw Denmark's contribution as verging on ethnocide. The physical lifestyle of the people had been changed too quickly. Their thoughts and attitudes had been overtaken and now lay stranded a generation or more behind. Denmark had created a trade and transport monopoly, developed her mining interests and offered the people Tuborg Lager instead of tuberculosis. 'Their policy of assimilation has been without regard for our culture, trying to make us into a less degrading step-brother rather than helping us to establish our status as a proud nation with a unique tradition.' It was an argument I was to hear again later from the North American Indian, the Aborigine and, to a lesser degree, the Maori – where combinations of greed and some genuine concern for welfare had left the indigenous people demoralised, poor, dependent and without an identity.

Epling had been to university in Denmark. He was a qualified dentist but worked as a shop assistant. It was his personal protest. As a Greenlander his salary was linked to their lesser economy, and his earnings would be half those of the Danish dentist working here alongside him. He saw himself and his people as second-class citizens in their own country. (His views were extreme but they were also widespread. Denmark had made mistakes, but merited more credit than was usually given. It was easy to be wise with hindsight, I thought – but you still shouldn't complain about farmers with your mouth full.)

I asked if there was anything left of 'old Greenland' and the Eskimos. He corrected me. They were called *Inuit* now. It means 'real men,' and their language is also known by this name. 'You should try to get up to Thule, but don't expect too much. The Inuit still hunt with a harpoon but they have central heating and fridges, and may learn karate like the rest of the world.' He wished me luck and we parted.

At the office of the KGH (Kongelige Grønlandske Handel), the Royal Greenland Trade Department who run the monopoly on all transport and supply ships (and expect ten per cent of each cargo to be stolen), they said the first boat to Thule would leave in three weeks. There was a ferry that afternoon heading north as far as Jakobshavn. When it left at 4 p.m. I was on it, straining to find my destination on a highly stylised sketch map which kept the secret to itself.

It was a mysterious country, full of simple contrasts and striking similarities, wide open to misinterpretation and encouraging back-handed compliments. One-sixth of the population were Danes, five-sixths were native Greenlanders. And one-sixth of Greenland was free of ice.

Figs are good travelling companions. The taste leaves me impartial but the seeds get stuck in my teeth and provide hours of entertainment trying to dislodge them; just the thing for the long journey it turned out to be. When we reached Jakobshavn the following afternoon two fishing boats pulled out at the same time. The one heading north was covered in flags and balloons, with people singing and cheering on the deck. The one heading south slipped quietly and unobtrusively around the nearest headland. They were evidently two football teams returning home after meeting halfway for an important game. The north had won.

It was hard to see where any level ground for a pitch could be found, but I made my way through the usual collection of houses perched in impossible positions and surrounded by dogs, and walked a few miles down the coastline to the icefjord. The sight of the most active glacier in this hemisphere left me both physically and mentally breathless; the bay was filled with a conglomeration of ice shapes rising to three hundred feet above the sea's surface for five miles across its width. The glacier advanced thirty-three yards each day (more than the Swiss ones move in a year) and annually calved seventy-eight million tons of icebergs into the sea. (I met a party of scientists, Grønlands Geologiske Undersøgelse, who were counting them.) Every few minutes there was the sharp report like the daily one o'clock gun salute from Edinburgh Castle as the offspring fell away from the main body of ice, slowly creaking, groaning and jostling in discomfort.

I pitched my tent overlooking this awesome panorama and sat on the world's most beautiful campsite. And in my deep contentment I felt sadness. Must life always contain this element of dualism, where the opposites go hand in hand and extremes flow so easily from one to the other? The peak of joy was mined with sorrow and one vital step separated the highwires of strength and weakness. We were not allowed to remain still. Emotions were a flux with dividing lines that could disappear, making it possible to be so deep within one realm and then suddenly to have crossed into the depths of its opposite. I was filled with melancholic happiness. All this beauty and privilege seemed too much for one person to bear alone. A pleasure shared was a pleasure doubled – but there was no one to share it with me. It was obvious that I had not yet come to terms with loneliness.

Nor with the mosquitos. It was a surprise to find them here at all but they thrived in the swampy ground and were colossal. They were non-malarial but it was only in such negative terms that one could say anything good about them. Certain fossil studies have shown that they were even more numerous in the past and there is a theory that this may account for the mysterious and sudden departure of the Vikings from Greenland. The mosquitos were hell-hounds with a bite much worse than their bark. Quick, persistent and bold, they displayed no sense of fairness in where or when to bite. Even the less skilful exacted a final irritation by perishing as a bloody smear on my skin or by falling into my tea. Yet I had to admire their ability to fly up a flapping trouser-leg while the occupant was walking along. They made camping miserable and each morning my face felt like a bean-bag while rows of mosquitos rested on my tent walls with the successful smiles of the well-to-do. It was certainly no place for a kilt.

The next few days were spent trying to get some special pictures of my tent. It had been given to me by Vango, a Scottish manufacturer, on condition that I would send back photographs of it in dramatic settings. There were certainly plenty of those here but low cloud shrouded the hills and ruined the backgrounds. I imagined

God up there putting the finishing touches to the mountain-tops and, rather like an impatient Pope waiting for Michelangelo to finish painting the ceiling, I hoped it would not take much longer. When the shroud was raised, the landscapes were spectacular but I soon found that there was a practical campsite and a photogenic one and the two seldom coincided. The photogenic sites involved erecting the tent on the edge of cliffs, over rocks, in partial bogs and on attractive windswept ridges – simply to fit it into the right setting. After pitching and striking camp six or seven times each day and spending much time trying to eradicate every crease and wrinkle, at last I was satisfied. Several months later Vango replied:

Dear Alastair,
    On the whole your trannies are excellent and I will be using some of them. If you will forgive a little constructive criticism, note the following:
1) Several shots have a magnificent background but the tent is very small. I sell tents, not icebergs . . .

Sometimes it's hard to win. But it was a good tent. (Other people do actually sell icebergs. Carrying a guarantee of being several thousand years old, inland ice is exported to North America for those extra-special cocktails. But this ice does in fact have a different molecular structure and gives off an angry 'fizz' in the glass at its premature thaw.)

As I was walking back to town over an area of rocks, my lenscap fell off and disappeared down a hole. I reached deep into it and suddenly recoiled in shock as I found myself looking into the eyeless socket of a skull. While staring this grim guardian of my lenscap in what had once been the face, my hand guddled around in the dark area of what had once been his knees, and then someone coughed. Two local women stood gazing solemnly at me and one slowly shook her head in reproachful disgust. I withdrew my hand, smiled weakly and pointed at my exposed lens but the task of explaining the situation in sign language was beyond me. Just as they seemed convinced I was callously rearranging the bones of their great-grandfather to pose him for the camera, I managed to locate the lenscap and held it up triumphantly. One muttered something and the other spat on the ground and they went off, leaving me lying in

Jakobshavn's historical cemetery, still holding up the lenscap like the brandmark of a graverobber.

It was in Jakobshavn post office that there was a notice about the Aussivik. This was the traditional cultural festival of the Green-landers. Each year they used to come from all over the country for a week of singing, talking and just to meet old friends. It was a small affair now but that year it was to be held nearby at Qutdligssat. It was said to be a special place, and a boat was leaving that same afternoon.

The town was on Disko Island and the little boat took ten hours to get there. It was an uncomfortable journey in the choppy sea and having to sit under the hostile stare of two great-granddaughters.

Qutdligssat was built on stony moorland that descended in a steep but smooth curve from a high craggy-edged plateau which, even at the end of July, was still heavy with snow. It comprised perhaps two square miles of rust, decay and dilapidation for this former coal-mining town was now dead and silent. Except for these two weeks in the year.

The settlement was created in the 1920s and grew to become one of the larger towns in Greenland with two thousand inhabitants. Its pretty setting was an impractical site from which to transport the coal, with unusually shallow water and frequent adverse winds, and when the coalmine's profitability began to decline, the Danish administration decided to abandon it. This meant closing the town as well for there was no alternative source of employment. The inhabitants were given three years' notice to leave and where poss-ible were rehoused in the town of their choice, but the people felt betrayed and the whole affair became a bitter source of resentment against the Danish. The emotional departures continued until 1972 when the last people left and the town was bought privately for scrap.

When we arrived I wandered amongst the houses that were scattered in random disorder; some were undamaged except for a door hanging from broken hinges, others were missing certain sections and crying out for nails and a few had given up altogether and had collapsed. It looked as if everyone had left in a hurry with a chaos of letters, plans and receipts strewn about the offices. The store was littered with rubbish although brand-new spare parts still lay on the shelves. The two mine entrances were outside the town, cut horizontally into the hillside. A gentle push sent a skip running smoothly along the rails to come to a halt at a junction damaged by the intentional rockfall that had blocked both tunnels. The burial ground was nearby, indistinguishable from the rest of the hillside except for its simple white crosses and abundance of faded plastic flowers – and this, paradoxically, was the only part of the town that did not sadden me with its lifelessness.

Several hundred young Greenlanders arrived over the next few days and filled the town with vitality once more. There were meetings and discussions and then in the evenings they played music on whistles, skin drums and electric guitars, fired by the noisy generators they had brought as well. They sang on until well into the nights.

I left before the end and on the way back to Jakobshavn my thoughts returned to the night before the Aussivik had begun. I had wandered into the empty meeting-room and was astonished to see the words of a song written by an untidy hand, in English, pinned to the wall. I stood under the skeleton of a hunting kayak hanging from a beam and by the light of the midnight sun I read the following:

The Saga of Qutdligssat

The Danish came to Qutdligssat
hoping for black gold
They dug the mine through ice and snow
not caring for the cold
They've left here now there's nothing here
the miners are no more
Gone to Godthåb, Jakobshavn
to look for work once more

The work was hard the hours were long
trying to make it pay
But with no harbour near at hand
how's the coal to be got away?
By barge to ship they ferried it
to be taken to the South
To Godthåb town and Jakobshavn
and the places round about

Though the miners worked so hard
their efforts were all in vain
In the sixties the experts spoke
and then the decision came
Close the pit and close the town
the people shall move away
to Godthåb town and Jakobshavn
to live for the rest of their days

The town is bare and empty now
the people have gone away
The church the last remaining link
will soon be on its way
Qutdligssat has paid the price
the Danish lust for gold
Broken homes and broken lives
a town that has no soul

Tes
Miki

(I found the church two days later – it had been re-erected in Jakobshavn.)

The young people at the festival represented mainly the political left. Amongst these ruins of the past which, however uncharitably, they saw as a fitting symbol of their unhappy association with Denmark, they sought hope for complete independence. Their ideas were blatantly impractical but they called their land Kalaallit Nunaat, the land of the Greenlander – and it was obvious that they were thirsting to have it back.

'Nø. Nø røøm.'

'There must be a place in deck-class, isn't there?'

'Løøk.' Scandinavians had adopted this abrupt, self-deleting mannerism. 'The ferry is føøl. Bøøked up før twø weeks. Løng waiting list. Nø røøm.'

The news at the KGH office was depressing. In a few days the first boat up to Thule would leave direct from Holsteinsborg and the only ferry that would get me there in time was føøl. The helicopter service was also fully booked. Somehow I had to get onto that boat.

When it duly arrived, my plan was to try to scramble aboard in the confusion when those waiting to meet friends usually stormed the barriers. Fortunately they obliged and I was in the first wave of welcoming arms to reach the side of the ship but when they stopped, I carried on enthusiastically and managed to nip over the handrail. On rounding the second corner I walked into a ship's officer and was simultaneously grabbed from behind by the purser who had spotted me. He demanded my ticket. I replied in French. This had the desired effect of being incomprehensible and lessened the anger with which he ordered me off. Making my way despondently and slowly back to the gangway I suddenly found myself alone. No one was escorting me. This was the only boat . . . A swift glance around showed an empty corridor so I disappeared into the first door, only to confront some of the crew in their quarters.

'. . . er, *excusez-moi* . . .' but this time my spontaneous schoolboy French only offered me pens of aunts on tables, until the third repetition of 'loo-keeng' provided the inspiration; '. . .for zee W C. Oui, zat eeze what je loo-keeng for.' I added an asinine grin.

The nearest sailor screwed his face up into a frown and directed me to a door at the end of the passage. To my delight there was a lock-up inside that was not missing the bottom twelve inches of door, thus ensuring complete privacy, and so I just locked myself up. Two hours till departure. Two hours to survive. What the hell does one do in a public lavatory for two whole hours?

My first look in the mirror for some time revealed that my beard needed a trim. I did a painstaking job with a penknife, then tried to compose some poetry, attempted to decode the Danish graffiti on the walls and finally sat down to write some letters – while all the time imagining the entire ship being alerted to look for me and wondering how to talk my way out of this one, in French, with a British passport.

Over the next hour the doorhandle was tried fifteen times until the dreaded jingle of keys came and the door was unlocked from the outside. Fortunately the embarrassed cleaner apologised and went off but by then I felt my cover had been blown. I changed my clothes, put on a scarf, a woolly hat and dark glasses, trying to emulate an inconspicuous see-no-evil monkey, and went out on deck to mingle with the legal. There was a thick mist around us.

The air suddenly reverberated as the foghorn growled its low-pitched warning into the obscurity, sending a shiver down my spine and marking the end of my nail-biting wait. The ferry gently moved off with her stowaway undiscovered. But it was still impossible to relax. Would there be ticket checks during the voyage? Or at the other end? Were they looking for me? Should I confess? It was a nerve-racking journey but in lieu of being offered the price of a ticket, I was happy to pay the price of a conscience. I reached Holsteinsborg with a day to spare and walked off the boat undetected, although the purser directed a prolonged stare at the passenger who had apparently shrunk into a pile of winter clothing with the mild weather.

My tent was no sooner up on the outskirts of town when a local family approached and put up their tent alongside. They called me over and I saw that five adults had brought seventy-two bottles of beer for their picnic, and they had forgotten the bottle-opener. I offered one of them a penknife that Gunnor had given to me on *Westaland*, after showing me how to open bottles without damaging the blade. Edouard took the knife gratefully and I cringed as he used the sharp edge to lever off the caps.

We drank a beer while his wife and children tore into raw seal liver and one of his friends tried to sell me some sealskins. He took each refusal as meaning it was too expensive and when lowering the price had no effect, he would bring out another of lesser quality and begin again. If he was trying to match his sealskins with his impression of my wealth then it said little for my appearance when he confidently produced a mangy pelt that was riddled with shotgun holes.

It was getting late and having to check my washing was a good excuse to leave. Socks placed in any stream for a day with a rock holding them at the top of a small waterfall was my own very successful innovation. Unfortunately there were no such short-cuts for my other clothes which needed a lot of soap and scrubbing in the cold pools. I slithered thankfully into my sleeping bag, for it had been a hard twenty-four hours as a stowaway. But soon bullets were being fired over my tent. The *zing* sounds kept me awake, and flattened to the ground; Greenlanders love guns with an infatuation that increases with every drink, as does their choice of targets. I was beginning to have doubts about this beautiful country.

'Hallo! Hallo!' It was six-thirty a.m. and my doubts were con-

firmed. I refused the beer that materialised through my tent door and
handed over my knife, not caring how Edouard opened his own. I
was tired of playing pseud-confident to drunks. Where, oh where
was the real Greenlander? Or was he drunk or disillusioned too? Was
I merely chasing my own misconceptions? Trying to see the world
in terms of the myths I believed in and wanted to see, instead of
accepting a different and harsher reality?

In Jakobshavn there was a cleft in the rocks with a ledge over a
vertical drop down to the sea. In former years the old, the infirm and
the unproductive would hurl themselves off during hard times to
improve the chances of survival for the others. If the problems of the
modern Greenlander had to be solved by such drastic measures
today, I wondered just how long would be the queue at that
ledge.

Up north, then. Maybe it would be different up north.

At the KGH office there was another setback.

'Thule? (Nø, etc.) That ship has been rerouted. Now there'll only
be one boat going up north this year. The *Nolson*. She'll be here in a
month.'

My heart sank. It was always a month. How could I get around the
world when everyone always delayed me a month? I wanted to pack
it all in – but no, that would have been the easy answer. The man
behind me saw my disappointment.

'If you've got to wait a month, how about a job? You can probably
have mine. I work on a coastal cargo boat. We go up and down the
coast calling in at every port. Ideal way to see the country. I'll ask the
captain if you like. I'm going on leave.'

Feeling a bit bewildered by the speed of developments I nevertheless followed eagerly. The captain of *Sudviking* was a small plump
man and as I watched the discussion through the window, he did not
seem too keen. Shakes of the head. More talking. A shrug. A long
stare at me. More discussion. A nod. Then my friend came out
smiling.

'Whew! It wasn't easy, but he'll take you on. You'll get on fine.
Nothing to the job. The others will help you too.'

'It's all right,' I replied confidently, 'I've had a little experience of
tying knots, winch controls and signals, derusting, painting . . .'

'Good, good,' he murmured, 'but you won't need any of that. You're the new cook.'

'Cook? . . . but you never told me . . .'

'Nothing to it. Dead easy.'

'But . . . I can't cook . . .'

5 · An Arctic cook in hot water

Greenland waters are clear and deep, enabling large ships to travel close to the rocks and to use the many narrow channels between the myriad islands that litter the southern coastline. Some of them passed only a stone's throw away as we wove in and out around their edges and nosed our way through the jigsaw of broken pack-ice. Two small fishing boats had tagged on behind, using us as an icebreaker as they sat in our wake which was churned out from our stern as white surf that faded into a hazy-green line of bubbles and eddies, reaching out across the blue sea to touch the icebergs and set them rocking with ponderous reluctance. One of the smaller bergs was upset from its point of balance and it slowly lurched over to find a new equilibrium, scooping up water on one side and letting it tumble over to the other as a series of cascades that glistened silver against the sunlight. And those mountains, always those towering mountains, separated by glaciers that had been halted by the thaw as they crept down to the sea, poised above us like cream caught oozing over the rim of a bowl. For all this country's faults, here was nature at its best.

Down in the ship's galley the new cook of *Sudviking* surveyed the shelves of jars and packets with labels and ingredients in foreign languages and the freezer which was full of a surprising and unrecognisable variety of dismembered species. In this dismal scene it was nature at its very worst.

My name was suddenly called over the loudspeaker by the captain, requesting to see me. He smoked cigars continuously and was accompanied by a permanent cloud of blue smoke that obscured most of his features except his eyes which he skilfully managed to maintain above the smoke-line. His serious expression only disappeared when this smoke-line rose and got into his eyes, making him cringe into a semblance of a smile. Thus disadvantaged and feeling distinctly naked in my corner of clear air, I tried to conceal from his relentless gaze the large flakes of white paint that had been removed from his corridor a few moments earlier and were now stuck to my pack frame.

'Mr Scott . . .' He used the impersonal tone of a driving-examiner. '. . . Mr Scott, you can cook, can't you?'

It was a delicate situation and required an answer that was positive, respectful and yet evasive enough for later grounds of misunderstanding.

'Yes, sir. Of course. However, I may need some help with the dishes that are new to me. Sir.'

A fresh billow of blue afforded me some respite from his intense scrutiny and informed me that there were only three men on board to cook for, which was surprising for such a large ship. But if that was the good news, the bad was whale.

'You'll find it up on the deck,' said another puff which also despatched me to fetch it.

Up on deck there was no sign of a whale anywhere even after checking all the normal places you might expect to find one. The only member of the crew visible was welding so I interrupted his work and put my question to the pair of eyes that lay behind a visor with dark-green flaps for eyelids, wondering if the entire journey would be spent talking to either smoke or masks. He spoke no English but after drawing a whale in the air, the hand that had lost its incandescent glow pointed to some wooden barrels.

The first contained rope and the second had a thick crust of ice over the top. The visor nodded. Instantly going off the idea of whale I broke the ice and put my hand into a chilly brown solution of brine. Only after peeling my jersey back beyond the elbow did my hand find a large slab of meat the size of an encyclopedia that was black with white hairline streaks. Back in the galley the captain handed me a recipe book, and I was forced to point out that it was in Danish – it was then that he began to realise just how much help was going to be needed.

By evening the meat had been soaked all day in fresh water and boiled for an hour, which had done nothing to change its appearance and only seemed to have made it exceptionally tough and dry. Whales seemed to do nothing in moderation. It was placed before the crew in much the same manner as a postman delivers a parcel, abdicating responsibility and with no knowledge of the contents. The cook quickly retired to the galley to await the consequences which were not long in coming.

'Where's the speck, Mr Scott?'

Wind-driven snow among the hills of the Faroes; Eysturoy

The glow of the midnight sun; Disko Bay, West Greenland

An old Inuit on his way to
fetch water; Qeqertat,
North-West Greenland

Pitching my Vango tent near
Umanak, West Greenland

An Inuit practising throwing
his harpoon. I was later to see
him in action hunting narwhal

Jakobshavn's houses are typical of the country that Eric the Red, a successful early estate agent, called Greenland

New World habitations and the Space Needle, Seattle

'Speck? Speck of what?'

'Speck, the blubber, Mr Scott. You've forgotten the blubber.'

'Is it in . . .?'

'Yes, yes. In the barrel, Mr Scott.'

Oh God. Up on deck I viewed the barrel once more with horror. The ice had reformed and yet even after I had broken through and reached down, there was nothing to be felt as far as my biceps. It was only after stripping off to the waist and immersing my arm up to the shoulder-blade in the freezing brine that I located some blubber, which took a further minute to extract from the hunks of salt at the bottom. This chunk of fat with skin on one side left a trail of brown liquid all the way to the galley as it dangled down from an arm that felt like an icicle. By the time I had washed myself and the speck, cut it up and brought it to the table, the room was empty. The crew had finished and gone. Releasing a long sigh that effused the last of my spirit I sat down, pushed away the cause of my misfortune and ate a few potatoes with my head hung low. The first day and already my popularity was losing points.

The following morning the atmosphere at breakfast was similar to the temperature of the whale barrel. The bread lay on the table in thick slices the way they had always been on *Westaland* and the way they should be – something to get your teeth into . . .

'Mr Scott? The bread's too thick. Cut it thinner in future, please.'

My apology was grunted through several inches of crust and marmalade and so I swallowed the mouthful and went through to do a better job in person. The captain then asked me to bring some more. One loaf was still frozen and the other had already been cut up into the same thick slices. As my knife tried to halve them, each one became so thin that it was either all holes or a loosely held-together collection of crumbs. I put what must have appeared as a plate of bloody-mindedness in front of the captain and went off to busy myself by drying the same plate for the next ten minutes.

'Come through and join us, Alas . . . er, what's your name?' shouted Peter, the friendly first mate. So I took my tea to the spare seat and told him my name although 'Alas' seemed more appropriate. 'You'll soon get the hang of everything,' he said kindly. 'Just takes a little time to get into the way of things.' There was a period of silence before the captain got up.

'Mr Scott.' That awful voice again. 'On this ship there is only one

green mug. *That* is the mug I always use.' He placed the blue one that
I had set for him heavily on the table and left the room.

I turned to Peter. 'And where does he keep his precious green
mug?'

Peter looked embarrassed. 'I think you're drinking out of it.'

The points seemed to slip away despite all my efforts to please and to
succeed. I was dealing with unknown quantities that refused to
respond to genuine concern and willingness. Optimism was not
enough for them; they demanded the know-how that was always
lacking. The series of culinary calamities increased until my confidence sank to its lowest and my smile faded to the gloomy frown
that also belonged to some familiar faces from the Faroes.

'Cods' heads.' I had to read the note that gave my daily menu once
again. Cods' heads? Surely they don't . . .? But they did and there
they were – a dozen faces of despair in a plastic bag. I hurried off to
look for Peter and found him up on deck using a rust-removing
machine of vibrating rods that created a cloud like the captain's, only
red.

'HOW DO YOU COOK CODS' HEADS?' I yelled into his ear which
was bunged up with cotton wool.

'Whose heads?'

'CODS',' I screamed, aware that it sounded blasphemous and yet
visualising another very human head. He turned off the machine.

'Cods' heads?'

It was getting monotonous. I nodded. 'Ahh! Captain's favourite.
Just boil them for an hour but don't let the skin go so soft that it falls
away from the bone.'

It sounded easy enough and an hour later I had twelve soft cods'
heads still intact as the crew sat down. There were nods of approval
and I mentally chalked up a few points in my favour. The captain,
however, had not appeared.

'He'll be down soon,' said Peter. 'He's got delayed with pack-ice.
You see, he's not just the captain, he owns this ship too and so he's
fussy over everything. Won't let me take it through the bad bits of
ice. He's not a bad type though, just a bit set in his ways. Drifting
around Greenland for so long goes for your head.'

I glanced anxiously down at the four eyes looking up at me from the bottom of the pot. It was going for their heads too and if he didn't come soon . . . but then Peter was called to the bridge and the captain duly appeared. To my relief they stayed whole while being served onto his plate and I was on the point of placing them in front of him when we hit some ice. The resulting jolt knocked me off balance, the plate slammed down onto the table in front of him, and the captain watched his favourite dish disintegrate into a mess of flesh and bones. I froze for a moment with my eyes closed and then turned on my heels and went out to the stern, wondering just how much a man could take – both the captain and myself.

We called in at every port and during the short stop-overs I went out to explore the new towns with the exhilaration of a reprieve from my labours in the galley and yet always having to return in time to try to transform some mutilated indigestible into something miraculously edible. It was true that there was nothing hard about the cooking; everything simply had to be boiled for an hour. The problem was knowing when something you had never seen before, let alone actually tasted, was ready as there was often a very slim margin for error between underdone and ruined. They ate all the parts of creatures that I would either have thrown away or eaten around. As each day brought a new town, so the daily menu began to sound like the ingredients for Macbeth's cauldron; lung of cow in Christianshåb, heart of pig in Julianehåb, liver of lamb in Frederik-shåb, wing of skate in Sukkertoppen, and meatball of elk in Arsuk.

Nothing was easy. Sausages came in one-yard lengths and it was only after Mr Scott had chopped one up into smaller and more manageable lengths that he was brusquely informed they are always cooked whole. He found it difficult to turn over three feet of sausage coiled up in a pan and when he succeeded he found it developed a twist and turned itself slowly back again onto the side that was already done. Lunch was twenty minutes late that day but the sausages were well received in spite of being burnt on one side, slightly raw on the other and of different lengths. Their relative success was due more to the person who had originally put them together than to the person who latterly tried to pull them apart. The new cook, aging rapidly, boiled the *rastofisk* for the statutory hour and did well, except . . . 'Mr Scott, you've forgotten the sheep's intestine fat. We always have sheep's intestine fat with *rastofisk*' . . . which might have been logical to one who knew what *rastofisk* was but the cook did not, and he was about to boil the *turrofisk* when someone caught him in time as *turrofisk*, of course, is always eaten raw, and he oversweetened the buttermilk pudding because that same someone said to add six tablespoons of sugar which was later denied as it should have been six teaspoons, and he was alone one day when . . .

'Alice . . .?'

Not even Peter, whose English was good but often inadequate, could pronounce the cook's name. Alice. Just a further degradation that the cook of *Sudviking* had to suffer.

'. . . Alice? Come up and help with the water-snake, please.'

So it was to be water-snakes next, was it? Nothing surprised the cook any more. He just followed instructions to the letter with whatever offering they put before him. He would gladly boil a water-snake for an hour if that was what they wanted. Or if they ate it raw then that would be just as agreeable. And if they liked their water-snake, boiled or raw, to be garnished with speck, served on thin bread or flavoured with a soupçon of sheep's intestine fat then he would happily oblige; so he, Alice, the cook of *Sudviking*, went up on deck to do what had to be done to water-snakes with the indifference and loyal servitude that had become instilled by ignorance, failure and the memory of a green mug.

'Is it in a barrel?' asked the cook.

'What?'

'The water-snake.'

'No, you're standing on it.'

The indifference vanished at once and the cook looked down at his feet with alarm. 'But that's a hose . . .'

'Oh? I don't know the word in English. Help me move it over there.'

A smile appeared on the cook's face for the first time in a week but it soon vanished at the thought of lunch which, like bad weather, was imminent. When they were finished moving the snake they went to the bow to look at the houses of Nanortalik which were slowly coming into view as the ship rounded a headland.

'You'll like this place, Alice,' said Peter. 'It's different. Although it's right in the south all the ice collects around it because of the currents and it's often inaccessible. The people are much more like the Eskimo because of their isolation. They're the ugliest people in

Greenland and also the friendliest. We'll have two days free here.'
'MR SCOTT, TO THE GALLEY, PLEASE.'
The cook ignored the loudspeaker. He seemed lost in thought. 'I'll
like anywhere,' he whispered mournfully. 'I may jump ship here –
and I'm going to change my name. Both of them.' He turned to face
the loudspeaker. Today was Nanortalik, and it was arm of squid.

Eric the Red would have had a hard time convincing Alice the Cook
that this land was green. Only the previous day at Narssaq (leg of
chicken) had it been truly green with pasture, wild flowers and
grazing sheep. Nanortalik had patches of grass but in general it was
like a bombsite. Large boulders had rolled down from the jagged
edges of the surrounding hills and now lay about the town, forming
the other half of lean-to houses in their appealing clashes of colours.
Most were tumble-down and the area was covered in cans, bottles,
plastic bags, paper, old car wheels, offal and the even less pleasant.
  I had not gone far when a German approached. He was an
ecologist staying there for a visit; he was in low spirits and just
wanted to talk to a European face. Mine seemed to fit the bill and I
was immediately accosted.
  'I come from a country where fifty per cent of our wildlife and
forty per cent of our plant life is dying – for ever,' he said with abrupt
directness. Swallows had changed their migration routes after centuries, he said, and we killed our soil with chemicals. He had come to
Greenland in the hope of finding some unspoilt part of the world
where people who lived directly from their environment cared for it;
but no, it seemed too late for the whole world. The problem was too
big, and those that cared were too small. He pointed to a house with
a pipe sticking out from its side, emptying the slops into the swamps
it had caused. They had washing-machines but nowhere to put the
dirty water. There was no sewage system here – the contents of the
lavatory were collected in a plastic bag each week in the same way as
rubbish, he explained, then the bags were slid off a chute into the sea.
Look at the cans, the litter, the plastic bags with 'Keep Greenland
Clean' printed on the side . . . He wandered off as suddenly as he had
come, leaving me to reflect on these depressing facts.
  Yet Greenland was getting into my blood. The excitement of its
raw character haunted my veins and its abused beauty still exuded

the mysterious confidence of a survivor. Greenland would survive.

As for its people, however, their survival was more open to doubt that evening in the Hotel Tupilak. The Greenlanders themselves had decided to introduce drink rationing in an effort to curb their chronic alcoholism, and this was the first day that restrictions came into force – but it appeared quite the contrary and as if they were intent on blowing the month's supply of coupons on the first night. They were going to go out in their accustomed style before having to become sober and meet the neighbours the following day.

Peter dug me in the ribs as a large girl passed. 'Plenty speck on her, eh?' I nodded but my attention was transfixed by the faces around me, fascinated by the hostility, the menace and the ferocity that radiated from a drunk Greenlander. A vulturish man with a narrow face, shoulder-length hair and a wart on the end of his nose which hung down like a drip and gave him a hooked beak, sat behind a table covered in unopened bottles. When he flung his head back and laughed, as expected, it was an ominous, mocking laugh, full of spite and malice. An apparition of a gypsy passed through the murk of cigarette smoke; tousled jet-black hair, front teeth missing, un-shaven and wearing one earring and a heavy leather jacket that was covered in unnecessary buckles, studs and Hell's Angel chains. It strained to cover his broad shoulders and to contain the latent power within – his volatile temper heightened the impression of a frighten-ing if not good prop-forward, had Nanortalik Rugby Football Club existed. The girls too wore outfits of leather or denim, and their harsh features suggested they were able companions of violence. If the land had imparted its wild beauty to the girls of Holsteinsborg, here it had dispensed only its wildness. I could not be sure that these people would survive, but they would certainly go down fighting.

The heavy beat of Boney M's *Rasputin* thundered out. A teenager was dancing continuously with any female he could find and once he fell over backwards and took ten seconds to get back to his feet, but his middle-aged partner had not even noticed that he had dis-appeared. She was in a daze. Her face was set in a fixed smile as she moved around with glazed eyes, dancing with anyone until they wandered off and left her alone, but all the time the smile never altered and never left her face. Then I saw her sit down and for a fraction of time, just an instant, the façade dropped – her expression changed and there was a look of indescribable sadness in her eyes.

Then with a few unsteady shakes of the head the grin returned, the mask was up and she was ready to face life one more.

As we walked back to the ship I thought of the look of sadness which had lurked behind the grin and felt that in this brief insight I had learnt more about the Greenland people than days of walking the streets would have ever taught me. These people seemed to have lost that 'fizz' which their ice had preserved for over five thousand years.

We wandered on into the embers of the midnight sun when I noticed some sealskins that were thrown into fine silhouette as they hung on a washing-line. My camera was always with me so I set it up on a tripod with the big lens. Peter wanted to have a look and he stood there mesmerised. He slowly turned to me and nodded thoughtfully. 'You see things that we do not see.'

It was a nice definition of a photographer. My ego was bolstered enough to board my floating kitchen once more to confront the hazards of the remaining journey.

We rounded Cape Farewell and the east coast showed itself to be every bit as creative as the west with its variety of mountains and even more generous with its icebergs. In Angmagssalik, whose streets should have all been posted as dangerous gradients, I climbed a hill to a small building where there was a trilingual notice which read, 'This is a radio station. It is vital to our communications. Please leave it in peace. Thank you. The Post Office.' On behalf of a cook I mentally made a similar request not to be molested as we took on new supplies of food, and to my relief the menu appeared to be the same as before except for a large white bucket that was sealed, unmarked and heavy.

Angmagssalik was an attractive town and typically eye-catching. The sea froze over and a jigsaw of ice formed around boats moored as wedges of colour. Like the houses, they flagrantly defied the decorum of a trichromatic world where blue and brown yielded only to the blackness of shadow. But soon we were retracing the long route back, revisiting every port of call, and I was ticking off each day that passed without mishap and calculating how many more I had to survive without discovering the contents of that bucket. It made me uneasy and my suspicions were well-founded, only its secret was even nastier than my fears.

My routine had fallen into place by then and it was very satisfying watching the land go by until Peter came down one day with news from the bridge. 'We've just heard the report on ship movements. Your ship to Thule, *Nolson*, left Denmark yesterday. That's three days ahead of her schedule. I don't think we're going to reach Holsteinsborg in time for you to catch her. I'm sorry.' It was a heavy burden. He turned to go but suddenly remembered something. 'Oh yes. You know that white container in the larder? Captain wants you to bring it in and open it. He'll be down in a while to show you what to do.'

I dragged the bucket through, my thoughts filled with the disappointment of missing the *Nolson*. I had gone through all this for nothing and lost the chance of visiting Thule. The seal broke easily and the lid came off. That had been my only chance of visiting the far north and now it had gone, all because . . . before me lay a small flock of sheep's heads. The hair had been singed off, the head had then been deep frozen and cut down the middle with a circular saw so that on one side you had a roadside sheep staring up at you and on the other a complete cross-section of the contents of the animal's head. I stood contemplating this grizzly spectacle for a moment. Sheep's head! – well, why not? We had eaten every other part of their anatomy except the normal cuts. The captain came in and showed me what to do. Boil for an hour.

When the hour was up I set them down on the table before the crew and was making a fairly hurried exit when they indicated the spare seat. Saying I was not hungry had no effect; they were obviously spoiling for some entertainment at my expense. I reluctantly sat down and began poking inoffensively at the face and then delicately chewed on a small portion of the jowl.

'Seems a bit overdone,' I said, getting up to go, 'I don't like mine overdone . . .' A hand grabbed me and pulled me down.

'They're just fine,' interrupted Peter, instantly losing a friend. 'Perfect. *Bon appétit*,' he grinned.

So, it was to be a test. I did my duty. It was not too bad once you got used to the eye staring up at you. The brain was unpleasant as it was full of bits of bone but fortunately sheep have only a small allocation of grey matter and what little these former numskulls possessed had been turned brown by an hour of boiling. After many excessively chewed mouthfuls there was scarcely anything left on my plate, save a hollow half of skull and I got up to go. The hand immediately hauled me down again.

'You haven't finished yet.'

'Yes I have,' I protested.

'What about the eye?' said my aggressor and smiles lit up around the table.

'Eye? You surely don't . . .' I sighed, and Peter gouged out the offensive organ, removed the black part and handed it to me. I hesitated, looked to the ceiling for divine intervention but none came, and put the eye in my mouth. My teeth made one bite to satisfy the expectations of those around me and then it went down in a gulp to ease the strain on my will-power. A loud cheer went up and the meal was over. In the eyes of the crew, their own eyes, their cook had achieved manhood – and probably very little else.

A week later we were leaving Søndre Strømfjord, a narrow fjord that stretches for over a hundred miles inland, with Holsteinsborg as our next stop. It was too late. *Nolson* had arrived there two days ago. But somehow it didn't seem so important any more, as I struggled with the inert powers of combustion that refused to keep my pipe alight and gazed wistfully at the coastline. The strata of the rock ran in different colours, following the contours of the hillsides in parallel veins and frequently rising and falling in deliberate curves around the scene of a past upheaval like the bold brushwork of an impressionist. Whenever my plans went wrong there was always compensation to be found in nature's artistry.

The next day Greenland's erratic shipping schedule worked in my favour and the *Nolson* was still there when we docked. After hasty goodbyes, which admittedly came easier than many, I rushed aboard the new ship. The captain instantly dashed my hopes. It was impossible to work my passage on account of regulation such-and-such, union laws, insurance small-print and contractual agreements – which seemed to cover most of the loopholes. The only answer was to buy a ticket as a passenger at the KGH office.

Here they said it was necessary to get the captain's permission before a ticket could be issued. I explained that the captain had sent me.

'No, you must have seen the wrong man. That wasn't the captain.'

Back to the ship. Less than an hour to departure. The same man, slightly angrier, affirmed that he was the captain and that he could do nothing until KGH had issued a ticket. Back to the office.

'Hmm! You'd better see him again, he is mistaken. He must sign a paper first.'

An extremely irate captain phoned the office and after a short, sharp monologue, I was returned to the office on the half-volley yet again.

'What's the problem? Why is it so difficult?' I asked in breathless gasps.

'Well, we don't know the procedure. You see, no one in this office has ever issued a ticket to Thule before.'

They managed to sort it out in time and that evening I watched more of Greenland slip by at the start of a four-day journey, deck-class, heading north. I was wearing a new jersey which had been handed to me with the minimum of fuss and ceremony, for the donor was a man of few words and much smoke. Nevertheless, the four words that had accompanied the presentation, 'Thank you, Mr Scott', had come carpeted in bursts of unfolding blue and had sounded deeply sincere. Perhaps he had even liked his cods' heads served as an Irish stew, for he had also privileged me with a rare smile.

6 · Timeless in Thule

Weighing 30·4 tons and known to the Eskimos as *Abnighito*, it was found up here in the far north-west of Greenland. Denmark allowed New York City to keep this, the largest meteorite to be exhibited by any museum, and many years later was privileged to be the first country to receive a present of moon rock from America. Meteor Island is near Cape York where there stands a tall pillar of stones sixty feet high as a memorial to an American. The plaque at the bottom reads: 'Robert Edwin Peary "The first to lead a party of his fellow men to a pole of the earth" April 6, 1909. During 25 years of persistent and courageous work in the Arctic, he also determined the insularity of Greenland and discovered the Cape York Meteorites. This monument to his memory is erected here in 1932 by his wife and children in grateful recognition of the devoted services of the Eskimo people.'

Four Eskimos and a negro were with Peary that day in 1909 when his eighth expedition was finally successful after eighteen years of effort. Their journey across the polar ice covered a total of 950 miles and took them fifty-three days, but the news of their conquest did not reach the world until five months later. Peary's achievement was challenged by a fellow American, Dr F. A. Cook, who claimed to have reached the Pole a year earlier, and the controversy flared for some time before Cook's contention was discounted, along with other of his myths and frauds.

The monument was visible from our ship after three days of uneventful travel. It was with growing apprehension that the cold-conscious Scott of the Arctic watched the increasing quantities of ice. He had already heard of two less encouraging discoveries. The well-preserved remains of an expedition and their dogs, missing since the last century, had been found in the nearby 'Fjord of the Dead', and the bodies of an Eskimo family that had been naturally freeze-dried when they perished five hundred years ago had been discovered further south near Umanak – chilling testimonies to the severity of this climate. We were going up to the 78th parallel, eight

hundred miles north of the Arctic Circle, where the winter temperature could drop below minus 60°C and the sun disappeared for four
months. Now it was mid-summer but the warm days could change
quickly as there was less than a month between the last snow shower
of the old winter and the first flakes of the new one. *Nolson* was
visiting all the small settlements in the area and then going south to
Iceland before returning to Denmark. The itinerary was perfect for
me – except that, the way things stood, I was not on it. My ticket
would take me to Thule, the third stop, and unless I succeeded in
working my way onto the crew despite a captain whose kindness
was obscured by regulations, the prospect was a long cold winter.

Aboard the *Nolson* the privilege of rank entitled the captain to
three pillows in his bunk, an officer had two, and all the rest had one.
In my opinion (despite an obvious bias and only one pillow), a good
cook was the second most influential person in the hierarchy of the
merchant navy when it was afloat.

Orly, the cook of *Nolson*, had worked on British ships and could
imitate accents from Aarhus to Falster as easily as from Arbroath to
Falmouth. His cooking won such acclaim that most of the crew
would sneak down to the galley at some time or other to request
their favourite dish or to slip him a backhander in exchange for
some rationed luxury from the bonded store. From this he progressed to become ship's news agency, agony aunt and oracle of
philosophic humour; all of which were adequately housed in his
bulky frame. At times his words seemed to flow as if merely to
entertain himself and the subjects changed with each eddy of thought
until they became lost in a backwater of silence.

'I don't want to be rich,' he said one day to nobody in particular.
'Money doesn't make you happy. No, sir. I just want to be wealthy
enough to be miserable in comfort.'

Silence.

'You know? When I first met my wife, she told me I looked like a
Greek god.' I tried to visualise him as a deity that had forsaken his
ambrosia for Carlsberg Lager, pivoting his sixteen stone over a ball
of dough. 'Last time at home we had this flaming row and she said
now I was just like a goddamned Greek.'

He seemed to find silence excruciating.

'Yeah, Denmark's going to hell. Still, at least we're going first-
class.'

To begin with I went down to listen to him as it was boring being an inactive passenger. Then I helped with odd small chores until one afternoon Orly didn't have time to clean the kitchen floor and so I did it when he was away. The mess boy then went down with flu and gradually I found more and more opportunities to help although never asked to do so. This led to Orly putting in a good word to the Chief Steward, who decided not to charge me for my meals, let me have an empty cabin though my status was deck-class, and even became friendly enough to show me a picture of his wife. She was attractive but a far cry from the top-heavy lass that had been tattooed on his forearm since his bachelor days. Things were slowly happening.

We reached Dundas, the American air base, whose most distinguishing features were copses of radio masts on every hilltop. It was a closed area and my permit did not allow me entry but the Americans made me welcome and said they had nothing to hide as they did nothing except drive around all day anyway. *Nolson* took on a landing-craft in tow to use later for transporting supplies to the villages, none of which had a harbour. It was also to push away icebergs that drifted towards the ship when it lay at anchor.

My duties increased but the captain was apparently still not reading between the lines of my ticket and his rules when he said one day on passing, 'Well, you'll soon have to find yourself a nice Eskimo girl for the winter, won't you.' He laughed, but I only managed a weak smile out of politeness.

The scenery was very different here. The rugged mountains had gone and had been replaced by low hills with flat tops and rounded ends. Their uniform grey colour was interrupted in places with ribbons of reddish rock and their smooth polished appearance was broken only by the occasional cliff. With so much rubble and scree scattered around and over them they resembled great piles of gravel. Above them and in the distance a white cloud lay sprawled along their tops, its lower edge forming a clearly defined straight line. It was only after looking at this for some time that I realised it was not a cloud but the permanent ice-cap; the great body of inland ice (five-sixths) which pushes out its glacial tentacles that slowly wriggle down to the sea.

This was now the land of the Inuit, the old Eskimos, who had found a refuge here in the shadow of an American airforce base (and also in certain remote parts of the east coast). Thule (Qânâq) was the principal town with a large proportion of southern Greenlanders living there and running businesses and services. The Inuit lived in scattered settlements in the surrounding area. We stopped at one of these, the small hunting community of Moriussaq which seemed deserted that day. Its graveyard had one solitary white cross on barren land riddled with stones. I left the ship to wander around and came across the skin of a polar bear which had been shot recently and was stretched out on a frame. Beyond this was the bloated body of a sled-dog, sitting up on its haunches, its head cocked to one side, still attached to the cord that had hanged it. The school-teacher came along while I was staring at this gruesome sight.

'Why do they do that?' I asked.

'It's very rarely done now and they aren't supposed to. It's just someone who still does things the old way. Some say the fur of a hanged dog stands better for using on the hood of a parka, others say it avoids damaging the pelt, and it also saves a bullet for a hunting trip.' He invited me into his simple wooden house for a *kaffee-mig*. The contents were not simple; a 35 mm. camera outfit with several lenses and a motordrive unit, a pocket dictaphone, calculator watch, a portable radio-cassette . . . He saw my surprise and nodded in the direction of Dundas.

'Duty-free zone,' he explained with a Southern States accent from the same source. He had come here from the south to fill a temporary vacancy in the school but liked the lifestyle so much that he was hoping it would become a permanent position.

After coffee he let me try his kayak. These were traditionally made by the women and the ability to do it well was an important quality that a hunter looked for in choosing a wife. Some kayaks are still made of a wooden frame bound together with thongs of hide rather than nails and covered in greased sealskins, but most are now made of canvas. This is painted white to be less conspicuous to a seal underwater looking up at the surface and also to blend in amongst the ice. The paddle is short and remarkably slender with blades that are only four fingers wide. This cuts down the risk of noise by splashing, is less tiring for long distances and is sufficient for propelling these craft which are much lighter and more manoeuvrable than their glassfibre descendants. The paddles were originally made from single pieces of driftwood which further restricted their size and design.

Kayaks are still the most effective craft for hunting because they are silent although they are often taken out to the hunting grounds by motorboat. Seal is the staple meat but this is supplemented by whale, walrus, caribou, fish and seabirds. Little Auks are particular favourites but an adult needs six or seven to make a meal. The Eskimos cut the skin around the head and then peel it off in one as if removing a sock. They eat all the flesh and squeeze the intestines clean before sucking them down raw like a length of spaghetti. Inuit cuisine is even simpler than boiling for an hour.

I paddled around the area cautiously, kayaks being more cramped than the canoes I was used to and just as unstable, but it was an exhilarating, unworldly feeling to float amongst those great menhirs of ice with their shades of blues and greens dropping down into the depths. The ship's horn pulled me back to reality and I had to return and move on to the end of my ticket.

Orly was tenderising some steaks with blows from a hammer that might once have belonged to Thor when I arrived back to start washing the floor for the second time that day.

'You'd better have a piss on the ice when we reach Thule,' he said suddenly. 'Everyone does. Yes, sir. Got to leave your mark in life somewhere. Lasts for years.' The hammer blows continued. 'Nearest you'll ever get to immortality,' he added, some of his godliness returning.

The inevitable pause.

'Wouldn't wash the floor if I were you. The captain liked his lunch today so I persuaded him to let you replace the mess boy until he gets better – just for a week, mind you. He's still going to drop you off at Thule at the end of our circuit.'

'Really . . .?'

'And you're in luck – they've added Qeqertat to our schedule. We're on our way there now.'

'What happens there?'

'Nothing at all as far as we're concerned. No women, no pubs, no beer, nothing. You might like it though. They are real Eskimos. They are hunters. It's one of the few places the narwhal come to breed. Poor sods.'

I jubilantly put the mop away and went off to the ship's library to see what a narwhal was.

The skin of these small whales is either black or speckled with white, and they reach a length of twenty feet. The males are linked in myth to the fabulous unicorn because of their upper canine which extends straight out from their blunt head to form a single spike that can grow over nine feet long and weigh 180 pounds. It is textured like deer antler but has a spiralled twist running all the way down its length like a tapering corkscrew and is solid except for a short hollow section at the base where it joins the skull. The exact purpose of the male's spike is not known but it is believed to be used for scraping up crustaceans from the seabed.

The book gave no explanation of how the female procured *her* crustaceans but doubtless she was managing well enough somewhere in the vicinity as we approached the settlement on Harvard Island late that night in thick mist. A powerful searchlight was directed out over our bow as the ship inched forward but all it achieved was to show just how abysmal the visibility really was. The bridge was in darkness with one figure at the controls and two others who monitored the instruments and constantly called out depths and distances to a fourth person. He stood in a faint pyramid of light, pencil and dividers in hand, and was bent over a chart from which most of the usual information was missing. Black lines denoting the coast frequently dissolved into vague shades of blue, and some areas were blank save for a question-mark that looked small and embarrassed. He continually glanced at a rough hand-drawn map alongside and called out bearings with what could only have been optimism. A decision was made. The anchor suddenly plunged down with a deafening roar as the heavy links of its chain hammered the deck. The noise abated and then silence returned to the village in the mist where the narwhal hunters lived.

Dawn came and with the increase in light filtering through, the mist began to lift until it had cleared the tops of the surrounding hills which had been veiled from our view. There it stopped and hung suspended as a theatre curtain for the drama that was about to unfold.

Qeqertat was a hamlet of twelve square houses, each with a little porch tacked on around its doorway and patches of flamboyant colours on its walls where the paint had managed to retain a grip. Outside every dwelling stood a wooden platform where meat was kept. Seal heads stared glassy-eyed amongst the entrails and vital organs of other creatures while pools of gore lay on the ground below them.

There was no fresh water on the island and an old man came down to the edge of the sea with an axe to hack off a lump from a stranded iceberg, taking it back to his house to let it thaw over a bucket. He walked slowly on shaky legs, and his shoulder-length white hair wavered in the sea breeze, matching the wispy polar bear fur which encircled his wrists. There was something noble in his deeply tanned face, much wrinkled by the endurance of many long winters.

Kayaks rested at an angle near the water, their bows held up in the air on sledges which served as stands and their decks cluttered with the essentials of the hunt; a rifle in a pouch was strapped to the front deck alongside a spare paddle and the harpoon, which were both tucked under two retaining loops. Attached to the harpoon was a strong nylon cord which lay in coils on the spraycover above the hunter's lap. It ran around behind him and the other end was connected to a sealskin float (complete with flippers) sitting on a low wooden tray to which it was loosely tied. The rear deck also held the heavier harpoon that was used only if the rifle malfunctioned, to stab the whale repeatedly until the *coup de grâce* had been delivered.

All forty villagers were gathered on a hillock to watch their year's supply of provisions being unloaded. These Inuit were no different in physical appearance from the Greenlander of the south, except for being more weathered. They were small and powerfully built, and their faces displayed broad, mongol features with that same rugged wildness. Their clothes were just as colourful but substituted extra thickness for ornamentation and style – in winter they would wear more skins and furs and take on our accepted image of an Eskimo. They spoke a different dialect which could be understood as far away as Alaska and their vocabulary contained more than twenty-seven different words for *snow*. Each word had a specific meaning to describe the snow's characteristics, how it would affect travelling and whether it had a practical use, such as for building a snowhouse.

A figure suddenly shouted. The Inuit turned their gaze out to sea as he pointed to a distant group of icebergs gossiping together in the middle of the bay, where a school of narwhal had just appeared and were leisurely humping their backs in graceful arches through the water. By the time I looked towards the kayaks once more, their stands were empty and six figures were paddling furiously away. They reached a smaller iceberg ahead of the whales and waited for them to pass before approaching from behind to make their strike.

The harpoon was launched into the air by using a hand-held baton which effectively extended the hunter's reach and the final flick gave the harpoon greater distance and thrust. As the harpoon flew through the air the cord was whipped up from the coils in his lap and the hunter had quickly to release the float behind him – this was the most dangerous moment for the hunter and usually fatal if he became entangled. Survival time in these unforgiving waters was approximately three minutes. The cord was connected to a point half-way along the detachable head of the harpoon which, if success-ful, embedded itself under the tough skin of the whale. The shaft was designed to fall off with the first sideways movement of the whale after impact. This left the head free to turn sideways in the wound when the cord was pulled taut by the drag of the float, making it impossible to dislodge. The whale was slowed down by the trailing float and was forced to come up for air more often, spending longer on the surface as it became weaker. The hunter collected the harpoon shaft from the water and followed the float, sometimes for over an hour, waiting for his chance with the rifle for a shot to the brain. He had to do all this from an unstable kayak.

The hunters disappeared from view but after some shots were heard, a group of women left in a motorboat and soon returned towing two narwhal behind. The hunters gradually paddled back and the two successful men set about dismembering the whales in a set pattern of cuts as they lay beached in shallow water. These narwhals had no horns for they were both females; their upturned mouths seemed fixed in permanent smiles as the water around them turned red and large slabs of steaming meat were taken away and spread out over the surrounding rocks. The skin was like polished marble both in colour and to the touch – it was rich in vitamins and fetched the highest price in the meat markets. Some children came down to cut bits off and began eating the raw skin.

'*Mat*-TOCK,' grinned a youngster, almost spitting out a piece with the final emphasis as he handed me a bit. It was tough and rubbery. They called it Eskimo chewing gum and it was easy to see why when I was still chewing the same tasteless morsel an hour later.

'*Mat*-TOCK,' I repeated, almost spitting out mine.

He pointed at the narwhal: '*Keel-eel-ooo-wuck*', and after I had repeated this too, he ran off with a smile that was as broad as the word was long and as happy as the upturned mouth of its meaning.

The whole family came to help. Children carried meat up to the platform by their house on a form of stretcher. Women disregarded the blood that covered their clothes as they used their special knife, the *ulo* (a semi-circular blade like a miniature shovel with a short T-shaped handle that fitted snugly inside the hand), scraping sinew from muscle to use for sewing thread. The remaining meat was laid in a hollow on higher ground and then covered with stones, forming a cairn to mark the spot of their winter larder and securing it from foxes and dogs. Not all Eskimos had fridges.

I lent a hand, for hard work is the quickest means of winning trust and friendship. The Eskimos seemed to welcome a newcomer in their midst and more so when he too had blood up to his elbows. They joked and often had to rest in fits of laughter, much of which was obviously centred around the stranger struggling with vast cuts of whale. But I felt honoured to be the butt of their good-natured humour, which was a token of acceptance.

It was a gory spectacle and yet the skill with which these people had caught these large creatures with implements they had fashioned from wood, sealskin, caribou and walrus tusk could only be admired. There were some more modern materials evident; one hunter used the inner tube from a car tyre as a float, another had an aluminium harpoon head and the tips all had steel edges, but it was still one man in a flimsy boat against one whale. The rifle only ended the conflict more quickly for both sides after the prey had been captured with a technique that was as old as the art of hunting itself.

These people were not to be compared to the commercial whalers of other countries. They were not driving the whale to extinction in selfish and desperate efforts to extract what revenue remained in an industry that was dying through exploitation and indiscriminate greed. These hunters were doing no more than they had always done by taking a few whales as a necessary supply of food for the winter months ahead. Local conservation measures nevertheless restricted the annual number of kills to one hundred, and all these had to be made first with a harpoon – a policy aimed at ensuring the quota went to the traditional Eskimo rather than to wholesale hunters armed only with rifles.

Every part of the whale was used except the skull and the backbone which were left to litter the beach. Nothing was wasted, not even the small unborn calf that was removed from its mother's body. It seemed sad that it would never get the chance to arch its dorsal fin gracefully through the waves. The villagers cheerfully nodded their approval when I took out my camera (and added blood to the barrels of my lenses which were already suffering from salt water spray and grit). I photographed the baby narwhal as it was carried off, smiling like the rest of its kin, to be fed to the dogs.

The work came to an end and one of the hunters invited me to join the group in his house, where his two youngest children were sitting over a bucket in the only room. Blood covered their faces and their forearms, and they chewed on the raw meat with obvious relish. This hunter had been to the North Pole a few years earlier and was justly proud of it, showing me pictures of the Italian expedition that he had accompanied. The room contained some chairs, two metal-framed beds, three tables, a cupboard and a stove – otherwise it was bare. A crude oil lamp had been fixed to one wall and separated a picture of the Danish explorer Knud Rasmussen from another of the Virgin and Child.

I took out my map to show my host where I came from. He raised his eyebrows, his features registered understanding and his chest suddenly expanded. He beamed and emitted a throaty warble, the unmistakable vocal equivalent of bagpipes, and used signs to ask if I played. I nodded and went through a short mime of inflating and squeezing an imaginary bag while my fingers rippled along a make-believe chanter. Another hunter copied my actions and indicated that he practised as well. I was puzzled. Could he play the pipes?

'No, no,' came the reply, conveyed with strong shakes of the head. He broke into a rollicking grin as he grabbed the nearest woman and wrapped her in his embrace.

'Ekimos don't play bagpipes' – his gestures were self-explanatory – 'but we use a similar technique, and identical fingering.'

When the howls of laughter died down they asked if I was married. I shook my head and a young woman with teeth like the keyboard of a broken piano, more black notes than white and even more missing, leapt up to rush me through the motions of dance. I playfully offered her my ring and they were all cheering and clapping when it suddenly occurred to me as a sobering shock that I might actually be committing myself to my partner by some ancient tradition. So I excused myself from the next dance on the pretext of being short of breath, hoping to indicate that I would make a feeble hunter and that her ability to make a good kayak was of no interest to me. After some tea, which was mostly concentrated sugar, the hunters gave me surprisingly weak handshakes and we said good-bye.

I made my way down through the skulls and vertebrae that lay scattered over the beach and paused for a moment to glance back over my shoulder. It had possibly only been my imagination, but amongst the smiling faces at my departure was one that seemed to falter, giving the impression of uncertainty and perhaps even regret. An indistinct movement at the window caught my eye, and then I turned to head for the ship. As the light began to fade, the curtain of mist took its cue and started to fall lower and lower . . . the white cloth covering the hills, the glaciers . . . lower and lower . . . finally obscuring the little village of Qeqertat from the eyes of the world once more, as it had probably done for centuries.

Thule's twin streets appeared to emerge from the sea, running up the hillside of glacial morraine like the tracks of a gigantic vehicle, and around them lay the unappealing warehouses of its businesses and public buildings, very much as if they had fallen off the back. Amongst them was the world's most northerly post office, and I eagerly went to collect some long-awaited mail. It was one of the special delights of travelling to receive a rare letter and each one felt like an extra Christmas. The man behind the counter seemed surprised.

'Poste restante? Oh no! We don't keep any letters here. People are always writing letters to us marked "poste restante" knowing they'll never be claimed and just wanting them returned with our postmark on them. So now we send all letters straight back. Sorry. Next please.'

There was no one actually waiting behind me and I was not sure if his 'next please' was an automatic response from busier days or a device as devious as the spurious letters, designed to avoid further discussion – but my letters had been returned home and that was that. It was a disappointment but it reinforced my determination to be aboard the *Nolson* when she headed south at the end of the week.

We moved on to Siorapaluk which had no post office and did not disturb the title of the one at Thule with its own eminent claim to being the world's most northerly permanent habitation. I had been given the name of an Eskimo who had been on Sir Edward Shackleton's 1934 expedition and when I showed the name to a man who stood in the doorway of a white house, he explained in signs how to find him. He pointed to the landing-area, touched his hair and then the wall and finally tugged at my jersey. I found him at once for Canutos Inuterssuaq had white hair, wore a jersey like mine and was down by the sea. Although he was now seventy-five years old he led me back to his house at a spritely walk. He wore kamiks, the thigh-length boots made of sealskin on the outside, lined with the fur of polar bear and Arctic hare on the inside, and tied at the top to prevent water from entering.

One area of the floor had been designated the kitchen and his tiny wife adopted a remarkable posture as she prepared some tea on a primus, surrounded by a conglomeration of utensils, jars and packets; keeping her legs rigidly straight she bent down until her head was near her ankles, and her arms swept around the place gathering cups and plates and buttering hardtack biscuits. Canutos proudly showed me a letter he had recently received from Lord Shackleton, almost forty years after they had last met, and he was so thrilled that it was now framed. He made me very welcome but was more intent on trying to sell me some of his hunting trophies, which was understandable in an area where gullible visitors were none too common. Canutos was beaming happily when I left, no wiser about Shackleton's expedition, carrying a set of undersized and overpriced walrus tusks under my arm.

Hurrying back to the ship, I stopped to ask a man the time. His English was perfect and, to my surprise, he explained he was Japanese. His features were indistinguishable from those of the local men and I later heard that he was reputed to be the best hunter in the village. He had come here as an engineer with an expedition six years previously, married a Siorapaluk girl and had only been back to Tokyo once for an expenses paid interview. When he answered my question, he confirmed something that I already knew.

'I don't know the time. I don't wear a watch. Here we have no time.'

I knew that Greenland only began up here in the north where the maps all said that it should end. Here were the people that had retained the special sparkle that was missing in the south. I knew that the real Greenlander was alive and well. (And I knew that nothing was safe from Japanese imitation.) I thanked him more generously than his simple answer might have deserved, and returned to the ship with a feeling of accomplishment.

The crew had made a rare visit ashore to buy souvenirs that would hold no memories for them but would prove they had indeed been to this country, and over the following days their excitement mounted at the thought of returning to a civilisation that had 'time'. My own concept of time lay somewhere in between that of the sailor and the Eskimo and yet it was with mixed feelings and a growing awareness of how much of the world there was still left to see that I went to consult Orly about leaving this small corner of it before the spell of the north ensnared me as it had done the hunter from the Orient.

Orly was admiring the new parka he had bought. 'You ought to get yourself one of these. Warm, by Jove! They're a portable Sahara. Yes, sir.'

Silence.

'By the way, the mess boy is better. Pity, isn't it?' He paused for a moment and changed voices. 'But dinna fash yersel', laddie.' (Vaguely Arbroath.) 'Oi've got a plan oop ma sleeve.' (Unlocated.) 'FOR HELVEDE.' (East Storstrøm, as he pricked his finger on the staple that held the label to the sleeve.)

If I had turned the world upside-down to get to Thule then Orly and the Chief Steward (one pillow) had to turn it back again to get me away, but they succeeded in persuading the captain that by now the ship really needed me. After signing a mass of incomprehensible papers I became a crewman for the fourth time and earned the right to my own modest headrest aboard the *Nolson*. It was a relief to be moving on to complete my large circle as we steamed towards Iceland through a sea that was as silver and heavy as mercury. Cape Farewell suddenly appeared and disappeared, and then my last glimpse of Greenland had gone.

We encountered the usual storms on this restless part of the oceans which sent strange vibrations through the ship, transforming it into a tuning fork as the bow crashed down, throwing pans around the galley and making plates shudder in their piles. My metamorphosis as a sailor was complete and I felt no ill effect except for the problem of trying to wash my feet one evening in a hand basin that was uncomfortably high off the floor. Having lifted one foot almost up to my chest to get it into the basin I was contorted into the stance of a doubtful stork when the boat gave a severe roll. This seemed to move the basin several feet higher up the wall and left me at the top of a steep incline. As my arms windmilled in the air my heel managed to retain a hold by hooking itself over the basin's rim – until the boat abruptly increased its angle still further, my heel slipped and I bounced backwards across the cabin in a series of ungainly hops before tripping over my shoes and ending up as a heap in the far corner. The others were suffering too and the mess boy, who had possibly not made a complete recovery, lost his balance on some stairs and the captain's vol-au-vents lived up to their name and resulted in a bas-relief plastered to the wall.

'Did you whistle?' Orly asked accusingly (in the lore of the sailor to whistle at sea is to whistle up bad weather). He eyed everyone suspiciously as he conducted his witch-hunt until the journey's end.

The storm did not interfere with the drinking parties every night when even the seasoned old sailors downed their schnapps with dilated pupils and a flinch of the shoulders. If I believed that the Greenlanders had needed to be shown how to drink then they could have found few teachers more dedicated than the Danes. Yet they were fine people and my debt to their kindness grew bigger by the day until my inevitable departure at Reykjavik. Events had moved so fast that the moment took me by surprise and I was again lost for words when Orly came to shake hands. It didn't matter as he did the talking as usual.

'Well, you take good care of yourself.'

Silence.

'That reminds me . . . you sure you didn't whistle?'

It was strange being back in a familiar city and yet it made me feel as though I did not belong here any more. My goodbyes had already been said to Iceland. The pull to move on was still strong and that same October day found me sitting in the waiting lounge of the airport with a ticket to New York.

The chairs each had a small coin-operated television set on the arm-rest but the only programme was a cars 'n' cops thriller which a man in the adjacent seat was watching. I decided instead to put a coin in a box that provided a taped commentary on Iceland, to hear what I had missed on my last visit. 'Press the language button of your choice,' said the instructions alongside five unmarked buttons. My choice was unlucky and a foreign voice suddenly spoke to me from a speaker hidden somewhere behind the dense leaves of a rubber plant. It was so loud that a man reading his newspaper nearby folded it away with a pronounced sigh and moved off to another row. The whole set-up must have been designed for the partially deaf simpletons of five undisclosed nations and was obviously broken, for the sound steadily increased of its own accord. I began to long for the serene silence of Siorapaluk as the public address system above my head was announcing a flight to Luxembourg while on my right the wheels of Kojak were shrieking around an endless corner and on my left, the virtues of the country were being extolled by a rubber plant which had by then worked itself up into a frenzy and was screaming at me in Spanish.

When I next recollected my senses, it was to find myself in a plane staring at a brown paper bag, instructions on how to bail out when we hit the sea and a booklet on how to enjoy the flight. My mind was on other things. It was hard to believe a year had gone past since my kilt had caused a stir that first night in Akureyri. A year spent in the isolated areas of the Arctic, almost void of human life, and a year in which I had hardly spoken my own language. Suddenly, ahead of me lay a completely different culture, an area where man came in millions and although he probably still did not speak my language, it would hopefully be much more intelligible.

My knowledge of America was scant. I remembered Orly the cook's earthy opinion: 'The States are the most impressive, most beautiful, the biggest, ugliest and the shittiest place I've been to. They've got everything. Lots to love, lots to hate.' I decided it would just be best to wait and see for myself. The postponement was made easier by the frequent arrivals of Coors Rocky Mountain Beer, and my apprehensions were removed with the empties. As the hostesses increased the mileage on the drinks trolly, all the time we were hurtling along at 739 feet per second towards the New World – and their uniforms appeared to get tighter by the minute.

My travels in North America

7 · One Big Apple
and the view from a truck

Three days after my arrival, I wrote home:

Flying over NY at night was a sight more like the active volcanoes I thought were behind me in Iceland with hot points of light covering the ground as far as the eye could see, fiercely lit cores of activity connected by burning trails of tangled roads that crossed the cooler glows of the suburban embers.

The immigration officer admitted me until 20th December, obviously not caring where I might be spending Christmas but just making sure it wasn't in the USA. I dossed down on a chair to pass the night and the next morning went into town on the subway which had been totally repainted in blotches of wild colours, both inside and out. I asked if it had been done intentionally. 'Sure, the graffiti kids spend hours getting it just right,' I was told.

Emerging from the Arctic, from the airport at night and from the tunnels of the subway into NY at rush hour I felt like a pea in a gutter with the deluge of humanity bearing down on me. Compared to Thule this really is the other end of the world and I can see why it's nearer the bottom. It must just be culture shock. My eyes moved higher and higher up a million panes of glass on all sides until my head was cricked back as far as it would go and I glimpsed a small square of sky at the top before someone pushed me; 'Hey! C'mon buddy, yer blockin' the sidewalk', and moved me into this tundra of tar, concrete and glass. I may be one of the last people to have got there but none of the earlier arrivals appears to have left.

The sidewalks swarm with a cross-section of the world; Hassidic Jews with straggly beards who walk stooped forwards with their hands held behind their backs, squinting over the rims of thick-lensed glasses as if desperately examining the ground for a one cent piece squandered by a careless Scot; there are timid Chinese and brash Indians; whites to fit every norm and every exception; and the blacks who outnumber all the others – in their clothes of the ultra-cool and casual, floppy felt hats, squashed pumpkin jockey caps and denim waistcoats, they jive down the streets to the soul music of their minds vibrating rhythm in everything they do. The hairstyles reflect the same exotic extremes of colour and character; over-grazed stubble of the convict, centre-line tufts of the Krishna-Cherokee, braided tassels of the Caribbean, starched bristles of the startled punk, shocking rainbows of the tinted trendy, luxuriant thatch of the Edwardian cottage and spherical cocoons of Afro-frizz. Floods of people and waves of cars, where any car less than eighteen feet long implies you are poor, misguided, suicidal or have recently been shortened in an accident. Jaywalking is like midday suns, only for mad dogs . . . and one rabid Scotsman who was cured very quickly.

The General Post Office appeared as a structural dwarf and a misfit of classical Greek pillars in hewn stone. Carved on its side in large letters were the words 'Neither snow nor rain nor heat nor gloom of night stays these couriers from the swift completion of their appointed rounds.' It was a long wall. Further on the mason had been made obsolete by a gigantic sign of moving lights with a more catchy message, 'I LIKE NEW YORK . . . HAVE A COKE . . . AND A SMILE . . . COKE ADDS LIFE . . . I LIKE. . .' and on it went, a visual punishment of lines.

It was hard to find a loaf of bread in the centre as the shops alternated between fur-lined this and gold-studded that with fast-food joints in the middle. Fair enough. Who comes to downtown NY to buy a loaf even if it is Vitamin D added, enriched with extra protein, nutritionally boosted and with more energy, which it has to be after the original goodness has been removed by being homogenised, purified, refined, of lower fat content and charged with factory freshness? Eventually I found a loaf of 'Mead's Fine Butter Honey Split Top Enriched Bread. Ingredients: bleached flour, water, corn, syrup, yeast, shortening (partially hydrogenated soy and cottonseed oils), cultured skim milk, vegetable mono- and diglycerides, salt, molasses, whey, dough conditioners (may contain: ethoxylated mono- and diglycerides, distilled monoglycerides), yeast nutrients (monocalcium phosphate, calcium sulphate, ammonium sulphate), calcium propionate, barley malt conditioners (may contain: potassium bromate, azodicarbonamide, potassium iodate), niacin, ferrous sulphate, thiamine hydrochloride, riboflavin', and then they added seductively, 'topped with butter and honey.' I decided the nasties we ate on *Sudviking* must have at least been healthy and wondered if a chain of fast-food sheeps' heads with a smile and a coke would catch on?

Went out to the Statue of Liberty and up into her crown where the summer temperature can reach 120°F. Took ages as the crowds caused a congestion around her kidneys, and climbing the spiral staircase in a kilt was worrying with people below the see-through grid steps. Scotsmen in kilts are rare here and yet their descendants are not. Every fifth person claims me as an ancestor, either pure blood or bastard. Were the Scots really so prolific, or is it something to do with the grid steps?

Then up the Empire State Building, long since deposed as the 'world's tallest' so they somewhat despondently clung to the 'world's most famous', but the views were worthy of either title. All around were the lesser skyscrapers packed tightly together like the spores from this mighty one, lacking only the constructor's sunlight or the investor's compost before they too rose as high as this architectural mutation of excessive growth. Down 87 floors in 100 seconds by lift, so they claimed, and out into the street.

The crowds eased slightly when darkness fell and the diurnal werewolves afraid of the night had locked themselves up behind burglar-proof bars in their penthouse dens. Yet the traffic still thundered along and the brief periods of relative peace droned with the nervous energy that makes this city's atmosphere so dynamic. The blue movies and peepshows of Times Square (which I had thought would reflect the sobriety of the newspaper) were in full swing and like the lights of the latest shows on Broadway, they tantalised and titillated those who had money, and just dazzled those who hadn't.

Blacks set up card stalls on the pavements and let their stooges win money with obvious tricks that became unfathomable the moment any passer-by had been drawn in and placed his dollars on the table – some dealers were only small boys but already man-eating card-sharks. When the cops cruised past they collapsed their stall and had vanished into the crowd within a second, using the darkness to best advantage. I don't know why but maybe this method of extortion is not as innocent as it looks.

Every few paces someone hassled me to take a leaflet, lend a dime, listen to his poverty or else a figure brushed past my back muttering '. . . smoke man? Loose joint – hash – shit – smoke . . .?' It's all here and if you want it you can get it, all except good bread and fresh water.

But there was fear in the people. They just kept on walking when you asked a question and you had to follow them until they realised you were not soliciting or pushing dope. If you confirmed it with a smile then they couldn't be more friendly, except in black Harlem where white honkies have a bounty on their heads, even rabid ones that wear sporrans.

A little old lady got on my bus and politely asked the driver if it went to Lexington Avenue. The driver did not like little old ladies. 'Do you see that sign up there? What does that sign say? Says 32nd Street, doesn't it? So that's where I'm goin'. Try the one behind – it happens to say "Lexington" on it.' 'Oh! I never saw it,' she said. 'You never will if you don't look,' he snapped. Then he drove off only to find a taxi trying to cut in. While still driving he flung open the window, stood up, pummelled the door with his fist and screamed out 'YOU STUPID PUNK . . .'

'The Big Apple' has its rosy side but it has its worms too. I'm staying at a YMCA hostel where my passport is held to ransom for $8 per night, and room 484 has the purpose-built severity of a filing cabinet. Three hectic but fascinating days here are enough for someone who is not a city person. Already I miss space, soft shapes, silence and Eskimos – so tomorrow I'll move on. My plans are vague as I want to be free to drift as invitations or suggestions come, but am taking the old advice and heading west, towards LA. Don't worry. I'll take care. At least there aren't any sea-cliffs for a few thousand miles.

Love

My letter tried to end with the feeling of confidence that I was lacking. Reports from other hitch-hikers varied from 'easy, no problems' to tales of violence and a first-hand account of an escape from a murder attempt. Even most Americans advised against it. The fear worked both ways to include not only the driver but also the hiker and yet when it had been overcome with a successful lift, hitching came into its own as the best means of discovering a country and of sampling its people. There was often the bonus of being sidetracked to special places only local drivers could know, and my visual impressions were accompanied by commentaries from a cross-section of their society. Opinions were expressed as blunt statements or were wrapped up in stories, leaving me to separate pretence from belief and fact from tittle-tattle. From this I would draw my own conclusions and make my oversimplifications. The world in a nutshell. Iceland was maybe cod, the Faroes were dangerously wonderful and Greenland came in significant sixths. How would North America – this other extreme beyond the grey area of Atlantic – appear through my tinted glasses? Hitching would I hoped provide a wide choice of criteria. It made travel all the more exciting, sometimes unnecessarily so. It was illegal on the freeways. But it was the cheapest way to cover large distances.

However, it could be a slow starter and after a morning of waiting beside the New Jersey turnpikes, a set of ten toll-booths where thousands of cars per hour paused for a moment, my travel philosophy began to falter. Feeling deflated I suddenly didn't know what I was trying to do or why. When a car did stop I leapt in so quickly that all my good intentions of cautiously trying to assess the driver's sincerity beforehand were instantly forgotten and I hardly even noticed that it was one of the rare undersized cars until we were off.

We left the freeway at the River Delaware. She wore a mantle of weed parted in the middle to reveal a négligée of algae, both in stagnant green. It was only then that the driver began to show some of the symptoms of an undersized car-owner. He became nervous, turned the radio on, then off, then on again, constantly glanced around and moved his hands about the wheel. His fingers trembled and his skin twitched like horseflesh bothered by horsefly and at each town he would say, 'Goddamn! Drugstores are all closed. Gotta get me some drugs . . .' His conversation turned black. Every subject I brought up cheerfully became dulled to doom, despair, famine, plague and the poor season the Philadelphia Eagles had suffered. He pulled my own spirits down so low that I asked to be let out, and my first lift ended. The manic depressive drove off having unburdened some of his woes onto one Scotsman who was left looking around for one, just one, smiling American.

One soon came along and he dropped me off feeling refreshed by his kindness at the entry to the freeway again, only to find the discouraging sign 'HITCHING IS A SAFETY VIOLATION PUNISH-ABLE BY A FINE.' Emotionally, it was becoming a bumpy trip.

A smart Lincoln Mercury with electric gadgets galore and seats that squirmed into different shapes at the push of buttons took me on across Pennsylvania's low undulating folds of land, thickly wooded with deciduous trees that had been denuded by frost. It felt a relief to be in the countryside again, away from cities and unfriendly signs, but this driver did nothing to ease my mistrust of the people,

'You've survived New York so now you're out of the worst. This area round Cleveland is the second worst – the armpit of the States. Mind you, there's Detroit, they call that "murder city", big racial problems, bad blacks and riddled with Mafia. Chicago's not so great either and then there's Albuquerque – that's "rape city" . . .' When he had exhausted his extensive knowledge of the great crime centres of the country, he turned on me in an aggressive manner as if I and my 'type' were the cause of them all.

'. . . and you hikers, you're just nothing but parasites on society. Why don't you bunch get a job and then you could afford a car instead of scrounging off us decent folk? Some of you haven't had a bath for months and the stories one hears nowadays, why half of you should be locked up the moment you set foot on a road 'cos you're a threat to our safety.' He stopped his damnation at a truck-stop only to resume it once more between mouthfuls of a meal, while I turned a deaf ear and drank a bottomless cup of coffee, marvelling at the system which seemed to give unlimited refills at no extra cost. Then he got up, handed me the bill and walked off saying that he was now going a different way which was no longer on my route. My head sank into my hands as I slouched wearily over a Whopperburger menu where the word 'whopper' went through a multitude of comparatives until the most expensive, 'superwhopperest', contemplating manic depressives, 'murder city' and a new species of host that successfully feeds off its parasite. I suddenly became aware of someone standing behind me.

'Y'itchin'? 't'aint legal 'ere. S' no molestin' ur cust'mers,' the manager said with abbreviated venom. It was hard to deny with a large sign that said 'WEST PLEASE' by my feet and he did not even wait for a reply in Oxford English but picked up my pack and carried it to the door. I followed behind my self-elected porter, not wanting to make a scene and not getting any opportunity, stopped to pay the bill and considered asking if they had a packet of biscuits. But what was the point? We didn't even speak the same language for my biscuits were their cookies and their biscuits were my scones, my crisps were their potato chips and my luggage was just being thrown outside. So I left with nothing but the irony of a receipt that a bored cashier had rubberstamped with the words, 'We are pleased to have served you, we hope you are pleased with our service. Have a safe journey, a nice nite – and hurry back.' The manager came back in, having troubled to take my pack to the furthest extremity of his juridical area and he didn't respond when I wished him a 'nice nite' too, nor did he appear to want me to hurry back.

The sun had set and dusk was rapidly absorbing everything save the noise of the traffic on the freeway. I stood a lonely kilted figure by the exit, hovering on the edge of the darkness and the floodlighting of my banishment, filled with terrible misgivings as I displayed 'WEST PLEASE' towards the armpit of the States. Things were not going so well.

A truck drew up. An enormous Kenworth. Twin sets of highly polished chrome exhausts ran up the side of its cab whose paintwork was ablaze with blow-brush flames engulfing it from every angle. Spotlights sat in every niche and were perched in rows, their crystal domes like pouting fantails on bars of stainless steel. It was overpowering.

'Are you'ze gonna geddin or aincha?' asked the charred figure of Nelson Brown, a small black man, leaning out of the inferno. I climbed up and up and inside there was a bed in an alcove, deep-pile carpeting from ceiling to floor, TV, fridge, kettle . . . 'What you'ze wearin' dat freaky gear for, man? You'ze darned lucky t'get you'ze a lift. What dey'se callin' you?'

'I come from Scotland and this is our national costume. My name's Alastair.' I wished I didn't speak so proper.

'Well, ah'll be . . . C'mon in man, welcome t'ma truck. Ah'ze goin' t'Houston, Texas, an' you'ze kin call me Nel, same as all ma frien's does.'

Nel was a religious man and ran his own furniture removal

business 'by God's grace'. He had recently donated a building to his faith for the purpose of starting a new church, to be called 'The Temple of the Deliverance'. It sounded appropriate to his job.

The CB radio went non-stop as truckers chatted and cut in on each other, throwing their codenames around as if in a game of radio scrabble: Buffalo Beaver, Tumbleweed, Ladybug, Globetrotter, Nervous Wreck, Who Cares . . . and the signposts seemed to join in, flashing past in our headlights and showing the way to Climax, Bethlehem, Kellogg, Paw Paw, Kalamazoo, Mishawaka and Kankakee. The miles fell away behind us as we drove through the night.

Nel picked up his microphone. 'Break one-nine, how 'bout it local?'

'Yea, go ahead, buddy. What kin I do?'

'We're lookin' fer fifty-five.'

'Well, what's yer twen'y?'

'We're westbound Kansas City on two-one-eight, just outta Fenton.'

'Gee, yer right behind me, buddy.'

'Mercy sakes, yer lookin' good.'

'Yea, we're truckin' real nice. Kansas City? Take the Baker Road exit an' follow fifty-nine south, then the forty-six west'll take you right on. Heard nothin' on bears there so looks like you got an open door . . .'

Then another voice cut in, '. . . My bird just barked so . . . yea, there he is, a smokie in the grass at the nineteen-mile yard. Better keep an eyeball out an' drop down to double nickels (fifty-five m.p.h.) 'cos' he sure looks hungry for them green stamps (dollars).' Then another asked for a ten-thirty-six (the time) and was told it was five-thirty (which was actually five-thirty) so he asked for a ten-nine (repeat) and five-thirty came again so he signed out with a ten-four whereupon Mamma Goose broke in with a one-nine to ask if the last voice was his old buddy the Sugarbug and because it was he asked for his twenty (location) and they chatted about hunting beaver (women) and Mamma Goose arranged to meet the Sugarbug around five-fifty when he stopped for motion-lotion (fuel) – and I suddenly appreciated the awesome problems of the Russians trying to gather intelligence in America.

At a truck-stop Nel led me to a table where there were some other drivers. One of them was chatting about Florida and said that they sprayed ice crystals over the streets at Christmas (at the rate-payer's expense) to have a brief white snowstorm in the heatwave. Another said he would like to go there as he could 'sure use a bit of sun tan.' I tried to swallow my laughter until tears welled up in my eyes and I felt about to explode. Then he turned to me and I released it when he winked, for he was as black as a midday shadow.

I was the only white at the table of five and Nel proudly introduced me to his friends. 'Do you'se see what ah got 'ere? Geeze, ah ain't never seen nothin' like dis on de road afore.' It was hard to work out if it was a compliment or not but when another told a story about a heavy night of drinking with a friend, I soon discovered that the triple negative was just the normal strength of denial.

'. . . So ah got ma frien' 'ome an' next day ee saze, "Wowee ma 'ead 'urts – an' it got bumps all over. Ah sure as 'ell ain't never got no bumps from no corn whiskey afore. What'ye'ze gone done d'me?" Ah saze, "Ah ain't gone done nothin', man. Ah wis jist tryin' take ye'ze 'ome over ma shoulder. Ain't no fault o'mine dat ye'ze so big an' ah'ze a bit short in d'arse but ah jist couldn't done stop yer 'ead bumpin' 'long dat kerb" . . .', and his voice disintegrated into a series of hysterical soprano whoops interspersed with splutters of giggles, and finally dissolved into moments of silence when his laughter was so intense that nothing could emerge, his mouth frozen open, his face puckled into a mass of wrinkles and his shoulders shaking wildly. Blacks have a capacity for laughter that is spontaneous and all-consuming.

As I looked around the other tables it was obvious that truck-drivers over the age of forty had become moulded into the same shape as a result of an unhealthy diet and an inactive lifestyle. A trucker's torso was conical with the broad base protruding around his midriff, caused by the upper regions of disused muscle slowly settling lower down through constant vibration to join the fats of excess French fries in forming the foundation of the driving/eating posture. The legs, so little used, had dwindled into absurdly fragile supports that sprouted from ornate cowboy boots of synthetic raw-hide. Sometimes he wore a suede jacket that did not even attempt the journey around his circumference and had Davy Crockett frills hanging down from the sleeves. The hands were loosely clenched grappling irons which grappled frequently with hamburgers, fitting them into an appropriately superwhopperest-sized mouth. Above it loomed a prominent nose that might have been the gramophone needle holding the truck to the road as it followed the dotted line groove, watched by eyes with the piercing sharpness of a stuffed hawk. The swept-back hairstyle, groomed into shape by rushing air from the ventilator while trucking through the night, disappeared into a large Wild West hat of so many US gallons (and less imperial ones) that was purposely tilted too far forwards the moment he entered a truck-stop. This rendered all frontal vision impossible and attempted to convey to those who did not see him trip on the doormat that he had just driven cross-country from the Big Apple to the Golden Gate with the same casual sideways glances that he was now giving the beavers who worked behind the counter. He had left his three hundred horsepower mount outside, tethered to a diesel pump. The very linoleum of the floor, slightly tacky with tomato ketchup, seemed to shake as the modern cowboy – the lifeblood of the great American transport system – sidled up to the counter to order candies and a coke through a hole in the side of his mouth where once a cigar might have been.

Nel nudged me back into concentration as a girl was taking our order for breakfast and she had to repeat the choice for me, with obvious tedium and a hint of a cold.

'We got boiled-soft-over-easy-scrambled-hard- (sniff) -sunny-side-up-scrambled-soft-boiled-hard- (sniff) -double-single-waffles-hash-browns-fries.'

A moment of stunned silence followed this onslaught.

'C'mon honey, ain't got all day.'

'A waffle, please,' I finally decided as it sounded intriguing and the least complicated in what was a lucky dip anyhow.

We drove on through St Louis with its attractive tall metallic arch that seemed to have no other purpose than to span the city as a silver rainbow, and on towards Kansas. The great farmland of the plains opened up before us and amply bore out an impression of truth in the saying that to put wheat in one pocket and sunflower seeds in the other was to have experienced Kansas.

Nel had a delivery to make in a small town. We drove along quiet side-roads to discover the charm of the back-country towns whose squat wooden houses had preserved the atmosphere of the early pioneering days with their individual simplicity. Some, however, were more run down and their brightly painted verandas and little slatted fences gave the air of a ribbon tied around the shabby sides of an old tea-box, trying to pass itself off as a treasure-chest.

A sharp noise in the engine brought us slowly to a halt amongst fields on the edge of town. Nel opened the bonnet and leant over deep into the works and fiddled around for some time. It was not a serious breakdown but it required special tools and a spare part, so he went off to phone a garage. An hour later he limped back, tired and dejected.

'D'aint no good dis area. Jist 'cos ah'ze black dey don't give no damn. Saze dey'll come when dey can. Saze maybe not even today. Jist 'cos ah'ze black. If ah wis white dey'd be 'ere in no time.'

'Oh come on, Nel. It's probably nothing like that. Maybe they're pretty busy or haven't got the part . . .' But he was not to be consoled.

'Dis is America, man. Dey kin get anythin' cross-country faster dan you'ze kin blink. Nope. You'ze don't know dis country. It's jist 'cos ah'ze black. An' ah phoned dat customer – she ain't none too frien'ly neither. Saze she don't want de load delivered in d'evenin'.'

We waited all day and no one came. Nel went off several times to see what was happening and returned more defeated each time. We passed that night in the cab and waited the following day until a mechanic arrived in the late afternoon. He soon completed the repair, ignoring Nel as much as possible and putting all his questions to me first. We set off in silence, both deep in our thoughts.

'You'ze better phone dat lady an' ask if we'ze kin come now seein' it's so late,' he said when we stopped at a phone. It struck me as a strange suggestion as he knew all the details, but he wanted to 'learn me de job.' A woman answered my call.

'Are you with the nigger that phoned earlier?' she asked. It was hard to believe the unkindness in the way she spat out the word 'nigger'.

'Look. We've driven a long way with your furniture. We've been stuck on the road for two days and we're tired. Do you want it or don't you?'

'Well, if you're with him, then it's OK. I just don't want no nigger turning up alone on my doorstep at night.'

'My friend is a better . . .' I put the phone down, choked with rage and my hands trembling. I understood why Nel had got me to phone. He was black and sounded black while I was white and sounded white. I found myself hating a woman I had never met as the image of Nel's heavy footsteps and his look of helplessness returned to me, flooding my soul with the same sense of injustice, the same feeling of despair, of shattered illusions – making me wish that I could remove this burden of prejudice, right a terrible wrong and, somehow, share his blackness.

We delivered the furniture as quickly as we could in a silence that matched the coldness of the owner and were soon driving on through the night non-stop for Houston. I was once more absorbed into the thrill of the trucker's life as we cruised along at eighty mph with breathtaking sensations of power and speed, of being supreme and unstoppable – it was all the fun of the fair only it was intensified and didn't suddenly stop when your money ran out. Motel signs rushed past in a blur of neon lights, low bridges stooped to remove our roof, gaps narrowed as we squeezed our way through the impossible, we wove to the right and back to the left across three lanes of traffic overtaking on any side that suited us for we were thirty tons of momentum and three hundred horsepower in motion that was faster and truly unstoppable. Trucks, trucks everywhere I looked, they were flying along the freeways in long lines, rows of coloured lights covered their contours and eighteen wheels were ceaselessly spinning. They had come a thousand miles and they were going a thousand more. America was on the move. Her cowboys were riding on with their love-hate relationship with a life they could not give up. Their truck was their home, their life, their job, their prison and they were only happy when they were cursing it, when they were driving and when they were being relentlessly driven. They swore they were going to give it up. They swore they would give it up fifteen years ago. They said it was one helluva life. They loved it. They loved to hate it.

The following evening we reached Houston. We exchanged addresses and Nel said he would try to come to Scotland one day.

'You'ze betcha. But ah ain't jist got me a family, ah got ma own army; nine littl'uns an' two dawgs an' ma missus so ain't easy jist t'up an' off like dat. But ah wanna try me on dat kilt an' dat dere 'airy sporran some day. You'ze take care.' The flaming Kenworth roared off. I was sorry to see Nel go, and knew we'd never meet again.

I found a bar on the outskirts of the city and went in to ask where the YMCA was. The barman stopped polishing a glass for long enough to look me over and then replied, 'Nah, she don't work here no more.' I found a cheap dive of a hotel instead, as the culmination of three nights without sleep began to take its toll and my energy seeped away.

It was still warm and humid as I tried to write up my diary. Two beetles patrolled the table-top and inspected the unemptied ashtray on each beat, while a large cockroach with feelers as long as his body performed handstands on the cornice around the ceiling. The fan did not work, the light gave out a meagre glow and the curtain was a dirty dishcloth with ragged edges, a torn corner and numerous large holes. It ran out optimistically from left to right for two-thirds of the window's width but not even at full stretch could it close the final gap. On the downward journey it didn't even try and gave up a yard from the bottom and hung there dejectedly. The walls had once been light-blue but a host of grubby hands had covered them with the brown impressions of their grime, and the carpet's original colour was lost amongst the stains, burns, holes and patches that were bare to the hemp. A drunk passed in the street below, singing noisily and muddling his words as if to scare my little room-mates, '. . . IS THISH THE WAY T'ARMADILLO . . .?'

And still the cockroach did his handstands. Surely he was meant for a better stage than this?

8 · Texas time and Las Vegas time

Houston, the boom city of America, was drawing many businesses away from New York and fresh arrivals were moving in at the rate of a thousand per week to add to the city's natural rate of population growth, and the confusion of the bus system. It had been dismantled and reerected elsewhere so often that not even the few locals without their own car knew if the next bus would materialise or not, despite being branded with the misleading slogan of 'Easyrider'. After an hour of waiting, new arrival 1001 for that week decided to walk and soon found he had a wino for company. He offered to show me the way to the centre and we passed the finger-lickin' good food bars and then a sign whose purpose was less well-defined but which announced the truism, 'How come people who snore always get off to sleep first?'

My guide soon began to falter, stopping to take surreptitious swigs from a brown paper bag until finally the bag had been tilted vertically in the air to deliver one swig too many. He collapsed onto a conveniently placed bench beneath the words 'Jesus Christ is OK' written on a wall in spray-can paint as if to reveal a new theological discovery and to offer reassurance to the whole of Christendom. My guide seemed oblivious of the good news and he sadly sought his reassurance from a brown paper bag that could never yield enough and had no more to give.

The next moment he had been replaced by a very affable artist who readily admitted to having 'dropped out', as if that would account for his sudden appearance, wearing three jackets and boots held together by more string than my own. He had recently crashed his car, and had no regular work, lived off credit cards that he had neither the intention nor the means of honouring (claiming that debtors were not sent to prison here but could have their property confiscated – so he had none but his jackets), had just taken up Zen Buddhism and was thoroughly enjoying life. The outer jacket seemed to be the tool kit of his former car with spanners sticking out of every pocket, the innermost one kept him warm while the middle one held a supply of cigars. He produced two after carefully selecting them from ones with minor imperfections, offered me one and insisted I take it despite all my refusals. Mine wouldn't light. 'I think ya got the wrong end in yer mouth,' said my friend who knew a lot about cigars, and it certainly went better after that. So two figures, one in kilt, one in excess jackets and both in parcelled boots, walked into downtown Boom City smoking cigars that were large even by Texan standards. Grass-roots travel was not always hard.

Houston has endeavoured to put as much of itself as possible under large roofs, to create sub-cities within a city. Under one of these roofs is a climate-controlled shopping complex so large it is necessary to have a map to find your way out. Under another is a bank so long, a traveller's cheque has a daunting final journey before it can be processed – and the Astrodome has the largest roof of any sports stadium in the world. Without a special ventilation system, humidity and condensation would collect under this huge ceiling and a shower of rain would fall on the nine and a half acres below. Boom City's wealth originated from oil, beef and its deepwater port but now it has expanded to include everything from long banks to space rockets. The prosperity is reflected by the generous abundance of its street litter bins and the frequency of skeleton cranes which perch on top of most buildings. Houston is a small apple compared to New York, rosier and more polished because, with the exception of a few cheap hotels, it has not yet had time to grow seedy.

Over the next few days I found an elusive Easyrider out to the Lyndon B. Johnson Space Center where they explained how to go about getting to the moon in do-it-yourself layman's language and with a fascinating display of dismembered rockets for aspiring spacepersons to tiptoe over their 'No Entry' ropes, to stare at, fiddle with and prod. 'No Entry' signs are always provocative, particularly to high-spirited Americans, but tiptoeing, staring, fiddling and prodding are socially acceptable forms of trespass and vandalism.

It is here that NASA controls all space missions once it has been seen from a safe distance of eight hundred miles that Florida's Cape Canaveral has launched them successfully, and it is here that astronauts are trained and equipment is tested. Figures walked around with clusters of limp wires clumped to their heads, having just been disconnected from a machine to fetch a cup of unscientific coffee. The less fortunate guinea-pigs of inanimate technology lay concealed in a test-chamber the size of a warehouse from which all the air had been drawn out except enough to fill a ping-pong ball and while one of its sides was heated to 280°F, the other was simultaneously frozen to minus 250°F. If it still worked then it was viewed suspiciously over a few more unscientific coffees before being repeatedly returned to this twentieth century rack until it finally disintegrated. The few exceptions received an expert's reluctant grunt of approval and were moved along the line to the next sinister warehouse. How fruitful all this was could only be imagined, but the guide pointed to the GMT digital clock, accurate to one second per century, and said, 'If there is nothing else we can do, we can tell you the right time.'

There was a moon-buggy which might well have been developed from the prototype that I had watched an Icelandic farmer drive around in the seventy-nine per cent wasteland with his hen and manure a year before, and there were dozens of distracted observers hunched over more coffee and their own television screen. They monitored tests of everything from a nut and bolt being ripped apart to the reaction of a strawberry blancmange under colossal atmospheres of pressure. I left the display feeling closer to the moon than to the centre of Houston where Easyrider missions lacked simulation and appeared to have been abandoned. I reset my watch to be correct to within one second per century; but then I remembered it was accustomed to lose five minutes every twenty-four hours.

My journey slowed down its frantic pace and yet continued, with a lift from a girl who was such an ardent man-hater in spite of, or because of, having a small son. She was undoubtedly a burn-her-bra type and would have done so had she not been in such obvious need of it, but then that was exactly the sort of observation she would have expected a man to make. Her lift was followed by one from a nuclear physicist who believed that the British led the world in techniques of atomic waste disposal, but he let me out before he had time to reveal where they were putting it all, and a short wait ended with another car and the company of a lecturer at the world's richest university in nearby Austin. His conversation centred around my well-being in the hereafter and he was the first of many to slip a small copy of the New Testament into my hand as we parted, with the best possible intentions – and just in case I had missed the writing on the wall in Houston.

The lecturer took me to San Antonio which has preserved something of the Spanish flavour from its history as well as the small mission where, in 1836, 188 Americans withstood the siege of five thousand Mexicans led by Santa Anna for twelve days before they fell on the thirteenth and were all killed, including the legendary Davy Crockett who died fighting with his rifle as a club. The Mexicans were later resoundingly defeated when 'Remember the Alamo' was called out as a battlecry to inspire the Americans to avenge that massacre.

America's past might not be as deep as that of Europe but because of this many of her historical landmarks have remained remarkably untouched since her decisive events took place, leaving the visitor with a greater feeling of their original atmosphere and a more tangible grasp on their significance. Bullet-holes in a wall, broken cartwheels from a pioneer's wagon and the streets of a mining ghost town bring history alive in a way that defies an overgrown hillside with the impressive name of a medieval battle. The little mission seemed to echo with gunfire as I was thus defending America's heritage in my mind, when I overheard two people whispering behind my back (Texans even do that loudly):

'I think it's cute that he's dressed up in his native uniform.'

It seemed prudent to move on before I was taken for a Mexican.

My hitch-hiking confidence was growing especially now that cities were almost non-existent in the immense expanses of open land that astounded me. Two days were needed simply to drive across Texas but I made a good start when a van pulling a trailer stopped for me. A friendly family indicated a car sitting on the trailer and said it was the only space they had, which was fine by my modest standards. So I hitched my first and only lift in a car all to myself without having to do any of the driving for the 250-mile trip. I relaxed back into the seat of my express sedan-chair and watched the scenery go by. This was the life.

Towns were spaced at thirty-mile intervals so that the early homesteaders who lived in between were never more than fifteen miles from a source of supplies. This was the furthest they could comfortably travel by wagon if they had to return home the same day. Each town was centred around a large building of ornate

stonework which stood alone in the square, the austere words
'Court House' chiselled on its best side. Sheep punctuated the
scrubland in places but it was shared mainly between cattle ranches
and the oil industry. Gas pumps covered the whole area, standing
like giant crows, endlessly rocking their bodies up and down and
pecking their beaks at the ground as they drew the gas up and fed it
into a matrix of pipes. Then both cattle and oil crows became more
scarce as the scrub turned to savannah, and disappeared altogether
with the gradual advent of desert where only sagebush, tumbleweed
and cactus seemed to thrive.

The Roberts family invited me to spend the night in their house
and fed me a meal that more than justified the Texans' reputation for
exaggerating everything to the extreme, and it was accompanied by
their natural and raw wit.

'How do you like your steak done?' Ma Roberts called through
from the kitchen.

Pa Roberts never gave me a chance to answer. 'If it's Aberdeen
Angus he'll take it as it comes. Just remove the horns, wipe under the
tail and it'll be fine, love.'

Families like these were hard to leave but the next day it was
another truck that took me on westwards. The driver was over sixty
and had just driven eighteen hours with stops only for meals.

'You ever seen a pacemaker?' he asked suddenly. 'You can take a
look at one right here, as this little bird just keeps me tickin' along',
and he unbuttoned his shirt to reveal a bulge over his heart as if two
matchboxes had been placed underneath the skin. I shifted uneasily
to the edge of my seat as he accelerated back up to seventy-five
m.p.h. For the next five hours all my concentration was on trying to
hear a tick that would indicate my driver's life-support system was
not giving up. The inevitable truck-stop provided a welcome break
and I sank into a chair on my own while a truckers' conference
sprang up around the room as they discussed the world's problems
over plates of eggs. The threats of communism, an oil crisis,
inflation, racialism and all other areas of human strife were solved
'over-easy' with a wave of the fork and an extra dollup of ketchup to
leave the world sunny-side-up. If only the White House would
invite truckers to a working breakfast . . .

Suddenly I realised my driver had gone. The warnings of other
hikers raced through my mind . . . Keep your luggage with you at

all times; avoid putting it in a car boot if possible – drivers may lock you out when you leave the car and roar off with your pack still in their boot. Beware truck-stops if your luggage is left in a car – your host may slip away or excuse himself to visit the restroom, and make a premature departure instead . . . Panic-stricken, I leapt up and dashed out, only to find that the driver's truck was in fact still there and he was making a long telephone call. The shock of thinking I'd lost all my belongings was so intense that it took me some time to recover but I vowed there and then never to leave my camera case alone anywhere – it contained my passport, money, traveller's cheques and my health certificates as well as my camera equipment. That case was my reason for travelling and my sole means. It was to become my ball and chain in many ways over the next four years but, except for one terrible occasion, it was never again to leave my side. We drove on to El Paso and I clutched my case the whole way.

The Rio Grande river has its source in the Rockies in Colorado, runs down to El Paso and from here to its mouth on the East Coast it forms the boundary between the United States and Mexico. Mexicans who have entered the United States illegally have always been known as 'wetbacks', having had to swim the Rio Grande to sneak in, and at this time there were believed to be about seven million of them currently working throughout the country without papers. Many were caught and sent back but they just returned again, for even the lowest wages here were better than no wages in their homeland.

It was cold waiting for a lift at El Paso. Winter was steadily approaching and already patches of snow lay on the desert sand. It was an incongruous sight and forced me to reconsider where I should go. Perhaps it would be best to find work for the winter months, but would that be possible in an area flooded with cheap labour?

'Hi! Happy Turkey Day,' said a man with a smile to tame a buffalo stampede. Larry Stones took me north through two hundred miles of desert known as the 'Journey of Death', past the town of Truth or Consequences (renamed after a television programme) where Geronimo used to bathe in the hot springs, to his adobe house in Socorro, New Mexico. I joined his family for the traditional meal of

turkey to celebrate Thanksgiving Day, commemorating the early
pilgrims' relief at having survived their first year. I felt the same
about mine.

The Stones family typified the generosity and overwhelming
hospitality that I came to believe was a national characteristic of
Americans. Within a week they had found me a job with a local
farmer and had opened up their home to me, a stranger, for as long as
I wanted. It was shared with a St Bernard called Lil Bit and Adrian
the goat (a nanny, but this had not been immediately evident).

I worked with the Mexicans, one of whom had walked every pace
of four hundred miles to get here, digging ditches, clearing drains
and sorting chilli peppers which stung our eyes. The work was
tedious and I learnt Robert Burns' long poem 'Tam O'Shanter' by
heart although many of the words were as meaningless as the
Spanish of my colleagues – but this helped to pass the time and to
suppress my guilt. It hurt me to see them sweat as much as myself.
They earned twelve dollars a day and I earned fifteen. We were both
illegal and both being robbed but they were brown, inarticulate and
three dollars less likely to cause trouble.

Our boss was a jovial, rotund man who frequently slewed over to
one side and excreted a vile gob of dark saliva, letting it course
pleasurably over his lips before it fell to the ground. He confided that
I was the only hiker he had ever come across who 'really' wanted to
work, and because of this he had actually created a job for me. I liked
him and was flattered into condoning what was a virtual slave trade.

'Y'know, Al?' he said, chewing tobacco packed so tightly around
his gums that his cheeks bulged like a gorged hamster, 'Ah figure
y'er the world's first Scottish wetback.'

The Rio Grande at El Paso was no more than a ditch of 'wetfoot'
dimensions in a cement trough when my visa expired. I went down
to cross over into Mexico for a few hours and returned with a new
visa valid for six months. It was easier than officially applying for an
extension. The weeks went past in pleasant oblivion until a mixture
of wanderlust, milder weather and the first complete recital of Tam
caused me to don my tartan once more and extend my trail of wet
footprints over a bit more of the country.

They went north to Taos, a small village that was a popular haunt
of the hippies in the great 'love and peace' era of the Sixties. Many of
them still lived there. The car that gave me a lift was driven by a

businessman, an ex-hippy, returning to the area for the first time in ten years. He suddenly stopped to talk to a middle-aged woman with tattooed flora shrivelling on her arms. She was an old acquaintance. They blushed greetings and fell into conversation.

'Times have changed, man,' she said. 'It was cool living by your ideals but that didn't earn you any bread. I'm a teacher now. . .' and they reached back across a decade to recall the old days with more than a hint of nostalgia, but much fatter wallets. And I thought hippies never blushed.

The village of the Pueblo Indians, my main interest in coming to Taos, was as sorry as a lost ideal. It was an intriguing conglomeration of adobe houses plastered together in haphazard fashion on different levels and facing all angles. The style was based on the cave dwellings of their predecessors, the Anasazi Indians, but everywhere were little booths where Indians with pigtails sold tickets for exploring, experiencing and disrupting their old way of life. Tourists flooded their village and their privacy. This was not surprising as exploring, experiencing and disrupting are intensified forms of fiddling and prodding when 'No Entry' signs have been removed. Especially where history and culture are concerned. The Pueblo Indians appeared to have been vandalised, badly restored and then put on display.

A drunk and dishevelled Indian came by as I was waiting for a lift. He wore a blanket wrapped tightly round his head and kept it secure by clamping the loose end between his teeth. He stared at me for a while, seemingly bemused that my own headdress had apparently slipped to my waist, and then he released his mouthful of blanket to say that hitching might be easier if I 'tried to look normal'. This remark irritated me. It was unpleasant enough to have just been treated as a tourist, but immeasurably worse to have been regarded as a substandard one. My impulse to pick an argument with him was nevertheless stifled for it seemed pointless to banter words with a drunk, especially when his mouth was bunged up with wool. He tottered off to his troglodyte village and vanished shortly before a car stopped for me. But by then Taos had palled and I didn't ask my driver to let me out at the spot nearby where D. H. Lawrence lived and is now buried. We passed a reservation of Navajo Indians, the largest tribe in North America, where billboards were stacked along the roadside advertising crafts, fireworks and petrified wood for sale. 'Come and see a live buffalo – FREE', said one as an incentive and there stood the miserable specimen beside a group of heavy Indians. In all the decadence it was questionable who would have had the greater difficulty; the wretched buffalo trying to run away or the indolent Navajo trying to catch him? Scotsmen and Indians certainly had different concepts of normal.

A few days later I stood poised on the edge of one of the wonders of the world. It is not the deepest nor the widest gorge, but the dramatic splendour of the Grand Canyon is worthy of its reputation. Over two hundred miles of canyons within a canyon, it forms a scar across the land nine miles wide and one mile deep, created by the erosion of wind, winter and the Colorado river that surges through it. The pinks, reds, greys and blues of the rock reflect the weather and the level of the sun with the pastel shades of a moody chamelion. It is an awesome demonstration of the power of water and a humbling illustration of mankind's youth.

There was a mule corral at the top of the most frequented path down into the canyon, where a number of gaudy tourists and their riotous children were clambering on and falling off the long-suffering animals in outfits that combined Après Ski with Wild West to devastating effect. I hurried past to enter the peace of the natural world with its more mellow tones and, unfortunately, the suffocating reminders of yesterday's mule trek left behind on the track.

The range of climate within the canyon, equal to that found at sea level from Mexico to the Arctic, provides four of the world's seven classified life zones for 270 species of animals living there. The most common and courageous of these are the chipmonks. They beguile many a visitor with their gymnastic entertainment when he stops to peel off the winter clothing necessary on the rim or sits sweltering in heat at the bottom. Then their charm turns to brazen robbery and he finds himself separated from his unpacked lunch. (The little rodents took mine as well.)

Black clouds rolled over and the canyon darkened in response. Flashes of lighting suddenly lit up the immense rock walls and deafening crashes of thunder shook the air and rippled their way down the ravines in mocking echoes. Blattering rain fell out of stormy squalls and for an hour the elements came romping, tumbling and kicking in playful abandon through this formidable trench as if they too were boisterous children and the canyons their mule. It was a fitting display of accord between the tempestuous forces and the playground of their own savage creation.

The path back up to the top grew longer and steeper as the true scale of one mile deep became taxingly obvious. My rests became more frequent until the discovery of a rattlesnake gave me a new burst of energy that took me back up to the rim at last. I cast a final look over the spectacular view before being reminded of the mules once more and went off to collapse in my tent. My stove turned out a tasteless meal that was deliciously hot and left me reflecting on how wonderful it was to feel exhausted after an achievement, and how much more wonderful if you had not been soaked in the effort. Still, after thunder and muleshit it would be all downhill to Las Vegas.

The Hoover Dam stands at the end of the land of canyons, blocking the course of the Colorado River like a bulging grey cork wedged firmly in the gorge and forming a lake along the boundary of Nevada. The fortune of this desert state was founded in its silver mines, but in 1931 its administration had the ingenious idea of being the first to legalise gambling and its ancillary vices. By this means certain areas of unproductive sand were transformed into highly lucrative silver mines of a different nature. One of these was Las Vegas. All the electricity generated at the Hoover Dam probably goes to feed the gambling metropolis of the world, situated conveniently close nearby, for it is built entirely of lights that burn all day and every day. It never closes. It is afraid to close. Las Vegas feels threatened by the dam and is enjoying one long, antediluvian, last fling.

The casinos are spread out in various concentrations along over forty miles of streets whose artificial suns turn midnight into daylight and make Piccadilly Circus look like a defunct Christmas tree. Walls are covered with bulbs stretching up into towering signs and overhanging banners that become megawatt rainbows casting out candelas of violent spectrums – ambers and ultraviolets, magentas and limes, indigos and crimsons; shattering the night in patterns of waterfalls and eruptions that flash, vibrate and revolve; morse codes of duration, intensity and speed; beckoning, teasing and attracting like flames the moths. A cowboy forty feet high with a moving arm and winking eye shows you where the guys like him go to play; a clown eighty feet high clothed in a quilt of luminiferous patches gives a silent laugh through iridescent lips; a girl fifty feet high sits on a bar-stool undulating incandescent fingers along her high-voltage thighs to show you where even the cowboy would rather be, and electric warriors pulse in dazzling clashes, throwing down their bizarre gauntlets of abstract and geometric radiation to do battle in this microcosm of neon, halogen and mercury vapour.

Eternal day outside, eternal night inside. Gambling is nightlife and windows are the symbol of day. The casinos are dimly lit and without windows or clocks to create the illusion of an evening without end. They hand out free drinks, meals, coupons, even free cash and long-distance telephone calls that can be claimed over a period of time and after a cursory check by long-legged, scimpily-clad girls to see that you are actually a bona fide squanderer of your money while on their premises. For nothing is free, not even in Vegas. It is just expenditure with a different weighting.

The croupiers and dealers might be framed pictures on a hair-stylist's wall, with manicured fingers and eyes that cover the table and then secretly rove the room without ever losing concentration or coordination. Void of emotion, they carry the air of an undertaker, a solemn sense of duty, a haunting expectancy, respectful sympathy and the infuriating resilience of a punchbag. Only an occasional smile of commercial politeness is expelled from the features of cold suspicion. They are all rotated every fifteen minutes to try to prevent boredom and to break the regularity of technique, or luck, at any one table.

The payouts from squadrons of one-arm bandits are each accompanied by a flashing beacon and raucous klaxons as they spit out dimes, nickels and quarters. When the flow of coins ceases the noise continues and only stops when another coin has been inserted, thereby forcing the weak-willed to play on, or at least to return one coin – with ranks of these machines in their hundreds, every coin counts. Gamblers sit morosely in front of pictures of non-sequential rows of fruit and pull levers in a mechanical motion that reveals no pleasure; automata that whine playing with automata that whirr and chunk-chunk-chunk in monotonous chorus.

At the baccarat table eight thousand dollars had just changed hands in one game. I stared at these bigtimers trying to find a 'type', but there seemed to be no single strain of *homo sapiens* that simply looked like a gambler. There was an elderly university professor type, well-groomed, a pointed white beard, glasses, bald crown and wearing an absent-minded, distant look. Not always so distant as it frequently came to rest on the unescorted figure of a Mondays-are-washdays housewife turned *nouveau riche* (perhaps here) who sat opposite. She looked the most relaxed and natural of them all. The party was completed by a middle-aged man with an ugly nose who exuded a mixture of philanthropy with belligerence according to his fortunes. He was having all the luck and scattered tips generously after winning eleven consecutive games. He examined his new cards one by one in a pained ritual of suspense and either threw them forcefully back onto the table with curses, or else lifted himself up from his chair just high enough to drop down and add effect to a whoop of excitement. His young wife, mistress or friend for the evening acted as a groupie giving little screams of delight and imitation whoops with his, throwing her arms over his shoulders, giving short shakes and hugs, while her eyes never once left his pile of chips. Finally he excused himself and his four thousand dollars of winnings. 'You're leaving, sir?' the croupier asked in surprise and disappointment and then he bowed slightly and bade them good-night. His attention became momentarily fixed on me and I was dismissed with a surly scowl, but then Las Vegas could scarcely be expected to rejoice at the sight of my canny type. To wear a kilt was to stand in the shadow of its reputation.

So I went and lost some dollars to the bandits. The blackjacks' speed panicked my slow maths into bad decisions, and I lost some more. Gambling made a mockery of me, but I didn't have to prove anything. In the minds of the croupiers I was Scrooge with a locked sporran, but I was damned if I was going to change the image by paying Las Vegas's electricity bill.

At the craps table the drinks were arriving with greater regularity than fortune for a man who cupped the dice in his hands, shook them vigorously above his head and called out to the magic cubes, 'OK, this time darlings, a nice-big-eight, OK baby, let's go, a hard eight . . .' and he kissed the little darlings through his hands and hurled them up the table. 'Well, GODDAMN HAIL. I just can't seem to hit it lucky tonight.' He grinned stupidly across the table. 'It kinda looks as if I'm losin' more than I'm winnin'.' The banker smiled patroni-singly back from over his vast piles of chips to this man and his row of three columns which had just fallen over.

A woman rapped the roulette-wheel a couple of times before placing her little stacks lovingly on each square from one to fourteen. 'Yer gonna have to get some help to pay all I'm gonna win this time,' she snarled. The ball spun around the edge for exaggerated seconds before falling down, hitting a bar and jumping into the bowl – sixteen. 'Ah sheesh,' and she looked sick as she prodded and fiddled with her remaining tokens, clicking them up and down. She had another drink. 'This time we'll show ya . . .' and she rapped the wheel and built up her stacks to the same set formula once again. Eight. Not one of her biggest columns but she got some back and vibrated up and down on her stool lightly clapping her hands in childish glee. 'Ya see – we're gettin' goin' now . . .' When I next passed she had hardly any tokens left but was still challenging, taunting and threatening the bank with how she would soon clean them out.

I left the casinos to wander down the strip, amazed that a camera viewfinder could be filled from corner to corner with a panchromatic test chart of patterns by pointing even a wide-angle lens in any direction. For several hours I saw the city through a camera lens, marvelling at the interminable variety of signs which could be duplicated as mirror images by squatting low over puddles, and only tiring of the scene when the street constellations began to pierce and needle my eyes. During my wanderings I came across many chapels. They too had bright flashing lights but sermons were never preached inside as there was no room for a congregation; these were purely for weddings and at one-thirty a.m. they were all open, for they never closed. They were administered by profiteers dealing in promises not prayers, demanding payment not penance and seeking converts to the city's hedonic calling. Instant twenty-four-hour weddings here could be followed by instant round-the-clock separations four hundred miles up the road at Reno, the divorce capital. After all, marriage was just another gamble.

'Newly wed at the Hitchin' Post,' ran the chapel's sign where the happy couple posed for a photograph. 'Always open – all credit cards and out of state cheques accepted,' read another which gave more emphasis to the real interests at heart. The names of the chapels went on one after the other, some trying to make even me feel more at home: Gretna Green, Wee Kirk o'the Heather, Sweetheart Desert

Bell, The Chapel Around the Corner . . .

. . . So they gamble in a palace (of neon purple and saffron), drink to songs of showbiz from the past, offer their lucky hand to the peccable girl already clinging to it, share their drunken dreams in trances of orgiastic delight, exchange slurred vows in a master-charge chapel (with rings of neon emerald and scarlet), gamble on until and beyond the change in fortune, sign away any and every possession they have with the engraved silver pen of the pawnbroker (in neon gilt and platinum) for the extra chance to reverse their fate, and finally, when the pen is offered no more, when they've crawled the streets paved with gold that is someone else's gold, when they've willed their wealth to Las Vegas and found that it wants more, even their last breath, then perhaps 'Palm Mortuaries' (in neon rose and violet) can put that star against their name where the roulette-wheel (in sanguine red and eternal black) failed. Las Vegas has it all from grand casinos of dubious repute to entire ranches of distinctly ill-repute; a mecca of temples for the worshippers of fun, where every indulgence and fantasy is catered for to the vulgar extremes of excess.

Daylight comes. The city has died. The façade has fallen, the colours have faded and the vitality has gone, leaving a feeling of deceit amongst the sterile streets and the wire frame of an impotent cowboy. Through her transparent veil, Las Vegas, your young bride, has suddenly aged in your hands.

I rather liked the place.

9 · Eccentric California

Hitch-hiking in a kilt meant sacrificing certain accepted human rights, privacy being my foremost loss. For the major part being a tartan oddity was an advantage and I felt privileged to have a national costume that was so distinctive, well-known and practical (in doldrums, at least). Shy strangers found me more approachable and this led to many absorbing discussions, invitations, contacts and special treatment even from officials inured to the sight of countless normal visitors. Because of the kilt, many doors were opened to me that would otherwise have remained closed.

The price was the reactions of the others. Some openly pointed and laughed, some yelled out insults and obscenities and some even swerved their cars towards me or hurled some object in my direction as they sped by. These had no visible effect as I walked on, chin held up, eyes set in front, gritting my teeth. But inwardly they hurt more than I allowed myself to show and sometimes I needed to muster all my courage and damaged pride to put on my kilt the following day.

Others felt that their lift imposed an obligation on me to satisfy their perverse curiosity over my sex life, plying me in vain with questions of the most obnoxious nature about with whom, when and how many times as if desperate to know if I had something that they lacked and terribly afraid that they were missing out in life. They would find themselves still wondering and as alone as the gay whose hand wandered from the gear-lever to my knee, and suddenly found his handbrake had been pulled on. He was entitled to his life just as I was entitled to mine. I took my luggage and wished him well, but not with me. Certainly life was never dull in a kilt, on account of the unusual characters who crossed my path. One of them was the man who took me away from Las Vegas.

He passed as I stood in the scorching desert heat. He stopped in the distance, swung around and returned to draw up beside me. A window lowered to reveal the sallow complexion of a man whose expression showed distress at being irretrievably in his late seventies.

'Come on. I can't leave you here. Your face has already gone red in the sun.'

My face was always red but that was beside the point and I eagerly put my pack along the rear seat. 'Mind you don't crush William, now.' I looked around but there was no apparent sign of life that might answer to the name of William.

'Who's William?'

'He's the Teddy Bear in the corner.' He sniggered. 'I'm a bit eccentric.'

That much was evident, but William Sr seemed harmless enough because of his age. Simplicity was not a fault, so I got in. Unfortunately simplicity led to other faults. First he ate a doughnut and then some chocolates, laughing that his doctor would be furious as he had hypoglycemia and sugar made him tired. 'But I get tired whether I have sugar or not and I kinda like candies, so what the hell.'

The hell was that it rendered him insensible. One moment his conversation was lively and the next it was slow and lethargic. He refused to stop for some fresh air, saying the spell would pass but when his eyes were blinking rapidly in the struggle to stay open and his one-word answers had dwindled to silence, I offered to take over. He accepted and for several hours I found myself driving through Death Valley in a brand new eight-cylinder Cadillac with the owner asleep by my side.

Death Valley, just inside the Californian border, the lowest point on the American continent, is 283 feet below sea level. When Satan tires of molesting the fortunes of others in the casinos he comes here for his recreation and to relax in pleasant summer temperatures of 134°F on an area of rutted mud and salt-flats known as the Devil's Golf Course. The ground is too hot to touch and the whole area shimmers in a hazy mirage.

A long climb with stops for water from special roadside tanks as the radiator began to boil took us five thousand feet into the bare Panamint Hills and then down into the valley beyond where green fields of alfalfa grass lay under lines of irrigation pipes, spouting white sprays of water of which up to sixty per cent would be lost in evaporation. We passed Owen's Lake, a subtle blend of gentle hues in a dry bed of salt, having had its water catchment area drained by the one billion gallon daily thirst of Los Angeles. The old man revived before we reached the city limits and took over the driving seat as if nothing had happened. After quickly checking that William had not been crushed he began eyeing a bag of mints on the dashboard, tempting him on as we drove through a tunnel to suburbia.

Hitch-hikers have a horror of being dropped off at a junction on a busy freeway. They lose sleep at the thought of anything worse but few could envisage the unique nightmare of this city; the intersection of four major freeways that leap-frogged over each other in a stack of bridges four levels high, shedding their coils of interchanges to form knots of many round turns and multiple half-hitches. The nightmare was realised and I was let out in this frightening scramble, knowing full well that hitch-hiking on freeways was illegal throughout the country. (Some states ban hitching completely, others, such as California, permit it on lesser highways, and a few have peculiar regulations which only allow it if you stand back from the kerb and pretend you are doing something else.) Within minutes a police car had stopped and I was beckoned inside, feeling thankful to escape the horrendous stampede of traffic. The officer was sympathetic and put away his notebook for road safety violations because I was so obviously a naïve foreigner, and offered to take me to his parents' house. His family had originally come from Scotland and they were fanatical about anything that reeked vaguely of heather, the lucky white variety or otherwise.

His parents adopted me at once, whatever my reek, and (perhaps as a result of it) they lent me a shirt, tie and shoes with real laces and no string. Then they took me along as their guest to a cocktail party which was to be attended by the Mayor of Los Angeles and other city dignitaries.

My initial impression of the affair was that cocktail party people were nothing but tedious obstacles frustrating direct attempts to reach the food and drink. Then I was introduced to the Mayor of Los Angeles himself and I stiffened with pride as cocktail parties took on a new meaning.

'How nice to see a kilt,' said the Mayor of Los Angeles (to me). 'Tell me, what do you do?'

'Well, sir,' I said (to the Mayor of Los Angeles), 'I'm a traveller and . . .'

'Really! Er . . . do excuse me one moment please,' and the Mayor of Los Angeles was gone. Of course he was a very busy man.

I had taken another step nearer the food when I was accosted by a woman who complained about the high cost of medical care in the country as if I were partly responsible. '. . . and you know, we just live in fear, absolute fear, of suffering a stroke and let's face it everyone has a stroke nowadays, and I mean everyone, which would be fine, fine, if you could insure against it but we can't so we just have to sit it out . . .' I reached the table at last and not even the M. of L.A. would have dragged me away. It was a lordly feast and California took on an instant appeal – and it was all due to the magic kilt.

I reverted to jeans for the rest of the week to see the city. Los Angeles was a maze of streets that led off everywhere but seemed to take you nowhere amongst more than eighty-five cities that had joined together to form four thousand square miles of confused urban sprawl. By night they turned to a carpet of terrestrial lights that mimicked the celestial ones which remained unseen for much of the year beyond a blanket of smog. It had drive-in meals, bars, laundries, shops, banks, cinemas and even drive-in funerals where the service was conducted to mourners in their cars. There was an Interflora service which specialised in delivering unpleasant messages with crushed and withered flowers or boxes of smashed chocolates. One of the world's greatest libraries could be found within its limits as well as museums, theatres, art and culture for every taste, and also the 'world's happiest place'.

Here vegetarian dinosaurs grazed peacefully, their stomachs moving with every breath and showing no sign of automation except for endlessly chewing the same mouthful. Disneyland was a monument to good taste. It engendered the very best in everyone of any age, even the most cynical. It was not just for children like the small blonde girl who sat in the arms of a large Micky Mouse, with an expression of disbelief as she looked up into the smile of her hero. It offered everyone escape into a fantasy world and adventure amongst animated dolls – and yet it left one with the disarming suspicion that these machines had achieved independence. They were free-moving personalities whose energy was induced by emotions of their own. They were laughing and playing along because it was fun to discover that their creators were so eaily amused.

The influence of this great playground was apparent throughout the city but if Disneyland left me with the conviction that it would keep going right through a power-cut, the same was not true of all the affected areas. Without electricity, the suburb of Hollywood instantly jammed. The entrances to dwellings became locked, ornate fortifications refused to sink out of sight or jump to the side when their owners demanded and phoney bricks in high walls could not ask a caller to identify himself as friend or foe. Mayhem ensued inside when gadgets failed, swimming-pools would not clean themselves, air-conditioning declined to work on credit and there was no ice for cocktails. Anyone walking the street, however, could have no appreciation of the full extent of such calamities. To the passer-by, here were mansions of concealed luxury rubbing epaulets with prefabricated castles and parading fleets of limousines. And nearby was Universal Studios, equally dependent on power, where tour buses passed a building which burst into flames every three minutes precisely, crossed a bridge which collapsed and then instantly re-assembled itself for the next bus, drove through a parting in the Red Sea pond and stared at the tonsils of an attacking Jaws.

Los Angeles was a heavy bombardment of the senses. 'Love it or leave it,' said the bumper-stickers. I did both and headed up the coast.

California's gross national product ranks it as the sixth greatest economic unit in the world, and its scenery holds its own in similar ratings for variety and beauty. My aluminium photographic case, which was beginning to break through the thin disguise of khaki canvas glued to its exterior, was forever being opened and it allowed my camera to consume film with an appetite that was voracious, and yet satisfying. (An abundance of film was the one extravagance of my trip.) California is spectacular, from her mountains, waterfalls, deserts, orchards and farmland to her ragged coastline which provides headlands, cliffs and rocky islands as well as great stretches of sand and tall waves for the surfers. Wearing dark wetsuits they floated on their boards like small oil slicks waiting for the traditional seventh wave which rolled in with its chest puffed out, the plume of spray on its crest held high, rising higher by degrees as it marched in from the deep Pacific, plucking up a surfer and allowing him to balance on the top before the crest toppled and rolled over in a thundering crash of foam on reaching the end of its journey.

Elsewhere waves bounded through an assault course of rocks, surging over and around them, turning into white, hissing, steaming acid as they gnawed at the land before being drawn back in lugubrious defeat to make way for the aggressive attack of the next. Sealions sat out on the rocks basking in the sun with their noses pointing up in the air while somewhere around them were the sharks, which had become more of a menace in recent years.

South of San Francisco stood a strange house that had belonged to Sarah Winchester. She was born in 1839 and married the son of the founder of the mighty Winchester Rifle Company (also hardware and roller-skates). Their only daughter died a few days after being born and fifteen years later her husband died too. This tiny widow, only four feet and ten inches tall, went on a holiday to Boston and met a spiritualist who persuaded her that the lives of her husband and baby daughter had been taken by the spirits of all those killed by the guns that had made the family fortune. Her life would also be taken unless . . . unless . . . she were to build a house according to the plans that the spirits would give her. Each night they would reveal to her the new designs and the detailed work to be done the following day. As long as the construction never stopped, as long as the building was never completed, her life would be spared and allowed to complete its natural span.

She bought an eight-acre ranch site in San Jose and, bolstered by the $1,000 per day income from the Company, she proceeded to construct this house. At the time of her death it had cost fifty million dollars and contained 160 rooms, 10,000 windows, 2,000 doors, two basements, forty staircases, forty-seven fireplaces, fifty-two skylights, three lifts, forty bedrooms, six kitchens, thirteen bathrooms and one shower. Her permanent staff consisted of eighteen house-servants, thirteen carpenters, eight gardeners and two chauffeurs. If they disregarded the smallest detail of her instructions they were dismissed at once, and she constantly prowled around to spy on them through all those windows.

I tagged onto a tour and became as disorientated as if I were inside a Rubik Cube during a record attempt. The old lady who designed this extraordinary labyrinth was no architect and received her inspiration from ghosts in moments of terror. She had them build staircases that went around corners and rose up to an abrupt halt at the ceiling, others that led down and then up when they could have gone directly up instead – one had forty-four steps, seven corners and covered a distance of a hundred feet to climb a total height of nine feet. She built doors that opened onto solid walls and floorless drops, windows that looked out onto brick walls six inches away and a cupboard with shelves one inch deep. Everything came in thirteens. It was her lucky number and chandeliers, window panes, steps and every addition was reckoned to this figure. Posts were always fitted upside-down and some never even reached the ceiling they were to support, being used instead to hold the floor down with their weight. She had a lift that required a man to pump for fifteen minutes to raise her one floor, but she seldom used it.

She blamed the spirits for the 1906 earthquake and the section of the house she had been in at the time was boarded up and never used again. She changed her bedroom frequently and the staff never knew where she was sleeping. Many of them needed a plan to find their way around. Despite all the bedrooms and two chauffeurs she never allowed a single visitor and seldom left her house. Sarah Winchester died in 1922, aged eighty-three, and left a will in thirteen parts. It required 364 truck loads to remove her furniture.

It seemed to be by chance that I was encountering the eccentrics of California until I reached San Francisco, the most liberated city, and discovered it to be their capital. This city does not try to emulate any other, it knows it is beautiful, it knows it is doomed to imminent destruction (expected to be more thorough than that of 1906) by loitering on the earthquake line of the San Andreas Fault, and this seems to account for its carefree, generous and tolerant manner. The centre is spread around hills that take pride in their steepness, forcing the trams to haul themselves up on cables. Some relief from the steep angles is afforded by the intersecting streets which run along tiered levels like steps on a Mayan pyramid, and here the trams rest for long enough to spill some passengers and to let others jump onto the footrail and cling to the sides. Frisco gathers its suburbs in close as if pulling them up into folds to prevent them from getting wet in the sea that lies on three sides. Apart from this, it seems to show little concern about anything.

The largest Chinese population outside China lives here and they wander around in abundance as part of the cosmopolitan masses, amongst rollerskaters and those out jogging with headphone radios, a man walking in pink leotard, throttled by rows of pearls, and

another man, embarrassingly nondescript, who was exercising his
dog; he nimbly laid down a piece of newspaper in time and then
looked away with a smug expression as his squatting dog unwittingly did his part in keeping the city clean.

And then I saw her. She appeared suddenly, conspicuous by her
colour and movement – an old woman, whose liberal make-up
could not disguise that she was in her fragile years, came dancing
along the street in a trance, wearing a see-through smock over a red
swimsuit from which purple tights ran down to dainty green shoes.
Her tights could have been empty, so thin and sinewy were her
delicate little legs, moving like a whisper of a shadow, slipping
quietly along in her gentle rhythm, lilting through the crowded
pavements, through laughing teenagers and the elegant rich, past the
semi-naked half-wit lying masturbating in a gutter, being delayed
by students dressed up as chickens for a charities campaign, dodging
the drunk with outstretched arms seeking an audience for his
monosyllabic speech and the loan of a dollar, cutting in front of
sun-bronzed lovers in chintzy T-shirts and each with a hand in the
hip-pocket of the other, oblivious of perspiring tourists rotating
their street-guides as they stood lost and momentarily stalled in the
pursuit of wonder, ignoring two businessmen in suits sharing a
goodbye kiss, on and on, an aged nymph flitting amongst the
extrovert and deranged, fun-loving and misplaced, revolutionaries
and experimentalists, the fashionable, conservative and sordid, on
and on, in a somnambulist's waltz through the echelons of modern
society.

San Francisco is the free city. You have a place here no matter what
your bent. You can openly do what you want, be what you really are
or what you would prefer to be, or simply just try it anyway. It is a
hubbub of excitement, bustling with type and trend and with a bit of
the conventional norm thrown in for good measure. It even has the
world's first gay cemetery.

One-and-a-half miles out in the bay lies an island where once
newcomers arrived reluctantly. Now they eagerly crowd the wharf
waiting for a ferry to go there, and I was one of them. From 1934 to
1963 Alcatraz Island was the site of the dreaded top-security prison,
the most secure in the world, where 'incorrigibles' were sent. For
each prisoner there were three guards and these had to sign an
agreement accepting that the authorities placed no value on their

lives, should they be taken hostage. The rules were strict; prisoners were not allowed to talk to anyone for the first six years and their uniform jackets had to be buttoned up to the chin for the first eight years. Privileges, such as being allowed to clean the area outside their cell and to read books, could be earned only after so many years of good behaviour.

Any misdemeanor resulted in the removal of these special rights and possibly a spell in the solitary confinement cells – the Attitude Adjustment Centres or 'hellholes', depending on which side of the door you stood. The law stated that all cells had to have lights but it omitted to say that they had to work, so these ones did not. It stated that nineteen days was the maximum stay in solitary confinement but omitted to specify any interval between confinements and so prisoners could be released for one minute and then be returned for another nineteen days. They were kept in total darkness and were allowed one shower each week. Any further defiance and the inmate was stripped of his clothes, his blanket was removed, and he was thus forced to try to sleep on his elbows and knees to minimize skin contact with the cold metal floor and walls that encased him. Six days was usually enough for the mean attitude to be adjusted.

Our tour trooped through corridors and rooms painted in standard colours of official plainness or else left bare, our feet causing muffled echoes to fill the gloomy silence. We stopped in the dining room. The food used to be the best of any prison in order to discourage trouble or riots at mealtimes. Armed guards with tear gas at the ready stood watching on a balcony and made the prisoners pass through a metal detector at the end of each meal. Then we shuffled on and the voices of other guides pervaded the fortified chambers and caged walkways carrying harangues of unflinching fact.

Inmates were allowed one visitor per month (blood relative, wife or lawyer only), seven incoming letters and two outgoing ones each week, and the outgoing ones were typed on prison paper by staff after the contents had been scrambled to spoil any secret codes. The privileged prisoners read an average of seventy-five books in one year (the national civilian average was two and a half), the most common subjects being firstly law (preparing one's own defence and trying to find legal loopholes), secondly engineering and then sport.

Prisoners arrived chained together and wearing individual ball and chains. Not even in death was a prisoner considered harmless and corpses were also chained and guarded until they had left the island. There were several known escapes in the days when it was a military prison, and the most ingenious belonged to a convict who printed his own pardon in the prison workshop. He bribed a guard to take it to the mainland and post it to the governor, who came over personally and escorted him back to the shore, and freedom. No one ever made a successful escape from Alcatraz after 1934.

Al Capone, believed to have been the cause of over five hundred murders (and whose income for the year 1929 was estimated at forty-four million dollars), spent four and a half unpopular years here running a prison mafia and surviving being stabbed with barber's shears and numerous other murder attempts before being freed. Robert Stroud, responsible for repeated multiple murders, also stayed here after his execution order was commuted to a life sentence. He spent fifty-four years of his life behind bars and forty of these in solitary confinement. He taught himself five languages but is most famous for becoming an authority on birds and their diseases after finding an injured bird one day, which inspired his interest to read and learn more. The 'Birdman of Alcatraz' was, however, a Hollywood misnomer for Stroud never kept a single bird at Alcatraz where all pets were banned. His 'bird life' had taken place at a previous prison where his interests were found to be less innocent – he used the birdseed to make whisky, and spent his spare time writing pornographic novels about the guards and their families.

Alcatraz was closed in 1963 mainly because it was too costly to run (an average of forty thousand dollars per annum for each prisoner). There were no sewage facilities, and three million gallons of fresh water had to be brought out each month in twelve deliveries. Paradoxically, the most feared penitentiary in the land is now a 'National Recreation Area' and a profitable tourist attraction for those who, like myself, come to indulge in the temporary discomfort of being where the murderers once cowered when the three-inch steel door of a hellhole is slammed shut with a resonance that lingers on in the dark, cold silence.

The bay surrounding Alcatraz joins the open sea to the north of the city where the famous Golden Gate suspension bridge crosses the narrows at its chosen setting. This graceful span, supported by a web of cables that hang down from twin towers, is one of the world's chosen spots for those wishing to make a premature departure from it. Over seven hundred people have attempted suicide by throwing themselves down 218 feet to the sea below, and only twelve have survived as failures.

As I stood on the side of the freeway at the end of the bridge, the first car of the day stopped. My policy was to try to get the driver to answer a few questions as to where he was going, how far it was and how long it would take to get there – anything to give me time to evaluate his character. Although there was nothing objectively wrong, this particular man had disturbing eyes and in a brief encounter it was only possible to go on intuition. If there were 'bad vibrations', however inexplicable, then it was best to act on them. He didn't seem to have a destination of his own, was very keen to take me anywhere and became more insistent that I should climb in. Bad vibes. The gut-feeling said 'no'.

It was very hard to refuse a lift without offending whoever had taken the trouble to stop for me. Excuses to the effect of suddenly wanting to go in the opposite direction, wanting a longer lift or waiting for a friend always appeared feeble. I just thanked this man and said I preferred to wait for another car. At first it looked as if he was going to become violent but he drove off swearing madly. It justified my decision but with Alcatraz so fresh in my mind, I shuddered to think what he might have had in mind. The next car had three freaks in it who looked high on everything but happiness.

'We'll give you a ride, man,' said a clod of hair, 'only we need bread. You got bread, man?' I took advantage of the proffered excuse and had a quick look in my sporran.

'Nah, not me man, ah ain't any dough', and they drove off without any sign of appreciating my attempt at jargon or humour. I began to feel apprehensive about what curiosity the next car would contain but, as if to redress the balance, his vibrations were of the best.

There seemed to be no limits to the amount of kindness that was showered on me by many of the people that I met. They invited me in for meals, to stay the night, some insisted I phone Scotland at their expense, some took my address so they could write to my family and confirm that I was well, some would take me on sight-seeing trips or run me many miles beyond their destination and others would press me to accept some small present. At times it was so overwhelming, I asked myself why they were so generous.

It was partly in their nature, partly because of that universal bond of parenthood in which instinct moves families to adopt an orphan traveller as they perhaps hope others would their own son, were he in a strange land, and partly for a reason that this man revealed to me. He had once dreamed of just dropping everything and travelling but he had never dared to take the first step. Then he found that it was too late, his circumstances had changed and the opportunity had passed.

'I pick up hikers now to listen to their stories, to be able to live a little in their fantasy which is being realised and to help others do what I wish I'd done.' I was the empathetic link to a dream he would never fulfil. I admired his noble gesture, turning what might have become bitterness into an act of friendliness and so I talked and shared my experiences and tried to pay my way with words.

I was let out amongst some trees, still feeling guilty at my envied role and the responsibility it entailed, and therefore it took me some time to notice anything unusual about them. Then my head went through the same motions as on my first day in New York, tilting as far back as it could to look up over 300 feet to the tops. The Giant Redwoods grow only in California and the tallest tree in the world is here, reaching a height of 362 feet. Further south are the Sequoia trees which grow less tall but which put on more bulk, and amongst them stands the 'General Sherman Tree', the largest living mass on earth; the trunk alone weighs 1,385 tons, has a circumference of 103 feet at its base, contains 52,000 cubic feet of timber and is covered in fireproof bark two feet thick.

Beside a carpark was a sign with a poem in praise of the Red-woods, ending with the words 'Sink down, óh Traveller, on your knees, God stands before you in these trees.' He was not the only one to stand in the trees. The proprietor of a souvenir shop, hollowed out of the trunk of one living tree, was visible inside the open doorway. 'The world's highest single-room house,' fluttered his banner. Elsewhere were 'drive thru' trees with a tunnel piercing their base, a 'drive along' tree which had fallen flat (perhaps as a result of having previously been a 'drive thru'), and the 'Immortal Tree', whose title and sign were the inspiration of the nearby shop whose owner had obviously not yet had time to bore a hole through it. And toll booths were as common as those of the Pueblo Indians.

I wandered away from the road and found a spot in the tranquillity of the forest where I lay down on the grass amongst the ferns and let my eyes run up the red trunks to the green branches at the tops of these natural giants. The clouds scurried along as if trying to avoid the uppermost branches that swayed in the light breeze. Magnificent – and all from a tiny seedling that weighed a few thousandths of an ounce. There had to be some philosophy in it somewhere, but it escaped me. Instead I thought back to all my good fortune, and the words of a seasoned traveller I had met in Iceland. Now it seemed so far away.

'You'll meet many kind people on your travels,' he told me, 'and you'll never be able to return that kindness to them. All you can do is to pass it on to someone else another day – and what a wonderful way to create a better world.' It was true. In receiving kindness from others, whether it was given gladly, grudgingly, or as recompense for a share in my adventures, there was a tacit obligation to pass it on and to let it branch out and grow. It would all be wasted if it stopped at me. I hoped not to forget that debt.

And it seemed my obligation was growing, almost as high as these lofty pylons that were the world's tallest living things, and the world's tallest signposts for the bricabrac of their commercial termites.

10 · Noah's ark, Columbia's floods and Rainbow People

God may well live in the Giant Redwoods but He does not live a short distance away in Sonoma County. After a local landowner had fallen into debt and found a loophole in the law whereby he would not forfeit his land if it were willed to God, the court hastily convened a meeting and ruled that God did not legally exist in their county. I was glad not to be in the spiritual void of Sonoma when I camped one night on the wooded slopes of Lassen volcano. I hoped the surrounding trees would not prove godless, but would offer emergency recourse if the need arose. This was bear country and there were many gruesome stories of attacks.

Before retiring for the night I went out in the dark to answer a more personal call of nature than those continually being emitted from Bumpass Hell, an area of mudpots, steam vents and fumaroles further up the hill. A small shape suddenly got up a short distance in front of me and I froze, thinking that it was a bear cub, terrified that its mother would be nearby. The creature stopped, turned round and ambled off. It was not a bear but there was so little light that it was impossible to make out any features, so I followed and crouched down low to find another angle against the night sky. It stopped again and then seemed to puff itself up like a vain turkey until it was half as big again – a porcupine!

By the light of my torch it was not at all like a form of hedgehog as I had always imagined, but more like a thin piglet on stumpy legs, covered in the long black and white quills that increase its size when they bristle out as a warning. By lashing its tail against an enemy a porcupine becomes a dangerous opponent, and it has been known to kill mountain lions whose bodies have been found with quills that penetrated the eye and reached the brain. A porcupine is always grumpy even during its brief mating period which lasts only three days, and perhaps this is why. The beast has always been regarded as the best friend of the lost and hungry as it is easy to kill and the meat is good, but it is devilishly hard to skin. Porcupines have a hard time finding enough salt and they will gnaw their way through boots, spade handles or anything that has been in contact with sweat.

I returned to my tent and hoisted my food and boots high up into a tree and out of their reach, for I had heard that porcupines do not like trees. They were everywhere. Several more crossed my path and one took fright and shuffled off. To my surprise it went straight up a tree trunk in strenuous jerky movements that made its spines rattle, and me feel stupid. So much for my theory. I recovered my salty valuables and cached them under some stones, trusting that the weight-lifting ability of porcupines was less than their apparent expertise as steeplejacks.

The next morning my cache was untouched but my toothpaste and toothbrush had vanished from outside my tent. I packed up and walked off down the road under the blue sky of a perfect day, whistling merrily between discoloured teeth. Somewhere around me was a debonair porcupine with a sparkling smile and freshmint breath, and yet still grumpy; the mating season had been last week. It was one of those days when nothing was particularly important, to me at least, and it felt good simply to stretch my muscles and walk. Across hillsides and over their tumbling streams, and through forests awakening with the sounds and fragrance of a new spring.

My daily routine, such as it was, had become simplified into extracting myself from wherever I had spent the night, moving towards a loosely planned objective, finding food along the way and then a place to sleep. My only other concern was a minimum of one hour's light sometime during the late afternoon or evening for writing my diary and recording the details of each photograph taken that day.

When I was not the guest of an inordinate number of hosts (whose washing machines removed my bugbear of laundry) and sleeping in their homes, I would find a spot to camp. This was never on official campsites because they were the same as youth hostels – fine for company and hot water, but places to be avoided if you simply wanted to sleep. I preferred to camp wild, waiting until dark to conceal my intentions and then slipping off inconspicuously to put up my tent well away from a thoroughfare and, if possible – I noted for the future – porcupines. It became a form of trivial entertainment to look out of my tent each morning and discover my surroundings.

Apart from the common ones of forest, pasture and wasteland, I seemed unwittingly attracted to potato patches, the less cultivated sections of unfenced but private gardens and, one particularly comfortable night, the fairway of a golf course.

My pack usually contained enough food for a couple of days so that I could break off from my route on a whim and disappear into the countryside or linger at places of unexpected appeal. I rose at dawn and ate raw porridge oats with milk (tinned or fresh) and a chopped apple thrown in, and brewed tea on my petrol stove. Breakfast was always rushed on the days when there was distance to be covered. The sound or even the thought of an approaching car made me believe it would be the ideal lift and so my tent was bundled up still wet with dew and I set off, impatient to discover what the day would bring.

Hitching had become easy. It was no longer an uncertain means of reaching my destination, but I was always conscious of the danger that the driver might be dishonest or have motives other than kindness. My route was based on the recommendations of other travellers and those who gave me lifts, and on the notes I had made from guide books; areas of unusual people or scenic features, and sometimes just fanciful names that appealed because nothing was claimed on their behalf. Fanciful names often proved unmemorable, but there were exceptions. Bumpass Hell had just introduced me to porcupines.

I ate a small lunch (mainly bread and cheese, raw carrots or fruit) and left cooking to the evening when I concocted another bowl of endless soup from a packet, and made it stodgy by throwing in noodles, rice or baked beans. It was a diet totally lacking in imagination, variety and (this was the beauty of it) effort, but I ate to fill my stomach, and as quickly as possible to leave more time for writing my diary. It became an obsession and frequently a tedious chore to write at length on the day's events. Not just details of where and what – everything was noted; history, feelings, impressions of places and people, their mannerisms, jokes, opinions and tittle-tattle. I wanted not only to remember these things at a later date, but to be able to relive them in my mind. Each evening I would struggle to catch up with a backlog of as much as one week, using my pack as a stool and writing on my knees, sometimes under a street lamp and sometimes in the fading twilight, trying to decipher my scribbled notes on numerous torn scraps of paper. Writing what I saw became a useful discipline, for it taught me to look so that I would later have something to write about. Tiredness or darkness would always beat me, and I would find no time for doing any repairs. Sewing was a constant necessity; buttons to replace safety-pins, emergency stitches to arrest small tears and patches to cover the tears that had been left until too late. But sewing was a low priority and so, showing signs of wear and still with a backlog of diary to carry over to the next day, I would wander off unwittingly into another potato patch and sleep.

On this particular morning I wandered past banks of wild crocuses and daffodils, half-heartedly musing on possible destinations. There was Glacier National Park, Montana (recommendation), the Grand Coulee Dam, Washington State, and, with good planning, the Calgary Stampede across the border in Alberta (heavily underlined in my notebook).

The first car came along at midday when my shoulders were beginning to tire and it stopped without any attempt at hitching on my part. The driver was returning from the World Frog Jumping Championships where there had been three thousand entries, including a team that had come over from Ireland. Each frog was placed individually on a starting-line and the distance covered in the first three hops was measured. Its owner (also coach and physiotherapist) was not allowed to prod or touch, which some found a severe handicap, but he could thump the ground around it and yell encouragement to spur his athletic amphibian into action. None of them had beaten the prodigious world record of thirty-three feet five and a half inches, set several years earlier by a specimen two inches long. South African sharp-nosed frogs were evidently best at it. They even sounded streamlined.

'I was in Scotland once,' said the frog jumper. 'We went from France to see the windmills.'

'That sounds more like Holland. We don't have windmills in Scotland.'

'Oh yes. Well, we went to Scotland too. They don't speak English there. We couldn't understand a word.'

'That must be Holland. Everyone in Scotland speaks, er, a form of English,' I said, aware of the possible arguments involved. But he just went on.

'Yes, I know Scotland, not too well mind you. Hellish flat there but we had some nice cheese at a place near . . .' So I gave up and let him think that Ben Nevis had been levelled, that tulips flooded the glens from Cape Wrath to Gretna Green while Scotsmen adjusted their windmills wearing clogs with their kilts. Still, at least we made nice cheese.

He dropped me off on another quiet country road and then a rare moment in a hiker's life occurred. There were occasional lulls in my luck when drivers pretended not to notice me, but at that moment two cars stopped simultaneously and I was suddenly standing in the middle of a friendly argument as both drivers put forward their respective claims on me. One said he had stopped first, the other replied that he had seen me first, one said he was tired and needed company, the other countered that he was interested in Scottish clans . . . It appeared my opinion did not count and I could only turn from one speaker to the other as a slightly bewildered spectator in their game of verbal ping-pong. The clan man won and I got into the seat next to Sep Rolund, an elderly man with a straight white beard that came down to his chest. His small nose was scarcely able to support a pair of old spectacles with heavy round lenses and he wore a battered peaked cap.

'I had to find out if you were being treated properly in my country. If you've got some spare time I'd like to talk to you. My home is miles from anywhere in the woods. I don't live like other people.' And then he went on to explain why.

There was an infectious enthusiasm about his words and manner that made me want to find out more. I warmed to him at once. Here was a special character, one who was knowledgeable and who had thought about life, what it had to offer and the qualities he wanted from it. Sep seemed delighted when I agreed to stay.

'Good on you, Jock', and we drove off the main road onto a rough track that led to his hermitage deeper in the woods.

Sep had left his native Denmark when he was fourteen and had sailed the world with merchant ships. Everywhere he'd been held some special meaning for him; sampans in Shanghai, a piece of prune tart in Sydney, sunset in Valparaiso, riots in Cape Town and a ragged street urchin in Cardiff ('Jesus, could that boy sing, sweeter than a lark it was'), and he talked on any country and subject with under-standing and conviction. When his ship reached San Francisco he married a girl there and settled down as a furniture-maker.

'I've been lucky. My wife and I have only argued four times in forty-two years. Unfortunately each of them lasted ten years', and his long beard quivered with his laughter. City life soon depressed them and when tales of violence, discrimination and drugs came back from the school which their five children attended, they decided to leave and seek healthier influences for their children's formative years. They came to the Mt Lassen area in North Califor-nia by chance and spent a night in a ruined cabin. His wife hated it until the next morning when she looked out and saw the lake and forest. ('When do we move in?' she had asked. 'We just have,' came the reply.) So they had squatted on the land and resisted all attempts to oust them by the Forestry Service, which had finally given up and now simply chose to ignore them.

Sep had built their house in six months and they were happy here, ten miles from the nearest neighbour, without electricity and tele-phone and sometimes being snowed in for weeks on end. Their children, however, had not found life in the country so totally fulfilling. They had grown up and now lived in small towns, and some had even gone back to the cities. Sep and his wife were sad about that.

A pet black-tailed deer grazed in front of their large log cabin and when the door opened, out came two racoons, a skunk, two cats and a poodle; and then, as I neared the top of the steps up to the door, I was staring into the unfriendly eyes of a Great Dane. This dog soon bounded off to look for the other animals which had all disappeared except for the racoons – they were eating beside a stream and busily rubbing their hands in the water. Sep explained that they weren't intentionally washing their food. They simply loved to feel it and the sense of touch was enhanced under water. I was wondering what else might emerge from this Noah's Ark when his wife appeared at the door. She was a small plump woman with her hair braided into a Roman wreath of laurels, and she greeted me with warmth and mild suspicion, each having brief moments of predomination until her trust had been won.

'We enjoy company,' she admitted, 'but we don't miss it. We like animals more than people. That's why we came here.'

Sep was a master cabinet-maker and his workshop was full of intricately carved sections of a table which would sell for ten thousand dollars. Running his hand along piles of wood in the way others might stroke a cat or racoons might rinse their food, he relished the sensations as his fingers traced patterns in the grain. He often stopped in the middle of a job to let the wood 'rest' for a few months. Rushing was a sin.

'Do you know what separates true art from mediocrity? It's hard work. The raw ability, the natural gift to create is the same in a lot of people, but true art needs hard work to develop that gift. My big fault is that I'm a perfectionist, a slow one, everything has to be just right. The little details of perfection take time – and you don't get paid for them.' He squinted at me and smiled. 'But the artist in me adapts to the practicalities of life.'

As we sat in the sitting-room a zip and a hum went past my face, then more zips and hums and flashes of colour . . .

'They're our humming birds. We feed them sugared water and now they are dependent on us, but in winter they fly south to Mexico and change their diet to leathery tortillas. They leave our "great" country.' The word was slingshot in his mouth. His own experiences made him scoff at the image of freedom in America and he saw it as the 'land of the free, as long as you conform.' He said he was not a communist but he resented having to sign a statement to that effect in order to join a trade union. He had refused to do so because he considered his political views to be private, and had been banned from joining as a result.

Every room in the Rolunds' house appeared to be a library. They spent much time reading and discussing books, and scorned the media. They found newspapers, radio and television to be filled with trivia, diverting the mind from serious issues. They saw the world as plagued by religion and patriotism, the worst diseases in history. They no longer wished to be part of this world.

But their escape had not been complete. Around the walls hung rifles, axes, an old bear spear, a sword, various knives and several revolvers all spaced out at the distance of a man's maximum stretch. Sep explained that even here they were afraid. An isolated family in the neighbourhood had been murdered not long ago, and they themselves were not so young any more. It was best to take precautions.

We went on to discuss nuclear power and porcupines, how it was a pity the Incas hadn't slit Pizarro's throat the moment he arrived, and Sep asked what Highland Games were. I explained.

'Wow! You Scots sure go for the intellectual stuff, don't you?' He then told me about a Scot he had once worked with on a ship. 'Daft about soccer', he had been, and in Gambia he got to knocking a ball about at sunset as three hundred Moslem Mandingoes were out on their mats praying to Allah. The ball hit one of them square on. They all got up and things were looking nasty when the Scottish lad somehow got them to join in a game. The next moment the ball was whizzing all over the place, three hundred men were chasing one ball over the horizon of the flat desert – and they never came back till past midnight.

I spent the following days being shown the forest by a couple who knew all its secrets and who shared them willingly, as well as the much-pondered conclusions from the hours of reading that they loved. I was sorry to leave this unusual couple. Sep drove me back to the outside world.

'Good luck, Jock,' he yelled, and his beard could not conceal a toothless grin as he drove off to become a recluse once more in the forest of his self-imposed exile.

The road led up into Oregon and over the McKenzie Pass where jagged black rocks of lava flow cut across the hillside as a million solidified witnesses to molten agony. The trees on the land that had been unscathed by the flow grew dense, tall and strong, while on the fringe of this area of desolation the odd pine tree clung precariously to life, small and stunted. Out in the middle others had given up trying to squeeze some nutrition out of the rocks and were dead; their branches held out like arms in despair, their boughs shrugged in a plea of helplessness, skeletons bleached white in the sun and standing in stark contrast to the black, black ground that had defeated them. It too had a certain aura of beauty, for beauty came in many forms and could be both dead and startling.

Then on into Washington State where twelve dams block the course of the Columbia River, generating electricity and regulating the flow for irrigation projects. The Grand Coulee dam is one of them, second in size to no other concrete creation on this planet and, in its day, the greatest construction effort of all time since the Great Pyramid of Cheops (reluctantly admitted to be bigger, as is the conveniently forgotten Great Wall of China). It forms a barrier, 4,173 feet long reaching up to 550 feet above bedrock. The Grand Coulee dam was begun in 1933, and during the eight years of construction the workers were housed in the wildest and most lawless town in the country. Although it boasted thirty-four bars and fourteen whorehouses the men managed to spare some time for work and laid twelve million cubic yards of concrete, and their labour produced Lake Roosevelt, which tails back for 151 miles. The dam is most dramatic at night when the spillway is floodlit in changing colours, but I found the town itself disappointing, with all the boasted entertainment dried up.

Beyond the far end of Lake Roosevelt, in wooded countryside where old barns with Dutch-style roofs stood in meadows full of buttercups and the things that ate them, I first heard about the Rainbow People. Nobody seemed to know much about them but the locals were worried. They had taken over an area of forest and it was rumoured that ten thousand of them were expected to arrive for their annual gathering.

Hand-painted signs showed the way on every road in the region and guided me up a forest track. I was one of a multitude straggled out along the way. Some clutched boxes, one rolled his belongings in an old oil-drum, another wore two backpacks and was sandwiched between them, one dragged an Indian travois and a middle-aged Gandhi figure with a desert island beard longer than Sep's carried nothing but an axe.

'How long did your beard take to grow?' I asked, to open a conversation.

'Four months,' replied Gandhi.

'Only four months?'

'Yes, but that was twelve years ago.' He went on to explain that this was a peace movement and this their tenth gathering, where they came to hold talks, lectures and to recruit new followers. 'It's the most unorganised organisation in the world. We have no money but we are a big family and all our Brothers and Sisters have an equal say. We believe in freedom of expression as long as it doesn't upset our neighbour. We're not religions in any one sense; we recognise that there is truth in all religions and so our basic philosophy is to love our neighbour. We don't like the way the world is going so we are trying to set up families all over the world, ideally to include the world, where we try to live from the land, get away from a dependence on the dollar and revert to bartering with other families, to care for Mother Earth' – he shifted the axe to his other hand – 'and to create a Home for her peoples.' Gandhi was a computer programmer from Boston.

We walked on, accompanied by Rainbow People in patched jeans, shorts, nothing but scanty leather flaps tied around their waists, Jesus sandals and one limped along wearing a single climbing boot saying he had lost the other on the way from Florida. At least I didn't feel too out of place in my kilt, which was a bonus of the garment. It was respectable enough for sharing a gin and tonic with the Mayor of Los Angeles and it was way-out enough for tramping through a forest with a collection of misfits.

We reached a clearing which served as a parking area for a variety of cars, vans and buses, mostly in a state of disrepair or in that state closer to beyond repair, painted with flowers and the rallying-cries of peace. 'Welcome Home' said a large banner, and 'Welcome Home' said everyone as a greeting, for evidently any spot where the Rainbow People set up camp was home for all their followers. A man, totally naked, stood at the entrance to receive us.

'Hi! I'm Natural-We', and having introduced himself as such he began to criticise the world's egotistical orientation in a jocular and fairly nonsensical monologue about we-volution, we-valuation, we-uniting and we-thinking that became childishly boring until it suddenly struck me that he really was onto something after all. His welcome was also an invitation for everyone to shed their own inhibitions and restraints, to open themselves up to new ideas, to act naturally for once, to live and let live – or if they couldn't, at least to accept those who could. Or it was possible that talking intellectual gibberish was just an essential part of being able to stand naked before ten thousand strangers.

On the clearing were Indian tepees and other tents, horses grazing, camp-fires, groups singing and others casually talking in collapsed huddles. A conch was blown and its hollow shudder called everyone to a communal meal.

'If you have any money to give for the meal, that's fine. If all you've got is a smile, that's fine too,' said Gandhi. I gave both and so did he. There were sacks for all litter, each divided into their recyclable components where possible, and a copy of the Country Code was nailed to a post ('. . . take only photographs, leave only footprints'). The atmosphere was one of overpowering friendliness.

All types seemed to be here in even more variety than the streets of San Francisco had provided. Tramps, religious devotees, an accountant, a baker, a 'Love Israel' family, the pregnant, handicapped, clean-shaven, bald, hirsute, loners and lovers, found souls, lost souls, the hyperactive and alert, the dazed and the inert.

Were they hippies? The term is always used derogatively. They were certainly confused by a society whose daily contradictions were hard to reconcile, and they were disillusioned with its gift to youth of prepackaged dogmas on what is acceptable – some of value, others merely obsolete anachronisms. But in this sense there is surely something of the hippy in all of us. In varying degrees we share their dislike of having to accept the bad with the good and of being shaped into uniform citizens by the invisible restrictions of public opinion, wrapped into traditional roles by society's cling-film. Is the common reaction against the alternative lifestylers not merely sour grapes to those who regret having lost that opportunity to escape themselves?

The assortment of people here might have been worthy conformists, worthy nonconformists or unworthy hangers-on, but within this forest clearing, none of them was a freak. For 'freakiness', like beauty, lies in the eye of the beholder. The Rainbow Family recognised people as people, beauty as people. And that, as a fundamental principle, seemed a basis beyond argument.

Many of them had a rainbow painted on their face and they explained that it had several meanings. It was the symbol in Genesis of the promise that the world would not be destroyed as it had once been in Noah's time, it represented the people of all colours that were gathered in their family, and others talked of an Indian legend that said one day all nations would unite, would become one colour and would cross the Rainbow Bridge to the happy land on the other side.

So I spent a few days living out my own latent hippy dreams in an atmosphere of love and goodwill, while working on a plan to change the world and save mankind. Revolution was surprisingly and pleasantly addictive. Then I felt it was time to leave the Rainbow People. One afternoon I gathered my belongings, said goodbye to

Gandhi and set off back through the woods along a path which suddenly struck me as cold and full of danger compared to the environment I had just left behind. Something Sep had said came back to me.

'You know, Jock, I never used to have any respect for General Omar Bradley. Always thought he was inhuman until his autobiography came out. He wrote, "Ours is a world of nuclear giants and ethical infants. We know more about war than we do about peace, more about killing than we do about living." '

Were the Rainbow People the answer? Or would they prove as transient as the reformed hippies at Taos? I felt I needed to know more, or was there any more to know? Wasn't it enough to have experienced their feelings and to have learnt their simple philosophy? The threat of nuclear war, the collapse of society, bankrupt economies, the selfish craving of materialism, starving and increasing populations, the dependence on the evil-attracting dollar – all this versus Love Your Neighbour? The principle was perfect, but it seemed so small and vague in the face of so many enormous problems.

My thoughts then pushed aside the world's tribulations, for the ability to do so is the traveller's prerogative. Move on, find something different, avoid discussion, avoid commitment, avoid responsibility. I realised it would not always be possible and therefore it was best to enjoy this privilege while it lasted, strolling down a forest track without cares, the air heavy with the scent of pine-needles lying as a deep springy carpet below my feet and butterflies skipping alongside, also heading in the general direction of Alaska.

11 · In Glacier National Park I ran and ran, almost naked . . .

It was raining. The covenant of the rainbow seemed forgotten. Hitch-hiking in the rain was always miserable. The cold and damp slowly crept through my clothes and up my kilt. Every car looked less inclined to stop for fear of disturbing its cosy, dry interior with a cold, wet stranger. The puddles leapt up under the wheels and spray and fumes rolled over me – a final slap in the face as I stood shaking the drops of water from my hair in the wake of their departure. My kilt seemed capable of absorbing all the water that reached the half-fathom of its depth, growing heavier with each passing car and causing me concern that it might suddenly sink down to my ankles. Times like these were the other side of the coin from smoking long cigars in Houston and called on additional reserves of resourcefulness to obtain that vital lift.

Signs are often helpful to the hitch-hiker. 'PLEASE', '10 MILES ONLY' and 'HELP' have all proved effective. Written destinations are best left vague and not too distant so that there is a chance of a lift from those not going to your specific goal but in the right direction, and from those who might be discouraged at the thought of a stranger's extended company to a far-off place. Sometimes an absurd destination such as 'AUSTRALIA', or a touching greeting is best of all. Friends were very successful one December when they hitched together, one holding 'HAPPY' and the other 'CHRISTMAS'.

When such as these have evoked no response, turning the sign upside-down can turn up trumps as someone usually feels inclined to stop and point out your error, and getting a car to stop is ninety per cent of the battle. Once you have achieved that then all the charm of your personality, and not just that initial visual impression, can be used to show what a wonderful asset you would be to the driver's journey. Signs do not work well in bad weather. The ink tends to run and the visibility is often so poor that cars have to come closer to try to read the mess, and just bring more water.

Showing your national flag is a popular gimmick as drivers tend to feel more sympathetic towards a foreigner. Americans hitch-hiking abroad often show the Canadian flag, using the maple leaf as a flag of convenience as it is distinctive, and Canada has a good clean image. In my case the kilt was enough, although a surprising number of people never noticed it until I was inside their car. So they would not have recognised the St Andrews flag anyway. It could appear quite similar to the Skull and Crossbones.

Then there is walking. Many drivers feel that if you are making the effort to reach your destination then they will help, but if the hitcher is reclined on his pack, sleeping with his hand held out *expecting* someone to stop . . . to hell with him, let him sit there and rot. And yet there are others who always stop irrespective of your appearance or what you are doing, simply because they always stop.

Hitching is not just an art form. It is a whole branch of applied psychology, and with an understanding of the mind behind the driving wheel, the successful hitcher can really go places. Choosing a good spot to stand is essential. The best is on a straight road where cars have plenty of time to see you – preferably slightly uphill or with an obstacle (e.g. roadworks) where they have to move more slowly, and with enough space for a car to pull off the road safely alongside you.

I was on such a spot. When the next car approached I gave it the standard thumb out, not aggressively but relaxed and gentle, an appealing swivel of the wrist to turn that thumb towards our mutual goal when the vehicle was precisely at a comfortable braking distance, a mild tilting of the head to one side, a little shrug of 'Come on – how about it?' before changing it to an arms-out plea. These were accompained by a broad smile, cheerful but not idiotic, eyebrows raised in expectation and then a beseeching expression suffused with optimism. Finally, as the car drove past, a small nod was needed to show my acceptance of rejection, followed by another smile and a friendly wave. This last part was vital and often resulted in a car screeching to a halt long after it had passed, conscience touched by the reflection of a figure in the rear-view mirror that showed passive defeat with no hint of anger or insult. I felt like a bullfighter rising to the occasion with a performance that shone with professionalism, expertise and a practised hand. It combined style with elegance, immaculate timing with fluency, and evoked the perfect blend of

The Grand Canyon seen from the North Rim, Arizona, just before a storm hit this formidable trench

Las Vegas, a microcosm of neon, halogen and mercury vapour

A Rainbow man with ideas for the future. He and I and ten thousand others — tramps, souls lost and found, the hyperactive and the inert, an accountant and a baker — attended an annual gathering of the Rainbow people in a quiet corner of Washington State

View from a cave: North Falls on Silver Creek, near Salem, Oregon

The Fijian warrior who leapt towards my lens at the Calgary Stampede, Alberta

Nightfall, about fifty miles from Fairbanks, Alaska

My cowboy companions at the end of a working day; near Carrizozo, New Mexico

hope, pity and pride. It was indeed a performance that merited two ears, and possibly half a tail besides on account of the inclement weather, but this car did not stop. A wave broke over the champion's head like a 'boo' or the impact of a cushion from a hostile spectator. The next car, however, did stop. It was a police car.

'Look buddy, if you wanna ticket, I'll give you one. I don't wanna see you hitching within ten feet of the kerb. *Capiste?*' And the car drove off.

Why did the term 'buddy' always precede an unpleasant message? '*Capiste?*' Obnoxious peasant. Did I look Italian? In the rain, maybe. So I paced out the required distance, repaired my smile and tried to lean out over ten feet of grass verge to impress the traffic once more, without feeling much confidence.

Beside me stood the sign of an Indian reservation which announced, 'Fireworks for Sale.' I had often wondered why Indians and fireworks always went together. It was later explained that most states ban the sale of fireworks but Indian land is not subject to the same laws and so, in a reversal of history, they are now the main source of underhand firesticks for the white man.

A van that had passed five minutes earlier came back and stopped in front of me.

'My! Who could resist a smile like that?' said the driver and I blushed modestly as if it had been entirely unintentional. 'Come on in. The law told me to come and get you.'

Unbelievable! That policeman had bothered to stop and ask a friend to come back and give me a lift!

'Who did you say told you to come and get me?' I asked as we drove off.

'The Lord did,' he repeated.

Eight hundred yards later he stopped outside his house where an enormous cross was planted in a rose border. The words 'JESUS SAVES' sprouted from the blooms of 'Peace', 'New Dawn' and 'Super Star'. He instantly converted his driving seat into a pulpit and began to read from the Bible (Matt. 3:3) on his dashboard lectern. In a voice that dropped an octave and became a scratched 'Hallelujah Chorus' at only sixteen and a bit revolutions per minute, he read out the text. Every now and then he stopped to explain the obvious by repeating the same words in a different order. I managed to forestall my preacher with the gist of the remaining verses before he reached them, whereupon he handed me some leaflets. Each was a picture story which had done away with compassion and was a shock-horror approach to conversion. One of them depicted an average man who had died suddenly and was at his Day of Judgement. He sat before a cinema screen and watched the recorded highlights of some of the more enjoyable pursuits of his life, accompanied by a man with a big book. At times he was moved to cry out in little balloons, 'Oh no! Not that dirty joke, I never meant it', until at the end he was dragged off to hell by demons holding tridents. The final page was blank except for the words, 'The choice is yours. Saved. Condemned. Please tick the appropriate box.' I stuffed the leaflets into my sporran and escaped with difficulty. One bedraggled Scotsman, persecuted through his resemblance to Italians and heathens, fled gratefully into a rainy wilderness of firecracker-selling Indians.

It was still raining by the time I reached the town of Kalispell in the next of the northern states, Montana, after a five-mile walk and a lift with a fire-engine. My feet were wet and my boots were wobbling on disintegrating heels when I passed a shoe shop. A small side alley provided enough privacy for me to change into dry socks and a moment later I was surrounded by shelves of footwear. The sales assistant gazed at my boots gravely and asked me to remove them. She immediately picked them up and dropped them into a – 'trash can' was printed on the side of the container and although there is no difference between 'trash' and other terms for refuse, I would have preferred my faithful boots to have ended their days in a *dustbin*; 'trash' seemed a slight on their character. Thus stranded in my socks in the middle of the shoe shop by an excellent saleswoman, I watched as she laid out a selection of boots before me. She raved about the comfort of Wayfarers' honey-combed soles, enthused about the suppleness of Trailblazers (and bent them until the toe touched the ankle), and thought the Rocky Ramblers would look swell with my kilt because they were blue. I was uncertain which would be best but finally paid thirty-seven dollars for a pair of Trailblazers and a tin of waterproofer, because my kilt had no blue in it, honey-combed soles always wore through quickly and she had made me feel naked by depriving my feet of their trashy boots.

My new Trailblazers seemed to have an immediate effect. The weather brightened and so did my prospects. Cars took me in quick succession past Lake McDonald whose flat calm surface mirrored the Rocky Mountains of Glacier National Park. Here was mountain scenery in all its glory, where snow-capped peaks looked out over lush forest, and banks of wild flowers surrounded lakes whose limpid waters turned deeper shades of turquoise with the distance. At the top of Siyeh Pass another man stood on the lonely trail admiring the scenery. He ignored my polite salutation and continued to let his eyes feast on the view. His thoughts were murmured and faintly audible. 'This is the nearest I'll ever get to Heaven.' Without turning round, he slowly wandered off into a masterpiece of a landscape.

It was my idea of Heaven too, or would have been without the bears. The warden at the park headquarters warned me about the high risk of attack; someone had recently been badly mauled at this very campsite. Caravans were safe enough but those with tents had to camp inside a small enclosure bounded by a high fence. I was the only one there and, as I looked out of my cage, it seemed the ideal way for a zoo to be; the visitor inside and the animals free to approach for a closer look. It was not a pleasant feeling to be shut inside and it reminded me of a sign at San Diego zoo. 'Do not annoy, torment, pester, plague, molest, worry, badger, horey, horass, heckle, persecute, irk, bullyrag, vex, disquiet, beset, bother, tease, nettle or tantalise . . . the animals.' I knew how they felt when other visitors came up to my cage to stare at me, but at least I was not bullyragged.

The wardens gave a talk on bears that evening. Bears would normally avoid contact with man if they knew of his presence. Walkers were advised to ring a bell or make frequent noises when out in these woods to lessen the risk of rounding a corner and finding a grizzly bearing down on them; seven hundred pounds of solid muscle that could rear up eight feet tall, easily outstrip a horse over short distances and kill an ox with a single blow.

If you did come across one they recommended you stayed still (quick movements excited the beast), slowly backed off until you were out of sight, and then ran like blazes for the nearest tree. Grizzlies were unlike porcupines and could not climb trees. If the bear approached before you could escape, then the brave were meant to stare it in the eye, and the first to blink lost. Or else it was best to stand your ground as they often made a sham attack, veering off before coming within striking distance and disappearing into the forest. However, not always. As a last resort it was considered wisest to drop down, if you had not already done so, and to play possum in the hope that if you appeared dead the bear would no longer regard you as a threat and might depart after no more than a token swipe. There were exceptions and an old man once ran towards a charging bear waving his stick and shouting. He successfully scared it away but this was not regarded as foolproof, mainly because not many people had tried it.

Numerous attacks took place near a campfire, although it was not known if this was a significant factor in itself; but bears were definitely attracted to food left in tents and, strangely, to women in menstruation. But the most dangerous situation of all was to be caught between a mother and her cub.

'The normal litter comprises two cubs and they are born naked,' the warden explained. 'Bears bear bare bears.' Then he showed a map of the park and pointed out the sites of recent attacks. Almost all of them had been attributed to errors made by the victims, he said. A girl had been killed here as she had not put her food outside her tent. A man had surprised a bear in this area as he was not ringing a bell, and another had been illegally camped here – unfortunately he had chosen a grizzly's favourite spot to cross the river. But the most frightening case had been the year before when the victim had done nothing wrong. He had a back-country permit and was camped at Lake Elizabeth on the official campsite. His food had been placed well away from his tent but when he returned from a hike, he could see from a distance that the tent had been ripped up and his camp ravaged. He saw no sign of movement so he went down to take some close-up photographs of the damage, and that was the last thing he ever did. The bear was still there, maybe even waiting for him. When a spotter plane passed a couple of days later the crew raised an alert and rangers went to investigate. The bear had treated the kill as if it had been normal prey, eating some parts and burying the rest to return for it later. All the rangers found were the remains of some bones and one hand.

Any bear that has killed or attacked is hunted and destroyed. Those that frequent campsites looking for food are tranquillised, tagged and taken to a remote area in the park. If they return, then after the third time they are destroyed. 'Don't let me put you off bears,' said the warden. 'They're great creatures, but they sure need a lot of respect.'

When the talk ended a retired couple invited me back to their fire for a chat over some coffee. The previous night the warden had told them their fire was too big and had warned them to keep it smaller. This time they had been more careful. When he passed later that evening they called out, 'How's our fire tonight?' The warden stopped, peered at it for a moment and walked on.

'Looks like it's out,' he said, instantly erasing their obliging smiles.

'That was a depressing talk,' I remarked gloomily. 'Makes me want to stay out of the woods.'

'Yes,' said my host between snorts of breath as he tried to revive the embers, 'and I don't go for that bell-ringing stuff. Just seems to me as if you're sounding the dinner gong for every bear in the area.'

My dinner gong was a thoroughly washed sardine can with some pebbles inside it and over the next few days my walks were ruined by the constant noise of this infernal rattle. The scenery was always heavenly but there was no wildlife to be seen and after hours of shaking this can as if I were collecting on behalf of the RSPC Sardines, it seemed preferable to risk meeting a bear and at least be able to enjoy a short period of silence.

Late one afternoon, feeling tired and slightly hard of hearing after a twenty-three-mile walk, I left the central area of the park and tried to hitch away. By darkness there was no more traffic and I was on the edge of the park, still very much in bear country and very far from my protective cage. After selecting a site that was not on any obvious animal trail and hiding my food a long way from my tent, things felt a little safer – until I came across a smear of undigested red berries; the unmistakable droppings of the omniverous bear. I resolved to sleep with my camera flashgun and a box of matches by my side in the hope that there would be eight seconds to spare for the flashgun to charge its cell and for me to set fire to my shirt, in a double-barrelled attempt, as it were, to frighten off an intruder.

These thoughts were all disquieting, especially as that same day a man had been attacked on a trail only three hours after I had been walking on it. He had forgotten to ring his bell for several corners and had suddenly come upon a grizzly. It charged and came to within ten feet before abruptly turning off into the trees. He could not stop his bell from shaking as he ran all the way back to his camp. It would have been interesting to know what his religion was, as it appeared to work.

This led me to reflect on the religious leaflets still in my sporran, and on my impious reaction to them. 'Saved or Condemned?' they had asked. With a faint suspicion that I might have inadvertently ticked the wrong box and created another godless Sonoma County around my tent, I fell asleep.

I woke up suddenly in the middle of the night to a very strange wind. It came in short powerful gusts. Each one could be heard approaching, roaring over the treetops, and shaking my tent violently for a moment before passing on. Then silence, sinister and unnerving, before the next gust came. There was a distant peal of thunder, and then I heard it. Another noise. Close, very close. Deep, rasping, heavy breathing. Wide awake, paralysed with fear, I held my head up in the air, my body stiffened . . . listening. Low-pitched growls. How close was it? Ten yards? Twenty? 'Thud-splash.' It was at the pond. Thirty yards away then. Long, deep exhalations, almost a cough, a grunt, more splashing. Panic seized my muscles. Run. Half of me wanted to run, half of me wouldn't move. 'Thud-splash.' Snorting. Bear. Fire. Run. My God . . .

. . . Ha! Don't turn to Him now, hypocrite. You've blown your chances there, buddy. Ha! Reciting a little bit of Matthew? Worthless! Not enough. We gave you the choice. Remember? But then We were just a bad joke, weren't We? Or did you not really mean it either? Ha! Ha! You're on your own, sinner . . .

What was I to do? . . . Groaning sounds, a dull yawn . . . Maybe it was a moose? . . . '. . . attributed to errors made by the victims . . . A man was illegally camped here – unfortunately he had chosen a grizzly's favourite spot to cross the river' . . . Got to get away . . . Run . . . 'All they found was a hand' . . .

My mind was spinning, my heartbeat racing. Eventually the waiting became too much. The creature was not coming any closer, at least. Slowly I opened the tent zip and peeped cautiously round towards the noise. The moon cast a slight glow on the pond and ripples were spreading across its surface, but the cause of those ripples, still breathing deeply, remained in darkness. Crawling out of my sleeping bag and grabbing some clothes and my boots, I tiptoed away in bare feet, wearing only underpants, trying to stifle the urge to run, breaking into a fast walk, then a trot and then suddenly tripping. I fell over into the darkness and landed painfully amongst some stones. Branches snapped under the impact and new spasms of terror tore at my mind as I choked my mouth and throat to stop myself from uttering any sound. The distant breathing stopped. Had it heard me? Was it coming? What was it like to see a wild grizzly standing over you, lips snarling, teeth descending, three-inch claws slashing . . .?

But nothing came. The grunting resumed. I got up gently and tiptoed away once more. My feet were cut and bleeding by the time I reached the road, so I put on my boots and then ran and ran, almost naked, still clutching my bundle of clothes. Anything to get away. About a mile further on a bulldozer stood by the side of the road. Its cab was locked but the feel of metal and something man-made was comforting and I stretched out along its engine cover, the arms of the shovel acting as walls to my bunk. An elk suddenly walked out of the woods and caused another surge of panic as it passed close by, but then my fear gradually subsided. There was no sleep that night and when at last dawn broke, it came as one of the most welcome sights of my life. I returned to my campsite full of apprehension and making as much noise as possible, in case I should find one bear or more in my tent, like a nightmare reversal of the Goldilocks story. There was, however, no sign of my nocturnal visitor.

A car with its rear-suspension removed came along looking similar to a resurrected Greenland taxi. 'Low-riders' were a craze that had persevered among the local Blackfoot tribe, and four inebriated young Indians gave me a lift to the Canadian border. They talked about partying, drinking, brawls and a friend called 'Marty Eagle Feathers', while continually opening more beers. Cans were stacked in every crevice. When we had a puncture they were too drunk to know what to do so I found the jack in a bootful of empties, and changed the wheel for them. They were very grateful and gave me a beer. I presumed that, up to a limited number, it was the modern and disposable version of the peace pipe.

My arrival in Calgary was opportune and it was the week of its famous Stampede, the biggest rodeo of its kind. The traditional skills of the cowboy's work were incorporated into competitions with strict rules and enough kicks and danger to excite even the 'shootroosters' – the old rodeo hands who sat around the coral fence and criticised the cocky newcomers. Straps were tightened around the hindquarters of broncos and steers, and they were bullyragged until they bucked and exploded in a frenzy of discomfort. Their rider sat hunched up with only one handhold and tried to survive eight seconds of thrashing motion in a style that would lead to glory, and a handsome prize cheque. If his animal was not lively enough he was allowed a rerun on another whose strap had been taken in an extra notch.

Clowns ran about in tattered dresses with balloons stuffed down their chest, the permanent smile of their make-up disguising any emotion as they tried to entice an angry animal away from a fallen rider. Cowboys leapt from their horse at the gallop and wrestled an escaping steer to the ground. Others lassoed a calf from the saddle and left it trussed and immobile in the dirt within seven seconds of the starter's flag. Wagons ran races on wobbly wheels, wild horses ran amuck in a genuine stampede and were roped by gritty figures who were dragged through the sand. Lumberjacks hurled axes at targets, jousted on floating logs, then climbed, felled and cut up trees in flurries of sweat and sawdust. It was the Olympics of the frontiersman.

Spread around the main arena was a congestion of sideshows and displays. To the background of the 1979–80 World Champion Whistler warbling sweetly over the loudspeakers, crowds of cowboys, cowgirls, cowkids, and cowgeriatrics, who probably couldn't tell a stirrup from a rein, all walked about clutching armfuls of free literature ranging from pro-abortion leaflets to Alberta's grain yields for last season, carrying the same plastic bags of 'Old College Weed Identification Kits', chewing gum, tripping along in their high-heeled boots and losing their stetsons under low stalls. These distortions of John Wayne formed huge posses and hung around like redundant extras in a Marlboro commercial as they gawped through glass-covered cut-outs to see the internal organs of the latest New Holland TR85 combine harvester, watched the continuous birth of a calf on a video screen, pressed all the wrong buttons in self-operating displays, applied ice cream cones to their faces when patient exhibitors explained the role of pesticides for the umpteenth time and seemed relieved when they left and no longer had to concentrate, look interested or pick up more brochures. With smiles they moseyed into the riot of snackbars, coffeestalls, Fantashacks and booths of Broncoburgers before feeling spurred on to attack the shopping section with renewed vigour. It was all there. The miracle kitchen food chopper, the wonder knife, the amazing money wallet, the revolutionary cooking pan, the incredible spring-gun fly swatter, the marvel carpet cleaner, the sensational, the money-saving, the time-beating.

I went to the Livestock Hall where the lovely French Lop rabbit was unaware of these bargains as it sat under folds of its own fur, and in the next cage stood an odd bundle of feathers called a Cochin hen – both of them apparently pondering how to grow into coats which were still several sizes too large. Further on a crowd sat around a small showring. 'And this is the Welsh pony,' said the man with a microphone, 'the gentlest and most docile of them all, a delightful pet and great with the kids. In fact, when you send your kids off on this little pony you can be sure it'll be nursemaiding them all-lll the time and they'll come back safe and sound . . .'

An old man in a cowboy hat turned to his neighbour. 'You hear that, Joe?' he asked in a voice loud enough to overcome his own deafness. 'Horseshit, absolute horseshit.'

Beside some prize bulls there was a notice: 'Semen for sale. $12 per unit.' I commented to a man that it seemed a good price for such champion bulls. He agreed it was a good price. He went on to say that the owner would probably sell $20,000 worth of semen from each animal every year and volunteered the further bits of information that the risk of injury was too great to allow a valuable bull to mount a cow, semen was induced by electric stimulation and $3,000 worth might be produced in one ejaculation. His detailed explanation continued for several minutes, and after that I was more discreet with my comments.

Outside, I came upon a machine that bent one cent pieces into funny shapes as good luck charms. Its sign read, 'Due to Canadian law we are forbidden to deface Canadian currency – WE BEND AMERICAN COINS.' In the fairground there were all the usual unoiled centrifugal thrills or you could ride a mechanical bucking steer after turning its dial to the Richter Scale setting of your choice. The over-ambitious were landing in heaps all over the place. Sarcee and Stoney Indians strolled around in headdresses trailing gaily dyed feathers down to their ankles, which explained at once why the bald-headed eagle of North America is bald. And there was even a group of Fijian warriors mixed up in a mêlée of dance-fighting, firewalking and autograph-signing. One leapt towards my lens, his face partially blackened and glistening with perspiration – he brandished a spear and his wicked stare was magnified into disconcerting detail by thirteen elements of finest Japanese optics.

For a week the Wild West relived some of its past, leaving me slightly dizzy at the end when the flying hooves finally came to rest, the cowboys went home and the cowpats of the Calgary Stampede were swept under the presentation stage for another year.

Magnetic North pulled me on through more of the Rockies which were every bit as masterful as they had been around Siyeh Pass, and more liberally sprinkled with Stella's jay, whistling ground squirrel, bighorn sheep, long-eared mule deer and the occasional glacier. The car that took me to Dawson Creek, the start of the Alaskan Highway, was driven by a woman from Quebec whose English was confident but unreliable. I asked her what type of dog it was lying stretched out along the backseat, looking like a russet mixture of French Lop rabbit and Cochin hen, only much bigger. 'It's a cross between a Golden Retriever and an English Settler,' she replied innocently.

The Alaskan Highway was hastily cut through virgin forest in just over seven months during the last war when a Japanese invasion in the north seemed imminent. It runs for 915 miles to Whitehorse in Canada's Yukon Territory, and then on another 600 miles to Fairbanks. It is a gravel road but with considerable stretches now sealed and more being added all the time. There are still plenty of deep potholes and broken windscreens to add a touch of excitement, although perhaps not enough to justify the sense of daring that the 'Alaska or bust' signs of the modern pioneers might suggest, as they drive along in mobile homes with air-conditioning, television and refrigerators.

This road is notoriously hard to hitch-hike. Drivers are faced with the thought of a stranger's company for at least one full day (and possibly up to three days) of travel. If this company proves tiresome, their only convenient excuses for breaking the journey are the small settlements which lie at 300-mile intervals. I saw other hitchers already there, spread out in a long line on the edge of town, and some had been waiting for four days. They offered cheerless nods as I walked past, carrying on until they were no longer within sight. The traffic was equally depressing, being sparse and mostly fully laden. It brought back lonely memories of Iceland. The kilt would need all its power to win lifts here.

The cars travelling south were all friendly, for they felt no obligation to stop. They waved and cheered at this figure who represented the pride of youth, the epitome of the adventuring spirit, the personification of courage and determination. The northbound drivers, on the other hand, sank down deeper behind their wheel, regarding me as a good-for-nothing vagrant who combined all the worst of what the newspaper always said. I bore them no grudge. If our roles had been reversed, I could not even be sure that I would have stopped for a figure such as myself, a figure whose kilt was showing signs of wear and tear (two patches, 9,188 stitches), and who could have been mistaken for a drag artiste of no fixed San Francisco address.

Fortunately it still resembled a kilt and after no more than an hour of waiting, a young couple welcomed me aboard their VW van. My two-day lift to the Yukon began. They had travelled extensively and it made an enjoyable journey sharing stories as kindred spirits and sharing our food as goulashes of whatever we had. We passed through one thousand miles of forest which also extended from coast to coast across the width of Canada, the second biggest country in the world. Here was land relatively untouched except for the odd logging and oil exploration tracks that were no more than hairs on a carthorse's back. For much of the way the road ran below the tops of Jack pine, a tall tree with stunted branches, but periodically it emerged on rounded hills and we looked out over tracts of forgotten forest and tranquil lakes.

Everything disappeared from view when we exchanged dust clouds with each oncoming car and a shower of gravel reduced our speed to a crawl. Onwards through dust and Jack pine to a town where it was customary to deposit a roadsign with the name of your hometown on it, which you had stolen before leaving. A homesick GI working on the road had started it off and now thousands of signs bearing names from all over North America were stacked up alongside the road, threatening to engulf the solitary signpost at each end and absorb the identity of Watson Lake; and yet its name would never be lost because it marked the only dot on the map for six hundred miles. At a junction near Whitehorse we spotted a Bohemian waxwing (they had a birdbook). It flew north, the VW drove north and I headed south for Skagway on the coast.

This town was on the narrow part of Alaska, affectionately called 'The Panhandle', but the American customs I had to pass through to reach it were anything but affectionate. Their manner was rude and unfriendly as I filled in a multiple-choice questionnaire. I said nothing but instead, several small leaflets were left behind on the counter. They had similar boxes to be ticked, only the range of choice was more limited.

It was my birthday. I shared it with some horseflies that had vicious bites, mosquitos that were larger than those of Greenland but not as large as the supposed Texan ones that carried you off for later, and some harmless clickety-clack flying crickets. Over the adjacent fence were buried 'Soapy Smith' – a confidence trickster who sold soap and ran a gang that defrauded and waylaid the early gold prospectors – and Reid, the local man who saved the honour of the town when he shot Smith in self-defence, although he himself was mortally wounded in the confrontation. It was scarcely the ideal setting for a celebration but I opened the card that had been kept loyally unopened since my last mail collection point a month earlier.

'Twenty-six . . . and the world is yours,' read the caption. I swatted a mosquito as a horsefly bit me from behind and, looking over the graveyard, was not totally convinced I wanted it. But after a bowl of broth the outlook appeared more acceptable. The world was mine! It was just a pity I was having difficulty claiming ownership.

12 · Finding the gold
in the Yukon

On 17th August 1896, George Carmack and his two Indian friends, Skookum Jim and Tagish Charley, discovered gold in a tributary of the Yukon River. At a time when a good pan would yield ten cents worth of gold they had found a stream off the Klondike River that brought up four dollars worth with each scoop of the pan. They filed the first claims and the word soon got out. 'GOLD! GOLD! GOLD! MEN MAKING FORTUNES OVERNIGHT,' read the headlines and, fifty years after the famous Californian strike, the Klondike gold rush was on. Men from all trades and every part of the country flocked up from Seattle to Skagway between 1897 and 1898. So many arrived that the Canadian authorities refused to admit anyone into the Yukon Territory (the border lay eight miles inland) unless they were accompanied by enough provisions to last each member of their party for one year. These accounted for half of the average two-thousand-pound load the prospector had to haul by the time he had also amassed his mining equipment.

From Skagway they either took the longer but less steep route via the White Pass or went to Dyea and climbed the thirty-degree slope of the notorious Chilkoot Pass. Although this was a shorter route it necessitated making thirty or forty trips with fifty-pound loads to move belongings over the tops, and it took two months to cover the first twenty-five miles. Any animal was made to carry a load; sheep and pigs were burdened and teams of goats pulled sledges. Photographs taken of the Chilkoot Pass in the winter of 1897/98, when more than twenty-two thousand people crossed over, show a single long line of figures toiling up the steep slope in deep snow. So desperate were they to complete the many journeys required up and down that they were continuously bunched into a solid queue and jealousies ran high with the result that if anyone stumbled out of place or stopped for a rest on the gruelling ascent, the figures closed up and that man would have to return to the bottom and wait his turn once more.

On the other side of the pass they had to wait in tent cities until Lakes Lindeman and Bennett thawed and when the break-up came on 29th May, an amazing flotilla of 7,124 homemade boats and anything that could float set off for the next stage of the arduous journey. For those that survived the one hundred miles from Skagway to Whitehorse, including the rapids on the Yukon River at Miles Canyon where many supplies and lives were lost, it was still another three hundred miles from there to the centre of the strike at Dawson City. A measles epidemic claimed more lives, a snowslide killed sixty-seven in a single day and for most it was a trail of incredible hardship, waiting in bitterly cold tent cities, losing vital provisions, and only to end in the heartbreak of finding that all the claims had long since been staked. Some turned back after the Chilkoot Pass while others went to Haines where, for a fee of $150, Jack Dalton provided guides and permitted them to use 'his' alternative route which was easier but considerably longer and which he protected with his own hired guards.

Secondary minor rushes occurred shortly after this, most notably in north-west Alaska at Nome where gold was discovered in the seaside sand, and also at Fairbanks. But by 1900, when the dreaded Chilkoot Pass was bypassed with the opening of the Skagway to Whitehorse railway, the Klondike gold rush – the greatest of all time – had already lost its momentum. For those that struck it lucky, many struck it exceptionally lucky in this area which has produced over one billion dollars of gold and has been mined continuously ever since.

To this day the Chilkoot Trail is littered with many relics of the gold rush and Skagway has retained much of the old atmosphere in both original and restored form. While I was walking along one of the wooden walkways that surrounded a block of pleasingly rundown houses and a saloon, carefully skirting a hole in the broken boards, a car passed and several defamatory remarks were directed at my kilt. When the car returned a few minutes later I decided to turn my back on them and become interested in a shop-window full of porcelain prospectors and Yukon knickknacks, to avoid the inevitable comments. Something blue suddenly landed at my feet as the car passed and it was followed by a shout.

'There's a fuckin' present for you.'

A pair of relatively new, freshly laundered jeans lay at my feet. I looked at the departing car, down at this unexpected form of manna and then up at the sky, suspicious of being the butt of a higher, warped sense of humour until pride forced me to move on. I stopped after only two steps. There was surely a time and place for pride and on reconsidering the situation in the light of the only pair of jeans in my pack having patches even on patches and no less than thirteen of them in all (and the street being empty), then this did not appear to be right on either count. Pride gave way to more mercenary instincts. Possibly they thought Scotsmen wore kilts because they had not yet discovered Levis but whatever the reasons for this godsend, they were a comfortable fit and lasted long enough to amass a goodly collection of their own patches.

A ferry took me to Haines, set on a headland by the edge of Glacier Bay at the base of imposing mountains, where thousands of bald-headed eagles gather to feed on the salmon each October and where the Chilkat Indians carve totem poles and perform their recently revived dances. The dance group make the costumes and masks themselves, consulting books and the older members of the community to ensure authenticity. One mask I saw displayed a wide grin of real human teeth which the dentist had provided, and it made the puckered lips of the music conductor appear all the more pronounced.

There were no other coastal roads that joined the national network within four hundred miles of this part of the panhandle, so I left Haines the next day on the only road that wandered northwards. My kilt again evoked catcalls (but no more jeans) and, as is my destiny, more dogs became caught in ferocious passions of possessiveness at my intrusion. Mist drifted leisurely past the surrounding hills which were covered in white veins carrying meltwater from their snowy crests down through dense pine forests in a helter-skelter course to the shores of a sea loch, where driftwood lay scattered in careless abandon and brown strands of wrack snaked among the rocks. It all reminded me so much of Scotland. With catcalls still ringing in the back of my mind, a hint of loneliness returned but only as much as the hardened loner can feel, or as much as he wisely permits himself to feel. The beauty around me, although partly to blame for my feelings of solitude through the bitter-sweet memories it provoked, soon made me forget such transient emotion. I was just a *cheechako*, a newcomer to the Yukon. Those that had stayed here over a winter from freeze-up to break-up became a 'sourdough'; a reference to the way they used to make their bread with a natural yeast. I made my way to where it all began, to Dawson City, where the real sourdoughs and gold fever still live on.

Once a city, always a city and although Dawson City now has a winter population of only 670, it will never lose its status. It sprang from nothing to thirty thousand within two years, reaching a peak of forty thousand, second in size only to New York at the time, and soon became known as 'the Paris of the North'. A theatre, cinema, bars, can-can girls, hawkers and all ancillary services and forms of entertainment were attracted to share the fortunes of the lucky and to provide consolation to the others, all at a high price. The law was strictly enforced and gambling mostly took place out of the town limits in a suburb of tents and shacks called Lousetown, where the prostitutes lived. With so many still arriving and finding all the claims gone, everyone tried to earn money by whatever means possible; some even collected clothes that had never been washed but had been discarded only when they became unbearable to wear, laundering, repairing and reselling these, sometimes back to the original owner.

Today Dawson City consists of five main streets, unsurfaced, riddled with potholes filled by the rain into deep puddles, flanked by wooden walkways where weeds grow between the broken slats and whose ends waver in the air like springboards. Original façades are still tacked on the fronts of old wooden buildings, rising up above the corrugated iron roof of the shabby warehouse they are hiding, mixing with more recent buildings also of wood and in the same style and interspersed among the gaps of those which have not survived the Yukon River's floods. Others stand around in delicate states of arrested decay, supported by makeshift braces that are slowly retreating; roofs have sunk into concave curves; verandas droop from rotting beams; sheets of corroded metal rattle in the breeze; some have sunk to their knees and lean over at acute angles, saved from total collapse by a sturdy tree. Dawson City is a joyful shambles of decadence; history simmers amongst the crumbling spokes of cartwheels that dangle from rusty hoops in the under-growth; gold rush excitement exudes from every corner of its dilapidated glory; its faded signs conjure up images of the past and enhance the enduring charisma of a living legend.

Windy Parr, a lean and leathery character whose clothes might have once been discarded and then repaired, patrols the streets with horse and cart. Water drips from the cart and a sign flaps at the back: 'Salman for sale – reasable.' Impromptu musicians may stand at a corner, one with his foot on the bottom of an inverted metal laundry tub, plucking at a string attached to the tub and tensioned by bracing a broom handle – a gut bucket base – while his sidekick rattles the rib bones of a moose as if they were spoons. Prospectors walk by in mudstained hats and bushy beards and sourdough girls dance can-cans in a copy of the original theatre whose front rows are still called the 'baldheaded seats' after the old miners who used to sit there for a better view. Even the lightbulbs are specially made to the old design and none, it is said, has had to be replaced in over twenty years. Klondike Kate used to dance here after arriving at the age of nineteen with a dance group in 1899. Very pretty and full of charm, she did not become a callgirl as did most of the dancers but won the respect of all the community, and miners would bring their valuables to her for safekeeping. She left in 1904 to marry a man who ran off with her fortune instead and started the chain of Pantages Theatres. He was forced to return only five hundred dollars when Kate sued for breach of promise. She later married a trapper who wrote to her from the Yukon, spending each summer up in the north with him until his death. The 'Queen of the Klondike' died in Oregon in 1957.

With my tent pitched near the deserted Lousetown and my luggage hidden in some bushes, I went into town one evening wearing my most respectable shirt and a pair of relatively new, freshly laundered jeans. The sound of music led me to Diamond Tooth Gertie's Gambling Hall, the only legalised casino in Canada, which still thrives in a barn inconspicuous on three sides and modest on the other. A showgirl sang to the jinks of a honky-tonk piano as she slunk amongst the guests, openly casting seductive winks to the crowd with calculated measure to leave every man flushed in the belief that the last wink was above the call of duty and directed just at him and so secretly that no one else even noticed. She minced amongst the tables where waitresses served drinks in 1920 bathing costumes of red and white stripes, revealing, on the back of one particular girl, the tattoo of an eagle hovering in flight. A young prospector, his beard spilling over the lapels of a stained jacket with missing buttons, wore a deflated hat with a bullet hole in it and when we had each received our own personal wink from the singer and were free to speak, I asked him what had happened.

'Two winters ago ah was prospectin' out Lake Laberge way. Man! Was that rough. Ah'd been a week on ma own in silence – just silence an' the squeak of the snow under ma boots. It gotten so bad ah couldn't take no more so ah set ma hat on a stump an' shot it, just to break that goddamn silence. Then ah wore it in Shaky Sue's Sauna in Skagway an', well, it's just never been the same since.'

Dawson City also had the log cabin where Robert Service lived when he was working in a bank shortly after the gold rush, and here he began writing the renowned poetry which recalls so vividly the hardship, humour and nostalgia of the times – and which speaks for the Yukon itself:

Wild and wide are my borders, stern as death is my sway,
And I wait for the men who will win me – and I will not
  be won in a day;
And I will not be won by weaklings, subtle, suave and mild,
But my men with the hearts of vikings, and the simple faith
  of a child . . .

The early years were not easy for this poet and yet he remained optimistic. The words he scrawled on the cabin wall one day are still there in his original hand. 'Rebuffs are just rungs on the ladder to success.'

The first cinema in town showed silent movies, and eventually the first colour films of 35 mm. size with eighteen frames per foot, each frame being hand-painted to perfectly match the others. Films were made of cellulose nitrate, a dangerous and unstable substance and accordingly were never required to be returned to the issuing companies. Their disposal became a problem until it was resolved in 1929 by burying the piles of old films in an abandoned swimming pool where they lay forgotten until accidentally discovered fifty years later. Some had deteriorated beyond repair but others were being restored by specialists in Eastern Canada.

During my stay in the town, a selection of copies made from these original films was being shown in the museum. I sat enthralled as the

same pictures and captions lit up the room as almost eighty years
earlier when they entertained the original pioneers. The films were
accompanied by a pianist, Fred Bass, who matched the tempo of
the music to the scene, high twittering notes during a walk in the
woods and low notes crashing angrily when a figure silently cursed
and !!! x c p n o p !!! appeared on the screen. Fred had been playing
at silent movies all his life and he reminisced over some of his
experiences since he first began playing in 1911 at the age of fourteen.

An audience once became so spellbound during a fight scene that
one man rushed up to the screen to lend a hand to the hero, only to
have to return to his seat feeling a little sheepish after running into the
wall. On another occasion a man came and saw a film which had
three beauties going down to the sea for a swim. They crossed over a
railway track, undressing as they went, and were down to the vital
coverings when a train came and hid them from view. This man
came every day to every performance for a week. When the manage-
ment asked what he found particularly enjoyable, he said; 'You
know that train scene when those girls are undressing? Well, one day
that train's going to be late, and I'm going to be there to see what
happens.'

After the show I was walking along the street when two Indian
girls stopped me.

'Why do you wear a skirt?' asked one.

'It's not a skirt, it's a kilt,' I replied.

'What's the difference between a kilt and a skirt then?'

It was an obvious question and yet one that I had been dreading
because I had no idea of the answer. A gulp of air afforded me some
time to hazard a guess.

'You step into a skirt but the kilt is a wraparound design.' It
sounded an ingenious and very plausible theory.

'It can't be. Many skirts are wraparounds.'

'In that case it must be the pleats then.'

'But I've a skirt with pleats.'

'How about the pattern? The difference is that kilts are tartan.'

'Nope. I've seen women wear tartan skirts.'

The kilt's length, style and material were also quickly dismissed. I
was stumped for any more ideas until she turned up the bottom edge
and suddenly exclaimed, 'Hey! There's no hem . . .'

'That's it,' I said triumphantly, 'skirts have hems, kilts don't. All right?'

She smiled, nodded and they went off. Later I saw one of the theatre girls walk by in an ankle-length dress which possibly did not have a hem. It had to be a long, cotton, frilly, flower-patterned, wraparound, partially pleated Klondike kilt.

The sourdoughs in the Old Folk's Home were great characters as individuals, but they had always been free spirits and to find themselves aged, dependent and forced into the company of others was so alien to the lifestyle they had led that many just withered away in silence. The matron of the home saw me passing one morning and invited me in for a rest because my camera case looked so heavy. I sat near some old-timers gathered round a table, and several cups of tea warmed them into conversation. They talked about the miner who had come into town one day with a nugget of gold an inch thick, the size of a dinner plate and so pure he could bend it. He had shaken off those who'd tried to follow him when he left the town and each month he came back with more. They believed the mine was only a few miles from Dawson but the miner must have died and the secret went with him for one year he never returned. They talked about the gold rush entrepreneur who carefully hauled a cargo of eggs up here and sold them for two pounds each to the prospectors who were fed up with tinned meat. They were found to be stinking rotten. He fled pursued by an angry mob and only escaped with his life by leaving his bag of gold behind and swimming a river in full spate. They talked about the 'Mad Trapper', an American who had fled to these parts after murdering two policemen, and about Barny, also a murderer and the last man to be hanged here in 1932. One old man remembered all these stories as he had been a Mounty in the area for sixty years. He used to tip off the local bars when they were going to make a raid as he felt it was no crime 'to have a drop of the hard stuff in a hard climate.'

The scene was more lively in the El Dorado Bar where other local worthies were still enjoying enough whisky to make up for the climate. Crazy Pierre, a former American NBC carmeraman who had given up his job to become a prospector, sat wearing his hat adorned with twenty thousand dollars worth of gold nuggets fixed all around the outside. He said he simply liked the lifestyle here and did not care too much for money, but admitted that he occasionally got uptight when he realised he had just left his hat in his unlocked van.

The sourdoughs' raw humour helped to mellow the long harsh winters, reflecting the colour of the past and the peculiar bent that die-hard characters show for the unusual, particularly in the fields of sport and entertainment. The Yukon Territory was the venue for: the annual Great Klondike Outhouse Race (carrying a genuine privy); a 1st July Snowball Fight (even though every town is buried under deep drifts during winter, snow was hauled in two trucks from the distant hills to Dawson City for a summer fight at a dollar per throw), a financial failure despite great price reductions at the end of the hot afternoon to encourage participants; the first 'Miss North of the 60th Parallel' Nude Contest (five entrants) failed to start after the Mounties confiscated the trophy; a planned 'Miss Nude Mud Wrestling' Contest (to replace the above), prospects unknown but dubious; the Yukon River Raft Race (car inner-tubes made into anything from imitation stern-wheelers powered by bicycle-driven paddles to simple soloists powered by a puncture and enthusiasm), innocent and successful; and here in the El Dorado Bar was the world's most unsavoury cocktail – a drink containing a real human toe.

There was a commotion at the bar counter as Captain Dick ('Rat') Stevenson, sporting the inevitable beard and the butt of a dead cigar in his mouth, took a jamjar out of his pocket and showed it to a girl whose face contorted with revulsion into a flautist's grimace. The Captain's past was something of a mystery and he seemed happy to keep it that way but it was rumoured he had been a riverboat pilot in the eastern provinces. He was an enthusiastic though seldom successful entrepreneur who ran tourist trips down the river and dabbled in the odd venture on the side. It had been his midsummer snowball fight.

A few years back he had bought an old cabin in the area and in a dusty cupboard he had found a jar containing a pickled human toe which had belonged to the previous owner, a hardy trapper. After suffering frostbite while dog-sledding in a remote region, the trapper had become afraid that gangrene might set in, so he shot off the afflicted foot, kept one toe as a grizzly memento and lived to carry on trapping for many more years. The Captain, never one to miss an opportunity, had been reading some of Robert Service's poems and one in particular appealed to his imagination. *The Ballad of the Ice-worm Cocktail* related how a boastful English hunter on a visit to the area had been cut down to size when he lacked the courage to taste a drink containing a live 'ice-worm' which the locals eventually revealed was merely a piece of spaghetti in a glass of water. The Captain looked again at his jar and the idea for the 'Sourtoe Cocktail' was born.

The Captain was supposedly given fifty free beers each month for drinking at the El Dorado Bar as his cocktail had developed a certain infamous appeal in attracting customers. Those who wished to qualify for a certificate and entry to the Captain's élite club had to buy a cocktail of his or her choice (five dollars), allow the toe to be dropped in and then drain the glass until the instigator of this ritual had nodded his approval.

A cheer went up as the girl tilted her glass back and then the Captain retrieved his toe and wrote her name in a thin ledger. This toe was the second biggest on a foot, a putrid brown–green colour with a ragged nail and a protruding bone. The Captain held the vile thing out to me.

'This one's not as good as the other,' he said.

'Other?' I queried. 'Have you got two?'

'No, but this isn't the original one. The trapper's toe was better. Look – this one's got a wart on it,' he said, apologising for the blemish.

It transpired that a few years earlier a drunk had come along to try the cocktail and had accidentally swallowed the toe. The Captain, distraught at the thought of losing his free beers, hunted in vain for a replacement until he vowed that if a toe was not forthcoming by a certain date he would have one of his own removed for the purpose. The national press picked up the story and shortly before his deadline a woman in Saskatchewan wrote to say she was due to have a toe amputated soon. Some time later a delighted Captain received it by post.

'Hey! The Scotsman wants to try it,' shouted a voice.

My face paled. 'No he doesn't,' I said quickly, trying to laugh it off as absurd while my alarm increased. A knot of look-alike miners seemed to close more tightly around me.

'Oh-yes-he-does, doesn't he, Boys?' came the voice again, heavy with the menacing rhetoric of a pantomime. Beards nodded in agreement and my fate was sealed. It was sheeps' heads all over again, only human toe was far worse.

A drink was suddenly placed in my hands and the toe was dropped in, causing a splash that sent droplets up into my face. As I raised the glass to my mouth the toe became magnified through the liquid, its serrated nail, wart and tattered flesh assuming greater dimensions of horror. It had spent so much of its recent life in alcohol that it made no difference to the taste but it still added a necrophobic flavour to my mind. It seemed stuck to the bottom of the glass as I forced the liquid down in a single draft, providing hope that it might stay there until the glass was empty. But as the last drops ran out it suddenly fell and hit me hard on the lip in a spiteful attempt at a kick in the teeth. It was extremely painful.

A reluctant number 980 received his 'Sourtoe Certificate' with the words on the bottom, 'The first person to drink the toe in a cocktail called a Kilt-Lifter.'

The scene of the original strike lay a short distance out of town on Bonanza Creek, where every claim has yielded at least one million dollars worth of gold over the years. In the Yukon anyone could apply when a claim became 'open' and it was given to the first in line on payment of a registration fee of ten dollars. This entitled him to five hundred feet of river and a thousand feet of bank on both sides which remained his until he relinquished it or failed to do the minimum amount of annual assessment work (showing that the ground had been altered in some way through his efforts), which was a condition of the claim. He was under no obligation to minimise damage to the landscape in the interests of conservation. Many claim-holders leased out the land and charged those who worked it a set fee plus a percentage of the gold they recovered, although it was impossible to ensure that they declared all their takings. The government, of course, taxed these declared earnings.

Some of the old underground mines in the area had been reopened even though the first miners had exhausted the seams, for they had left pillars of natural rock to support the roof as they cut their way along and these pillars were made out of the original seams of rich ore. Elsewhere they had had to overcome the problems of perma-frost which keeps this land frozen solid the year round to a depth of several hundred feet below the surface. They used to light fires which would melt a small area, digging down and removing as much thawed earth as they could before repeating the process, and in this way vertical shafts were sunk down into the deposits. Their firewood was always so cold and slow to ignite that they had to apply the flame with a candle instead of a match. But most of Dawson's gold, which was of high eight-five quality (eighty-five per cent pure) or better, was alluvial gold, recovered from the river bed itself or from old water courses.

Gold is seven times heavier than stone and always settles as low as it can amongst the rocks and gravel. Panning for gold merely involves scooping up a pan of gravel and swilling water around gently until the lighter stones have been washed out, leaving any gold behind. The larger nuggets are called 'plinkers' from the sound they used to make when dropped into the pan; but they don't plink any more as most modern pans are made of rubber. The fine grains of gold dust have always been difficult to separate from the dirt; adding mercury used to be the most common method as mercury is attracted to and absorbs gold. On heating, the gold is released and the mercury can be used again indefinitely, but the vapour given off is highly poisonous. Nowadays other chemical processes are used.

The sluice-box, still the principal device used for recovering gold, consists of an angled trough where the dirt is dumped, and a gentle flow of water dissolves it, carrying particles down to the lower end where they pass over a mat and dozens of riffles – ridges and grooves like the surface of a washboard – where the heavier gold collects. Little has changed for the modern prospectors, except for the larger quantities they can put through using bulldozers, pumps and press-ure hoses.

Bonanza Creek was mile after mile of loose rocks and rubble piled up into huge banks, the tailings created by the old dredge mining vessel which lay deep in silt at one end, after fifty years of service. It had floated in a small pond while its endless chain of buckets ate into the bank, feeding the gravel to processors inside where the gold was extracted, and then disgorging the cleaned gravel out behind it. This great mechanical duck gradually moved across the land taking the pond with it. In 1932 it recovered 35,000 ounces of gold in 262 days.

'No Admittance.' 'No Trespassing.' The signs were everywhere and the suspicious and reticent miners whom I encountered made it clear that strangers were not welcome. One group let me watch their final wash of an area which had already been worked over at least twice by a dredger. They were consulting old log books and digging deeper at the exact locations of former high yields and their efforts seemed to be paying – although naturally no one would admit it. The best indication of a miner's success is the state of his equipment, and everything they had was brand-new.

Here it was then, the sight that all those thousands had come to see at the turn of the century. Nuggets as big as cornflakes were being plucked out as they tumbled through the sluice-box and soon my hands too were helping, lifting out real plinkers and dropping them into the tray as more and more rolled by amongst the lesser flecks, turning the water into a syrup of glittering colour, '*Gold! Gold! Gold!*', that mesmeric metal, the alchemist's dream trickling out of the gravel, '*Gold! Gold! Gold!*' and the fever was catching . . .

'*Get your hands out,*' snapped a threatening voice and I was suddenly looking into the malevolent faces of three angry partners. I apologised profusely, trying to explain that my excitement had carried me away, but the goodwill had been used up and their cold unblinking eyes followed me all the way back to the 'No Entry' sign on the edge of their camp.

I retraced my steps to Lousetown, wondering how much gold there was still left to be won, and how many men with the hearts of Vikings would still try. I thought of the haggard sourdough in the Old Folk's Home who scratched a lifetime of stubble on his chin, chuckling, his eyes glinting anew as he swore that the Yukon's reserves had barely been touched and that the Mother Lode, wherever she was, had plenty more to give. While the bearded figures who continued to sluice the gravel and hunt for pay dirt, gathered at Diamond Tooth Gertie's, shook their heads pitifully and bemoaned their lot. But I realised you should believe only half of what a prospector tells you. And even then not until it has been confirmed with your own eyes (but not with your own hands).

A less tangible factor was at work here amongst the wealth of characters who walked the ramshackle streets of Dawson City, bewitching me in the same way that it had bewitched them and also Robert Service when he wrote the final verse of *The Spell of the Yukon*:

> There's gold, and it's haunting and haunting;
>   It's luring me on as of old;
> Yet it isn't the gold that I'm wanting
>   So much as just finding the gold.
> It's the great, big, broad land 'way up yonder,
>   It's the forests where silence has lease;
> It's the beauty that thrills me with wonder,
>   It's the stillness that fills me with peace.

13 · Alaska –
home of the individual

If the Yukon River could cross the mountains to the south, it would reach the sea within fifty miles of its source, but with the lie of the land pulling northwards and then to the west, it has to flow on almost two thousand miles before emptying its rich waters into the Bering Sea. Its course splits Alaska into equal halves, traversing the vast tundra areas of marshland, lichens and hibernal flora that lie between the oilfields of Prudhoe Bay on the Arctic Ocean and the coastal mountains on the Pacific.

The ferry from Dawson City took me across the river. Indian fishwheels lay at anchor, their paddleblades slowly turning in the current as their wire nets scooped the water for an unwary salmon – the lazy man's method. During the short crossing, a man who simply called himself Hungry said he was about to drive the 450 miles to Anchorage, and he offered to take me there.

The ferry docked at the start of the 'Top of the World' highway which twisted through gently undulating and thickly forested hills to the border of Alaska; one-fifth the size of the rest of the combined American states and, much to the chagrin of some, twice as big as Texas. Alaska became represented by the forty-ninth star on the United States' flag when it joined the Union in 1959, although the land had been in American hands ever since it was purchased from Russia almost a century earlier. The 'lower forty-eight' states tend to ignore the fact that Alaska is a leading oil producer in the world, looking on it more as a neglected back-garden; not very useful, requiring great effort to visit and look after, but nice to own as an extra bit of land.

We passed the hamlet of Chicken which should have been called Ptarmigan after the state bird, but no one was able to spell it or could even be sure of the pronunciation. At Lost Chicken Creek and Gold Gulch bush planes were parked alongside the highway which also served as a runway. It was easy to believe there were more planes per head of population here than anywhere else in the world. And if there were also fifteen hundred square miles of land for every Alaskan, then it appeared necessary to have a plane just to find your neighbour.

It would take twelve hours to reach Anchorage but I was becoming used to the vast distances of this region, where you had to travel at least several hundred miles to reach the next town, and almost one thousand miles to find another that was appreciably different from the first. This aspect only added to my enjoyment of the land's untouched beauty. Travel is always thrilling when the world turns out to be something you like, and especially that something you feared had gone.

Both Canadians and Americans are usually more possessive about their own particular state or province than about their country, and Hungry saw himself primarily as Alaskan. He shared my enthusiasm for the size and emptiness of the land, and enjoyed its unique characteristics – except that exemplified in 1964 when an earthquake (Richter Scale 8·6) made the mountains ripple like jelly and left parked cars inverted with their wheels in the air. A gigantic tsunami, a seismic sea wave, ravaged the coastline, plucked boats from their moorings and smashed them in the streets. The tremors lasted for four minutes, claimed 115 lives and happened on Good Friday.

'That sure was the worst Easter we ever had. But it's a great life up here, always something different to do. In winter we drive on frozen rivers and you never skid as long as the temperature stays low. Ice only becomes slippery when it begins to melt. Anyway, we have to drive on the rivers. This state doesn't ration its gas, just its roads.' The Matanuska Glacier appeared on our left, squeezed out as a white worm of toothpaste from the hills that had been pushed closer together like segments of a compressed concertina. Against the dark valley, its whiteness was shocking.

'Plenty moose around here. In some parts of Anchorage they even come into people's gardens during the winter. It's quite a problem because a hungry moose doesn't scare easily and can turn real nasty. They love eating the young shoots of witch hazel, cotoneaster and apple trees, and nobody can do a thing about it because it's out of hunting season. It's also illegal to fire a gun within city limits, so they're doubly protected.' I chuckled at the thought of Alaska's sacred moose munching its way along the vegetable counters of the supermarkets.

'At Christmas we dry their droppings. Some folk burn them as a sort of incense stick – nice aroma too. Some decorate the droppings with evergreen leaves and we call it "moostletoe".'

'Come on,' I protested. Sourtoes in the Yukon, moostletoes in Alaska? It was all too much.

'It's the absolute truth,' he said indignantly, hurt that his word had been doubted. 'Alaska's not like anywhere else. It's the only state where it's legal to grow, possess and smoke your own marijuana, if you like that sort of thing. And in winter we have our own game, snowshoe baseball. Running's a bit tricky and the ball gets lost every time it lands but it's the real thing. I wouldn't live anywhere else. The rest of the world sits all day with a fishing pole and gets excited over a two-bite trout – that's all the meal they get out of it – while we can go down to the nearest stream and catch all we can carry in an hour. And with a permit to hunt, each year we can get nine hundred pounds of dressed meat, fresh and free. Yeah, here in Alaska we go for it, man. But hell, I hope you're not too impressed. It's already too crowded up here.' Another fifteen hundred square miles fell away, and there still wasn't a soul in sight.

Our conversation cut short the hours and the remaining half of the journey passed quickly. We stopped only for fuel and meals (when my driver amply demonstrated his name), and reached Hungry's home late in the evening. By then it was raining and I needed no persuasion to make use of a spare bed.

Few cities in the world are attractive in the rain, and Anchorage is no exception despite the surrounding hills and its open streets. The American states have all striven to select a relatively insignificant town for their capital and in keeping with this tradition, Juneau is Alaska's capital at the far end of the Panhandle, while Anchorage remains easily the largest city, its access for shipping not as advantageous as its name suggests as it is situated at some distance from the Gulf of Alaska up a long narrow inlet.

A few days later I was walking on the Resurrection Pass Trail which picked its way through the mountains and pine forests well to the south of Anchorage, passing lakes as still as rockpools, surrounded by the purple of fireweed and foxglove and with all the magic of the distant Yukon. Early on I met a group of forestry workers who called me over for fruit salad, and cake baked in an oil drum over the fire. I asked them about moostletoe. They swore it was true, but their broad grins were caused by more than the taste of the cake or mere politeness. So I told them stories about haggis, the creatures of Loch Ness and Iceland's resurrected shark sandwiches, which seemed appropriate in the absence of anyone who could explain how the trail had got its name. That was the only company I met, and all that I wanted, on the forty-mile trek, although two unexpected companions were to join me that same evening.

The streams were so full of salmon that they flowed blood-red, the tightly packed bodies filling even the shallows where their dorsal fins protruded above the surface. These sockeye salmon do not feed after leaving the sea and as their oil and body fat are used up on the last journey of their life-cycle, swimming up to two thousand miles to spawn in the river of their birth, they turn a deeper shade of red. Their meat becomes dry and stringy but is eagerly seized by bears and eagles which gorge themselves on this easy prey.

Still in bear country. I rattled a dinner gong once more until it was time to stop at one of the log cabins that were dispersed along the track. This one was beside a lake and had a rowing boat whose padlock became ineffective if a knot was untied.

That evening I was floating in the middle of the lake in a boat that had slipped its moorings, puffing away at my pipe and producing satisfying clouds of smoke as do bonfires on a wet day. This kept the mosquitoes away and somehow justified using three-quarters of my only box of matches. A sound on the far bank caught my attention. A mother and her young calf, whose gangling legs threatened to give way at any moment, stood there with the characteristic smiles of moose, suggesting they knew something about moostletoe which had yet to be explained to me. The calf waited anxiously on the bank while its mother entered the water until her back was no more than a shallow hump on the surface. She ducked her head under, the hump walked around and then her head suddenly burst up with the mouthful of weed she had found. Each time she ducked I rowed towards her in short burst of activity, timing it to appear motionless when she next emerged, and in this way the gap between us narrowed. When she surfaced her ears were erect, water poured off in rivulets and her round eyes stared at me in surprise as if someone had just woken her with a bucket of cold water. She then began chewing, slowing her jaws in moments of suspicion, tilting her head slightly to one side to check the alignment of the boat against a distant landmark, thinking, 'Did he move? . . .' and then her enjoyment of the weed became too much and down she would dive once more. It was a beautiful sight but eventually I entered her critical zone of fifty yards and she mouched slowly out of the water to the delight of her calf, gave me a long hard look while she chewed the last stalk of weed, and then sauntered off.

Inside the cabin was a visitors' book which contained some unusual entries beside those lamenting the poor weather, disappointment at finding the boat padlocked, and the teethmarks of mice.

'We are visiting Jehovah's Witnesses. Deeply regret that last night we had to burn copies of our magazine *Awake* to get warm enough to sleep.'

'Hard work chopping wood. I'd give my right arm to be ambidextrous.'

'As you travel down the road of life, remember to look at the doughnut and not at the hole.'

While I was reading this by candlelight, a timber wolf let out a long mournful howl nearby. It was a deeply moving sound that seemed to fit the isolation of my setting and yet it sent a shiver down my spine – even if it is claimed that there is no authentic report of this maligned animal ever having attacked a man. I bolted the door anyhow as it would be a pity to spoil such a good record.

The early part of the following morning was occupied with a clothes-washing session. Travelling light with only a few changes of essential clothing meant frequent washing. My kilt tended to stay remarkably clean considering what it went through but this was one of the times when it too needed a wash. I sewed the pleats into place using long tacking stitches on both sides of the garment as otherwise it soon lost its shape. Cold water and a bar of soap were effective enough with brisk rubbing and scrubbing, and the final rinse took place not so much when the kilt looked clean, but more when my feet became unbearably cold after standing in Moose Lake for five minutes. I tied my wrung clothes over my backpack to dry during the remaining walk but the kilt had to hang freely or else it dried with pronounced creases, and wearing it was the easiest solution. This wasn't too unpleasant – Faroese fishermen believed wool kept them warmer when it was thirty per cent wet – but it was still a relief to be rid of the damp feeling which persisted for two days.

It made a change to be a dapper vagabond, clean and neat (and damp) as I continued through the fine scenery of Resurrection Pass. This was just the sort of walk that made adventure worthwhile. But it seemed I was forever rushing on and leaving the beautiful places, the happy times and the special experiences that I had travelled specifically to find. Perhaps it was best to do so while they still held powerful significance and before anything soured their memory. The trail ended on the third day after following a stream that wound its way in bubbling cascades, meandering through forest glades lit up by fingers of sunlight filtering through the branches – and yet at a time when my feet felt bruised and no longer wanted to meander. A truck took me the remaining 130 miles to Homer.

This town was founded at the end of last century and was named after an early but otherwise insignificant gold prospector, Homer Pennock. It does not boast of having the second longest spit in the world but it has, jutting out four miles into the sea of Kachemak Bay. 'Kachemak' comes from the Aleut dialect and, like Reykjavik, means 'smoky bay' – the area is rich in coal deposits and smoke once rose from naturally smouldering seams. Garden vegetables grow well and the tide deposits enough coal along the shore to prevent the residents from worrying about winter fuel, which is possibly why they call Homer the 'Shangri-la of Alaska'.

Two fish factories are sited on the spit, with the usual shoals of sorrowful grins, and workers trying to paliate their boredom by prolonging another sandwich in the short coffee-break. They savoured every mouthful until it had gone and there was nothing for it but to go back to work, processing salmon roe for the Japanese market. Others had gone to a frail wooden lighthouse that had been converted into the Salty Dawg Saloon. It was a legend in the area on account of its age and the miracle of having survived the 220-foot tsunami that swept the coastline on that fateful Good Friday. The interior was a dark smuggler's tavern, a dirt floor of irregular bumps and hollows, a crooked bar counter and nooks and crannies over-flowing with keepsakes of the sea. These covered the walls and hung from the ceiling in such ponderous abundance that they threatened to bring about the collapse that had eluded the wave: thirty ships' lifebelts, glass fishing floats, flags, old bottles, a copper diving helmet, plaster-of-paris lobsters, pirate paintings and a portion of a human skull with the legend, 'The last person to give us a hot cheque.' Another sign hung from the heating controls of a radiator: 'Achtung! Alle Touristen and Non-Technischen Lookenspeepers, das Maschine Control is nicht fur Gefingerpoken and Mittengrabben oderwise is easy Schnappen Springenwerk, Blowenfuse and Poppencorken mit Spitzsparken. Der Maschine is Diggen by Experten only. Is nicht fur Geverken by das Dummkopfer das Rubbernecke Sightseenen. Keepen das Cottonpickin Hands in das Pockets so relaxen and watchen das Blinkenlights.' Alongside was the translation, 'Please do not touch.'

By that time it had become obvious to me that there was something unique in the attitude of the average Alaskan. Every challenge of the outdoor life could be found in this state, often in what was little more than an extension of each garden. Adventure and responsibility were offered, even thrust upon you at an early age. You could legally drive a car at the age of fourteen (with parental consent) and learned to hunt and use a gun as soon as you could safely do so. Alaskans displayed the confidence and enthusiasm that was summed up in one of their own expressions I heard over and over again: 'Go for it, man!' It was as much a state of mind as a figure of speech and the children seemed to grow up with this phrase ingrained into their senses as a catalyst for action.

At the bar I bought a drink for a young fisherman called Rumppo, at least that was how it sounded after our second or third.

'Helluva game this fishin'. Just when it's goin' good and the fish are there, the engine breaks, you lose half your tackle or bait goes up in price. Still, it pays the bills, sometimes. Had me a tooth fixed with a crown last month – shit, that's no joke. The old toothpuller's all right though, says he'll take payment in crabs. So that's keepin' me kinda busy now.'

I asked if it would be possible for me to go out with him on a trip.

'Sure, why not? Go for it, man.' Then he added wistfully, 'After all, this is Alaska – the home of the individual, and other endangered species.'

'It ain't as good here as it used to be now all them oilmen are comin' up here, and the tourists – pukers, we call 'em,' Rumppo said, lifting a spiky King Crab, two feet across from toe to toe, out of the cage.

'Were you born here?' I asked, hastily letting go of another.

'Hell no. I came up here to escape 'Nam.'

He stopped working and his face became serious. 'Don't get me wrong. I'd fight to defend my country. But that wasn't our war and no way was I goin' to be cannonfodder in someone else's . . . Don't suppose you ever heard of Beaver 55? They were an anti-Nam protest group. Well, they broke into the local office and burnt all the records so no draft papers could be issued in my area, but my name would've been called up soon enough so I just left and came here. And that was a federal offence. Meant I could never go back home again in my life. That wasn't easy, man. It cut me up real bad.' His eyes no longer focused, wrinkles creased his brow. 'I'd been here a couple of years and there were others too, livin' on an island. One day this navy patrol boat just appears outta nowhere. Must have been tipped off but we had no time to find a good place to hide. I was under an old cabin and they never saw me first time but then they checked again and dragged me out. Put chains round my wrists and ankles like I was some kinda animal and then they knocked me about a bit. They thought I'd been with Beaver, but I never had anything to do with them. They took me back south and I spent three months in prison and then they aquitted me 'cos of some legal hitch. I still feel bad about it. 'Nam left a big scar on Americans. Hurt their pride, made them suspicious of the leaders, made them feel betrayed, really shook their trust . . . Sometimes I think the only hope for man is for him to become extinct.' He pulled up a pot with the largest crab of the day. 'Wowee! Take a look at this sucker. He should just about cover that tooth enamel.'

Rumppo became more cheerful after that although the remaining pots produced only one reasonable halibut, and undersized crabs which he returned. That evening we moored against an old jetty in Jackaloff Bay, an uninhabited part of the coastline, and made a fire from the pieces of coal lying on the beach. Rumppo sacrificed some tooth enamel by cooking as much crab as we could eat, and then we talked on into the night.

The next day I decided to leave Rumppo and walk ten miles along a logging track to an old Russian settlement on the tip of the Kenai Peninsula. Russia once owned the whole of Alaska and although the first settlers never explored the interior, they trapped furs along the coast and built trading posts. America bought Alaska in 1867 for only $7,200,000 (less than two cents per acre). The sale was negotiated by the Secretary of State, William Seward, and because nothing was known of the potential resources of this land, it became known as 'Seward's Folly', 'Seward's Icebox', and 'Walrussia'. The discovery of gold soon paid back the purchase price many times over, and the strategic importance of Seward's Icebox as a military base became apparent when Japan occupied the Aleutian Islands in the second world war and threatened to invade the mainland. Now it is considered even more vital as the American-owned Little Diomede Island, in the narrowest part of the Bering Sea, is only two and a half miles from the Russian-owned Big Diomede Island. Russia and America stand separated by twenty-seven football pitches of sea.

The walk to Seldovia took twice as long as it should have done because a piece of string, vital to my own defences, broke and caused the sole of one of my Trailblazers to flap at the heel (soon repaired, more string) and because the wild raspberries and brambles were out in force. The bushes were covered with fruit, for Russians did not appear to enjoy the berries as much as I did.

A small cemetery rested on the edge of the village. White Russian Orthodox crosses with their triple bars, the lowest one sharply angled, were slowly being consumed by the advancing undergrowth. Only a goat showed any signs of caring for the place as he chomped his way along the weeds of one Olga Saracoff. Seldovia's wooden houses were built out from the rocks and squatted on stilts over the sea, linked together by an assortment of platforms, bridges and catwalks. This American village inhabited by former Russians and with the air of a Chinese shantytown appeared to have no connection with the superpowers except in name, and in fact it had very little connection with anywhere. Homer was situated relatively close to the north across the sea inlet but there was no connecting road or track around the seventy miles of forested and deeply indented coastline. Seldovia was crudely nailed together into prettiness but its appeal was quickly exhausted, and then its isolation became frustrating.

A fisherman was mending his net in bare feet, stretching the torn area against his toes which were curled through the mesh, adding to my conviction that the north-west observed some form of pedal fetish. He was not Russian but said there were several other colonies in the area, and then pointed to a group of girls wearing the bright clothes of gypsies, who had just appeared strolling along the street. 'There are some,' he said. 'They've all been here many generations now but Russian is still their first language. I'm told it's different from modern Russian but I couldn't say. Could be Greek for all I know. They're fairly shy. Keep to themselves most of the time but there's a lot of drinking and brawling goes on.'

They didn't sound too welcoming. I asked how to get back to Homer.

'Probably the same way you got here. Did you swim?' I explained about my lift. ' 's'pose you might find a boat that chances to pop in or there's a ferry in two days. You could try hanging around the airstrip for a bushplane, otherwise you'll have to get your flippers on and swim.'

The harbour was empty so the airstrip sounded the best hope. Although several planes did land and take off at sporadic intervals, none showed any concern for the optimist standing at the start of the runway with his thumb held out. A small helicopter then landed but the man who hurried out told me firmly that it was private and only for use by company employees. He disappeared, the rotor blades picked up speed again and the engine noise increased. Then the power was reduced. After some hesitation the pilot beckoned me over – and the next moment I had hitched my first lift on a helicopter. It took off gently, hovering for an instant; that wonderful little pause when a hulk of metal just sits in the air as if it were weightless and Newton had been wrong. We pivoted around and rose steeply into the air, accelerating forwards, nose down, tail up and with the exhilarating feeling of three-dimensional mobility. We cruised over the fjords where fishing smacks crawled as small black slugs leaving silvery trails of troubled water amongst the scattered islands, passing low over a glacier and an old trading post. Then the Salty Dawg Saloon appeared and we landed in Homer before my original smile had time to fade. As I left the craft and entered the turbulence below the spinning blades the smile disappeared at once as I struggled to find enough hands to pin down the rising folds of my kilt. The pilot was grinning and still shaking his head in disbelief when the glass bubble floated off once more.

The trip to Fairbanks seemed slow in comparison but equally entertaining. An elderly widow took me the first two miles.

'My! You're taking your life in your hands travelling with an old woman like myself,' she sniggered.

'I'm delighted to risk it,' I replied, for every mile and every lift counted, if not in distance then as a new encounter.

With two miles down and 358 left to go there followed a long wait in which I went through my repertoire of measures to relieve the boredom. My diary was brought up to date, *Tam O'Shanter* was imperfectly recited (twice) and stones were thrown at a can for over an hour, frequently achieving the three consecutive hits that in a personal superstition made the next car duty-bound to stop for me. However none of them seemed aware that they risked being chased by warlocks and witches as they sped past. I sat down again and took out my pocket map of the world. It afforded me the luxury of travelling more quickly and of planning grand schemes. My gaze wandered around the many holes where names such as 'Greenland' had disappeared at the intersection of four creases, and my attention became stranded on Newfoundland. The idea was immediately attractive. Yes, I would go to Newfoundland. And with another destination decided, there was nothing left but the onerous task of sewing on patches and mending my clothes.

My next car came, a Toyota. My driver seemed embarrassed that it wasn't a Ford but if I had no objection to a 'Japanese riceburner', then he would appreciate some company to Fairbanks. When we reached the turn-off to the highest mountain in North America, Mount McKinley (20,320 feet), he decided to make a detour to see it. As the number of cars allowed in the area was restricted, this meant taking a free National Park bus to complete the 180-mile round trip. America's National Parks are managed with an efficiency that is a lesson to the world.

Wildlife was plentiful, and we saw grizzlies, moose, caribou, marmots, eagles, a gerfalcon, and then caught a lucky glimpse of the peak itself. The sharp summit appeared momentarily, standing clear of the cloud that enveloped it, so high it seemed divorced from its foothills – and the angles that connected them in the obscurity seemed unlikely in the mind. The same Dr F. A. Cook who claimed to have beaten Peary to the North Pole by one year also claimed to have made the first successful ascent of Mt McKinley but the honour of this achievement was credited in 1913 to another American, the adversely named explorer Hudson Stuck.

We spent the night on the park campsite and continued our journey the next day. This man had been a bushpilot for over forty years.

'There's many good pilots here in Alaska, and many more dead ones. I've had some scrapes too. Used to do test flights for Cub planes,' he laughed. 'One day it was their latest model, a super-powerful brute, and all the directors and prospective buyers were there watching. Well, I completely underestimated its power on take-off and the next moment I'd done one hop, flipped it over and landed on my back. I crawled out with all the top brass running towards me and the managing director got there first, an angry scowl on his face. I dusted myself off and told him, "Even after a short flight I can tell it's just a fine, fine plane." ' He laughed again. 'They never did invite me back to try another.'

The first building of Fairbanks we came upon was a funeral home with a prominent sign: 'Undertaker and Crematory'. It sounded unwholesome, almost political. But the atmosphere in the streets was festive for a special day of celebration. To my surprise there was an active local pipeband and the Alaskan jocks were out in their kilts. Their band's emblem was a dancing polar bear with a blue balmoral and a red hackle. Several pipers were gathered around a man with a small instrument in a black leather case. 'Bagpipe Tuner. Made in Japan,' said the label.

'Hi! Welcome to the real Scotland,' said Frank Miles, the piper who had just been electronically tuned. 'Pity we haven't got a spare set of pipes for you. We're short-staffed today.' A brass band walked by on their way to play. 'Hey! You with the trombone,' shouted Frank, 'tag on at the back. Doesn't matter what you play, we need all the help we can get.'

A parade approached as the pipe band waited their turn. A very diminutive majorette, scarcely bigger than the mace she was juggling, led a squad of cheer girls chanting in unison and shaking colossal pompoms of coloured raffia. They highstepped to the fanfare of the brass band which included the unresponsive trombone player and a young boy apparently being throttled by the coils of a brass cobra. He puffed into its tail and emitted deep throaty noises through the gaping mouth poised above him. A dazzling beauty queen followed on a float and then my view was blocked by a large woman who walked past with a countenance to chill the blood of a sergeant-major.

'That must be her mother,' whispered Frank.

The performance of the pipe band was well received with clapping and shouts for more (particularly *Scotland the Brave* and *Amazing Grace*) from a crowd largely composed of welders and carpenters. They were up here working on the oil and gas pipeline projects. Frank (oddly enough, an electrician) invited me back to his house in the village of North Pole (centred around a toy factory), where I was introduced to his family and more of his inexhaustible humour. He relaxed back into a chair and lit his pipe which he seemed to smoke as continuously as an Icelander.

'I suppose people always come up to you and ask about your tartan, same as they do to me? A guy approached me once and said, "That's my tartan too. Why! You must be a Douglas?" So I said my name was Miles and that I had no legitimate claim to the kilt but merely liked the colour. He got all uppity, went through a spiel about the clan history and demanded to know where and how a Miles had come by his family tartan. I was fed up and didn't like the guy. I just told him, "We got it off a dead Douglas." He stormed off and later in the day my wife brought home the local paper and there was a picture of that guy I'd met. "Chief of Clan Douglas visits Fairbanks." '

His stories went on and even caused the grey hearthrug to give the odd shudder, where his scruffy terrier, Payday ('Everyone needs a payday'), lay as an indistinguishable bump among the matted tufts. When we talked about a friend who had his own plane I confided in him a scheme at the back of my mind. I had been hoping to get the chance to be dropped off in some remote area for a short while, just to see what it was like to be completely alone in a wilderness. I asked Frank if he knew of anyone who might help.

'Andy would take you, no bother. He's always flying off to fish somewhere. He's a bit suicidal but then you can't exactly be right in the head either. He's not here at the moment . . .' He paused and thought for a moment. The hearthrug stirred, unsettled by the rare silence. '. . . Tell you what. Why don't you come north with me for a few days? I've got to do a job for an oil company up at the North Slope so you could be dropped off and make for our log cabin in Manley. It's a neat place. Mostly miners there and each winter they sign a petition requesting the road not to be maintained so they can be snowed in and be on their own. I'll pick you up when I return and then we'll see Andy – if you haven't been cured of isolation by then.'

We set off the next day, driving alongside the Alaskan Pipeline which followed the contours of the tundra like a silver rope laid over the landscape until it disappeared into the ground, only to reappear in the distance as a delicate thread.

'Looks like a drunk laid it,' said Frank, 'or else they followed an old moose trail', and it did weave around in a quite illogical manner and even incorporated zigzags in its level sections. 'All those bends are to slow down the speed of the oil flow, usually after a hill, in case it ruptures the pipe. It's an amazing feat of engineering; forty-eight inches in diameter and eight hundred miles long. Where it's not underground that means there was a risk of melting the permafrost and causing subsidence, so they built it up on trestles and each support has its own freezing unit running all year round to prevent the ground from thawing. The pipeline can slide a foot on either side to cushion the effect of an earthquake and they even built special underpasses to allow the migrating caribou to cross underneath.' He seemed very proud of the Alaskan Pipeline.

When we reached a sign that said 'All vehicles to drive with lights on for the next 435 miles', Frank continued north towards Prudhoe Bay and I made my way to Manley, passing a signpost to 'Heaven, 17 miles', and a lonely cabin which had 'MEAN DOG' painted on its gate.

My own log cabin had real moose antlers on the wall and was in itself an ideal retreat. I cut wood to keep the stove burning, the coffee pot simmering and the oven hot for making sourdough bread from an old recipe. It refused to rise but contained no ethoxylated diglycerides from New York and was so tasty that it disappeared in a morning, and I had to make more. The evenings were spent on a lake propelling an open canoe in a spiralling course with a single-blade paddle. Beavers swam about with branches gripped between their teeth, frequently taking fright and somersaulting into a dive. The branches remained but they vanished with resounding slaps of their leathery tails as a warning to others of their kind, for they knew the price of their pelts.

All the time I was weighing up the dangers of being dropped in a wilderness with no chance of help should an emergency arise, and wondering if I should take the risk. The answer was a foregone conclusion because that all-Alaskan phrase had already become ingrained into my own way of thinking.

'Go for it, man!'

14 · Marooned in a wilderness – and a dash for Newfoundland

Andy was not the type to inspire confidence. He was a self-employed contract worker, owning and driving a much repaired bulldozer, mainly clearing land for building projects. He displayed the casual, carefree attitude of one well-accustomed to passing along on a trail of destruction. He had readily agreed to take me out in his plane but when Frank and I arrived at his house on the edge of Fairbanks at the prearranged time, there was no sign of Andy or his aircraft. We waited in a yard strewn with fragments of machinery and piles of rubble until Andy duly came back from shopping with his family an hour later. In his rush to apologise for forgetting about the arrangements, he flung open the car door without noticing a rubbish bin, knocked it over and added another scratch to what was left of the car's paintwork. But by then I had committed myself and it was too late for second thoughts.

'You're quite sure you want to go ahead with this?' Frank asked, thrusting a fishing rod and a book on edible plants into my hands and then, when I nodded, two moose steaks, a pound of Polish sausage and a bottle of beer. They subtracted a little from the 'living off the land' aspect but seemed a sensible precaution.

'I know just the spot to take you,' said Andy, 'but it's fifty miles into nowhere and it's bear country, so you'll have to borrow a gun.' He handed me an old twenty-bore shotgun with flakes of rust along the barrel and a trigger that rattled. 'It's not much but it might help. 'fraid I've only one cartridge left.'

'You'll just have to hope there isn't a queue of bears waiting for you,' said Frank, thoroughly enjoying the situation.

'What do I aim for if a bear does charge?' I asked.

'Just aim for the whole bear,' replied Andy, sandpapering the corrosion off the cartridge, 'no point in trying to go for a head, heart or a shoulder shot. Anyway, you'll have to wait until it's within ten feet if it's to do any good, and besides, it'll be all you can do just to hit it. There's no sights on the gun and from memory it pulls to the left. Remember to jump to the side after firing – grizzlies can run fifty yards after they've been shot dead.'

I held the gun with little enthusiasm. It seemed the only advantage was that it saved me having to shout 'bang'.

'Have you remembered to tie the loose wing back on the plane?' asked Andy's wife, disappearing into the house and wobbling with laughter.

'Just ignore her,' said Frank in a comforting manner. The Polish sausage seemed to develop jitters in my hand. 'Andy, show Alastair that photo of your plane.'

'Oh yes,' beamed Andy, and promptly returned with an album. There was a picture of my pilot standing beside a plane lying upside-down on the grass. The jitters increased. 'This was shortly after I got it,' he said proudly. 'It had brakes and my last one didn't, so I stopped it a bit suddenly. This is the one we'll be taking.'

I looked at Frank with severe misgivings. 'Maybe it's not such a good idea after all.'

'Nonsense, you'll be fine,' said Frank. 'You'll survive, no problem. In fact I can imagine us sitting here, Andy, and you suddenly saying, "My God! You remember that Scotsman I dropped off five years ago in bear country with one shotgun shell and food for two days – I plum forgot to pick him up," ' and they fell about laughing once more.

The plane stood on what looked like an old railway embankment behind the house, facing a tree as if it had only just pulled up in time. It was such a narrow embankment that there was no room to turn the craft, but Andy went to the tail, lifted it up and simply walked it around to face the right way. There were no markings to tell me what type of plane it was but it looked similar to pictures I had seen of crashed spitfires, and I think it was mostly homemade. The nose had a large dent on one side, several burnt patches on the engine casing and the single propeller was more like what you would expect to find under an inexpensive boat. The fuselage was mainly canvas, liberally covered with masking tape and with lesser gashes that had not yet been repaired.

'There she is,' exulted Andy, and I could find no words to reply, thinking that Frank might soon have a Dead Scott tartan to add to his collection. The seats were in tandem and Andy packed my gear around and on top of me in the rear one until I was wedged in. Then he felt unhappy about the weight distribution and spent five minutes reorganising it all until I thought that if it was that critical then maybe we should forget the whole thing. When it was all to his liking he noticed I wasn't wearing my safety-belt, so we had to unpack once more to find it and then retie the loose end to the roof with binder twine.

'You don't get airsick, do you?' he asked.

'Not normally,' I replied.

'Good. It can be a fairly, er . . . lively flight.'

My feet rested on the connection for the dual-control joystick, an ironic misnomer, my arm was pressed against a lever, and my legs lay over my camera case which sat on the wire that ran to the elevators at the tail. He said it was fine. 'Just keep your feet off that connection or I'll lose control and whatever you do, don't touch the throttle with your arm or when I turn the prop you could take off – and that would be a laugh, buried under all your gear in the backseat without a pilot.'

I sat there not daring to move as Andy went to the nose and gave the prop a few turns. On the third it sprang to life with a roar that sounded healthy. He got in, did a quick test of the rudder, flaps and elevators (which also made my knees go up and down), and then shouted, 'Here we go.' He whooped and we bumped forwards. In no time we were airborne. We climbed steeply, reached a small peak and suddenly lost some height, making my heart strain against my shoulders in an effort to stay where it had just been.

'Got to get some fuel,' he shouted and we dropped straight down, skimming over some electricity cables and then treetops were rushing past at face level and we were down in a small airfield where about fifty other kamikaze planes were parked. He pulled up by some ordinary pumps of Avgas.

'Just like a car,' he said as he filled the tank and did the self-service checks. 'Never hurt yourself in these. Our landing speed is only thirty-eight m.p.h.' He got back in, drove to the end of the strip, opened his door and stood half out. 'Anything coming?' he asked an imaginary control tower on a non-existent radio as he looked around. 'Hope not,' and we were airborne again.

The door suddenly sprang open two inches. 'Damn catch is broken. Don't worry, airstream'll stop it opening any more,' he yelled as we banked sharply to one side, the open door side. I wasn't worrying. I was at the back of a jerry-built flying machine, buried under my luggage, surrounded by levers I wasn't to touch, my knees being moved in unison with the controls, a Polish sausage slipping down my chest, and the main door was hanging open. There didn't seem much point in worrying as anything else would surely be a merciful release . . . and my delicate state of being was soon forgotten as we skimmed low over the moorlands; bogs, tussock grass and sparse clusters of pine; a ploutering moose; the broad Cheno River, unfordable; tracts of forest, and then the strange sight of a wrecked car riddled with bullet holes which the army had dropped there by helicopter for target practice. After forty minutes we landed on an old fire-fighter's clearing.

Andy took off at once, circling around and swooping so low over me that I automatically ducked and never thought of waving good-bye. The hum of his engine was swallowed by the silence, and a sense of emptiness crept over me. I stooped to brush off some strands of sticky cobweb that clung to the hair on my legs, while more stuck to my arms and floated around my neck – only I found there were no cobwebs there. The creeping sensations continued, and I knew then how it felt to be truly alone.

I wrote in my diary:

My pack was too bulky for the plane so everything was loose; tent, sleeping bag, cooking pot, fishing rod, the book on plants, food for two days, toothbrush, Frank's practice pipe chanter, a sheet of music (reel, *The Kilt is my Delight*) and a rusty shotgun. Bundled them under my arms and trundled off into the wilds like a *Punch* caricature of the great summer-holiday outdoorsman. Camped near a small river and went fishing as the evening rise had begun and trout were jumping all the time. No shortage of food for them; the mosquitoes were out in clouds with a vengeance, supported by those black midges the Indians call 'noseeums' – but you can seeum, though usually after you've feltum first. And the intrepid explorer has forgotten his repellent. Shame.

Spinning was not easy. My lure had aquaphobia and would grab hold of anything to avoid going into the water, even changing course quite considerably in mid-air under its own power. It would latch onto grass, branches, my jeans, the gun barrel, and finally embedded itself firmly in a stump that had grounded in the centre of the river. It was too deep to wade so I had to strip off and the bugs had a field day on me before I managed to leap in – ye gods! The water must have been ice a few hours earlier. I retrieved the lure, scrambled into my clothes (no towel), gave up fishing and decided I'd try to live from the wilds another day. Anyway, the Polish sausage needed to be eaten soon. I set up my kitchen five minutes from my tent in case bears were also attracted to Polish sausage.

It was dark by the time my meal was over. The moon found a gap in the cloud cover, forming a hazy headlight in the sky with a faint rainbow of colour around its edge. The fire crackled, hissed and spat out the odd spark of disgust, and then glowed with contentment until it had to repeat the procedure. The firelight turned the smoke from my pipe into a nebulous sunset red, creating the enthralling illusion of breathing fire, flames billowing out from my mouth. A distant bird called, there was a scuffle in the undergrowth and an insect rasped out its love song to some unknown, unseen, silent Juliet in the darkness. It soon gave up as Juliet remained unknown, unseen, unimpressed. Everything fell still. There wasn't a single sound. I was fifty miles from anywhere and it might have been a thousand.

Having covered up the fire with just enough earth to let it smoulder through the night and stay alight for the morning, I realised I had nothing to cook for the morning so put it out. I climbed a tree to hide my moose steaks and then made a second ascent to add my bottle of beer to the cache, just to be on the safe side. Funny – it seemed quite valuable now. I made my way back to the tent carrying my gun at the ready this time and forcing myself to sing to alert any bears; I felt like a rural drunk returning home in the early hours after a few jars at the local. I sang rather quietly at first as the sound of my own voice made me nervous in the darkness and total silence, but then my confidence grew and little by little my singing became louder. 'I'VE PLAYED THE WILD ROVER FOR MANY'S A YEAR . . .' The words of this gritty tune emerged in a bawdy voice and with such boldness that it took me by surprise. '. . . and I've spent all me money on . . .' They trailed off into a breathless hum as the overpowering silence made me feel that it had been a little too bold. Then I felt it was not loud enough for a bear to hear and began again, only to reach the same point, whereupon it seemed sufficient to carry me safely over the next fifty yards and I lapsed into a consolation hum once more. I was so intent on trying to detect the sound of snapping twigs or a sign of movement that I scarcely realised the same line was just being repeated over and over. I reached the tent at last, having forgotten what the rover bought anyhow.

I even took the gun down to the river and had it alongside me while brushing my teeth, when a sudden knocking sound made me clamp my teeth on the bristles and reach for it. I stood there aiming the weapon in the direction of the noise, trembling, telling myself, 'Safety catch off, let it come to ten feet, keep calm, what's ten feet? Until that bush, OK? Pulls to the left, or was it the right? Safety catch off, got to leap to the side . . .' After a while, and some abortive speculation on the probable course that a dead grizzly would take when shot with a lop-sided shotgun, it appeared to be a false alarm. Then I dimly made out a branch dipping down into the current, being caught in each surge and pulled back only to be released without warning like a catapult, making it hit against a stump. Sometimes it would stop for a while and then mysteriously start up again. With a sigh of relief I sat down on the bank – then instantly leapt up as I landed on something uncomfortable. I picked the object up and stood there, staring foolishly at my only shotgun cartridge which had fallen out of the breech a few minutes earlier. The wild rover went to bed but lay awake for a long time listening for noises, recalling the heavy breathing of a past disturbed night, and deciding yet again that he really didn't enjoy camping in bear country.

I was up early with the dawn but had no idea of the time. Finding some fishing line in a tree with an artificial fly on it, I cut it free after another cold plunge, replaced the obstacle-magnetic Mepps lure with this fly, and set off more confidently to catch my breakfast. The trees made casting impossible but with a flick and dangle technique I soon had several two-bite trout, but returned them as undersize. Then I saw a large fish and placed my fly perfectly before him. Five times he lunged for it and each time he missed. Just my luck to pick a dim-witted trout. On the seventh pass, *zap*, I had him. Once out of the water he shrank a bit but was still a nice size and looked even better in the pan. The meal was insufficiently cooked and the bony mouthfuls left me even more ravenous than before but having won my first bite from the wilds gave me a sense of achievement. With my belt pulled in a notch I went for a stroll, feeling better.

Bear droppings. Like bad telegrams they always came during a moment of contentment or modest elation. My clutch on the gun tightened. It was surprising what a false sense of security it provided and after yesterday's initial mistrust, today I felt a match for anything. Yet it also made me feel persecuted, turning me into a more dangerous but still inadequate threat; the object in my hand might be the final provocation to transform my potential victim into my actual killer. When one is unarmed one feels the need to escape and to avoid a conflict, but with a gun one feels the need to stand up and defend oneself with it. Guns narrow the vision, superimpose hairline crosses on everything one sees, and their effect extends with equal force to the President no less — only his weapon is bigger, and isn't rusty. That was what frightened me about my shotgun; a weapon in the hand rapidly became the only option in the mind. Nevertheless, at that particular moment I was glad to have it as bear droppings in the mind seemed marginally worse.

Having changed my image from the holiday outdoorsman through the rural drunk and wild rover stage to that of intrepid explorer, I took out my book of *Wild Edible and Poisonous Plants of Alaska* (New Revised Edition) and changed it once more to that of armed Sunday school teacher on a nature walk. There were two types of berries in the area but only one was marked in my book. High bush cranberries were abundant but I was told '. . . mostly used for making jelly. Some people object to the musty odour and taste but if picked before the first frost, just before truly ripe, the fruit is more acid and of better flavour.' But there was no information on how to make jelly and it wasn't the time of year for frost. Berries were ruled out as staple. My criterion of what was a keepable fish instantly dropped by several inches. After returning and rashly consuming both moose steaks and the bottle of beer, I lay back feeling replete but also as if my only shotgun shell had just been fired. Drifting into a pleasant siesta, I tried to forget that there were still five more days to go.

Some rabbits were hopping around that evening and when I later tripped over some insulating wire lying on a track (some wilderness!) the thought of making a snare came to mind. I stripped off the plastic coating and soon had a free-sliding noose set up along a rabbit run. I left it there and went off to look for more trout.

The snare proved very successful and I relaxed into a life of trapping and fishing, practising *The Kilt is my Delight* and doing the little chores of fetching water, collecting wood, washing and cooking, which seemed to become the protracted events in a full day. Wilderness time went nowhere. For once my camera was put aside and I didn't dash about trying to segregate rectangles of interest from my surroundings. I took only one picture and that was a rare shot of myself, just for the record. I dislike photographs of myself just as drunks dislike mirrors when they are sober – both seem to catch an unfair moment and produce distorted images, parodies of our benevolent view from the inside. But it wasn't so hard to pose between a rabbit and my campfire while the camera took the picture by itself, when I knew I wouldn't see the result for three years.

One afternoon I was eating roast trout and rabbit for the third consecutive day and wondering how long a body could survive on such a narrow diet and whether cranberries were approaching their prime yet, when a plane landed in the clearing. A man got out with his fishing rod and walked past but didn't notice me until I called out a greeting. He stopped, said nothing, turned round to scan the area for a concealed plan, nodded and went off still deeply perplexed. While I marvelled at the way Alaskans used planes as others used cars to pop out for an evening's fishing, it annoyed me that my privacy had been disturbed. After tearing off more mouthfuls of rabbit I saw *another* plane landing! This made me furious. 'Might as well have camped on the flaming runway at Heathrow,' I muttered to a disinterested rabbit.

When the planes had gone and it was *my* wilderness again I began to enjoy the isolation once more. It was a fairly safe compromise situation as long as I didn't injure myself, and while I felt disappointed with my inadequate knowledge of how to survive, these things could be learnt and it was reassuring to feel mentally at ease with the loneliness and the need to be independent. I set off cheerfully back to my tent, this time whistling for a bear-scare but reverting to song in case my other sound was mistaken for the call of a marmot, as bears also ate marmots. All risks had to be carefully considered when you had only one bang at your disposal.

Andy touched down a week later at eight a.m. (I guessed ten by the sun) and was surprised to be handed his gun, two rabbits and the intact cartridge. I was certainly glad to be rid of them. It had been a novel experience but my mouth was watering, as might that of an Anchorage moose, at the thought of all the food in a supermarket. Andy wanted a cup of tea so I brewed one for each of us. He threw his away after the first sip and said we'd better be getting on. I thought the tea was good and wondered what else the week had done to me.

As we flew back I asked Andy if he would like to be a commercial pilot.

'Oh hell, no. That would kill all the fun. Like making love for money', and soon we landed on his narrow embankment with the tree on it. It was an unusual concept of fun.

The idea of going straight to Newfoundland had come on sudden impulse and swiftly grew to assume such importance that I was seized by a mad urge to cover distance as quickly as possible. Travel became reduced merely to a destination; Newfoundland. The fact that it lay several thousand miles away on the other side of Canada was unimportant. All that mattered was to keep moving, day and night if possible, heading to the furthermost end to the road east; on and on, from one car to the next, eyes set on the east, seeking my satisfaction only from the miles that fell behind.

The lifts started with a red-headed Indian, driving a bread delivery van, who dispensed a joke with each loaf, saying a day without laughter was a day wasted. He said his father was Irish so that made him 'half-tomahawk, half-shamrock', and he gave me a loaf. An emigrant Scots couple took me on; an uncomfortable ride as they were a sinister duo, harbourers of prejudice, quick to victimise and eager to flow with the dangerous tide of popular opinion. They were merchants of limited bonhomie; 'Come in, come in. Ye'll have had yer tea and will'na be stayin' long, I doot,' said one screwing the top firmly back on a thermos flask as I climbed into their car. They offered me their jaundiced views, qualifying each statement until they had contradicted it and won my agreement, with the fawning confidence of sycophants. It wasn't their stinginess that I resented for that was as forgivable as simplicity or poverty. It was their pride in their stinginess that disturbed me. They couldn't see how it had pinched their vision, asphyxiated their reasoning and, worse, become their ambition. They let me out shortly before their next pause for a cup of tea. I didn't miss the tea but I wished these Scots hadn't filled my cup with bitter introspection.

An Edmonton University geological expedition took me 912 miles in under twenty-four hours and then I was travelling across the great prairies of Saskatchewan and Manitoba with a young organic farmer. 'I recently got two geese to be fattened up for the pot, but my family's making a fuss. Want me to give them names so I gets all fond of them and won't kill them. They plagued me so bad I relented. So now one's called "Lunch" and the other's "Supper".' We passed a community of Hutterites where Biblical times were being relived with modern implements, and men were working the fields dressed in suits as black as carrion crows. I was intrigued and wanted to learn more but there was no time to stop with Newfoundland beckoning. It didn't matter, for I was to come back and visit the Hutterites later.

Into Ontario and past the mining city of Sudbury, Canada's largest producer of copper, platinum, gold, silver and nickel. My driver pointed to the world's largest smokestack which is now enabling vegetation to regrow on the denuded hills nearby by discharging the smelter's daily four thousand tons of sulphurous waste high into the atmosphere so that it drifts over to Sweden and the United States to poison their hills and lakes as acid rain. 'Oh yes, we're generous,' he said, 'we like to share the effects of our wealth with the rest of the world.'

Through Quebec and into the Maritime Provinces where there was a roadside café that had never heard of an omelette. A Ford Transit van gave me my last lift, and after climbing in I noticed a stretcher in the back with a bulge under a blanket.

'Is it . . .?'

'Yes . . . I don't normally give lifts but you looked kinda desperate.'

When I left the hearse I was in the north–east Nova Scotian port of Sydney. An official with remarkable rubber joints was directing cars onto the ferry for Newfoundland by simultaneously pointing fingers, wrists, forearms and elbows in opposing directions and effecting independent beckoning movements with each adjoining section of the limb. The dash from Alaska had covered 4,826 miles in thirty-nine lifts, spanned seven time zones and taken eleven days. My urge for distance had been fully satisfied.

The 'Noofies' who inhabit the island that was formerly Britain's oldest colony and is now Canada's youngest province accept with good nature that they are the butt of North America's 'Irish' jokes – which are totally unfounded, although there are occasions when it is easy to see how the misconception originated. 'New Founde Isle' was first mentioned by John Cabot in 1497 but it was not until 1583 that Sir Humphrey Gilbert claimed it for England. The first settlers were fishermen who sailed over for the summer months each year. They came from Devon and Cornwall, collecting some Welshmen on the way to Wexford, where they stocked up with supplies and a few Irishmen to complement their crew for the long voyage. As a result, several words of archaic English are still in everyday usage and the accents still strongly reflect these areas (with the exception of the Welsh who must have gone home early) and are reinforced by a fast, soft-spoken speech of diluted rural North England tinged with Mississippi, a combination which is as baffling as it sounds.

Newfoundland is practically speaking closer to London than to Winnipeg in the centre of Canada, making it a chosen end-point for the trans-Atlantic records of recent history; the *Great Eastern* wonder ship laying the first successful cable in 1866, Marconi receiving the first wireless signals from Britain in 1901, Alcock and Brown's takeoff for the first non-stop flight in 1919; and it was also here that Churchill and Roosevelt drew up the Atlantic Charter in 1941.

My first lift was with Con O'Reilly, a late middle-aged, almost spherical man with a slobbery face and a bubbling sense of humour that shook the fat on his face and contributed to much of the slobber. We passed a figure hitching by the roadside and Con lowered his window.

'Oy'll not stop for you. You've got no kilt on,' he yelled to the bewildered man, seemingly pleased with the vacant response.

'Do you come down south to this part of the island often?' I asked.

'We're not sayin' that 'ere. That's what they're sayin' down north where they're as English as the Devil. Oy go all over so to answer yer question; yes, oy go up south and down north quite often', and he slobbered and chuckled again.

There was a sudden 'thwack' sound and Con lurched forward momentarily as his braces lost their rear hold on his trousers and sprang up, or maybe down, to grip him around the back of the neck. He ignored the mishap and slowly turned a deeper shade of red until he eventually pulled up on a corner in the middle of the road, looking highly volatile. There was a large expanse of lake beside us which provided a conversation piece while I helped to refix the clip, as his arms proved too short for groping around his bulk.

'What's the name of this lake?'

'That's a pond. We're not havin' lakes 'ere, we're callin' them ponds instead', and his braces contracted and expanded ominously as he laughed at my confusion. Despite their language the Newfoundlanders were extremely friendly, and Con readily agreed on the point.

'Friendly? By jingus, that's roight! But they're also half-simple.'

'Half-simple?' I queried hesitantly, expecting another idiosyncrasy. 'Is that from poor education?'

'Partly, but more as a result of two hundred years of leisure,' he smiled, honestly.

It was the opposite of the Alaskan attitude on this island where the interior was full of 'ponds' and only the coast was inhabited. Small villages of simple fisherfolk; boats moored with killocks – a wooden fork with a rock strapped between its prongs as an anchor; gulls screaming as the skulking mist; the occasional old cannon lying rusting in the grass; past and present resting alongside each other as accepted or ignored companions. 'Do it if you must but start next week' was the battlecry of the timeless and carefree people whose two hundred years of leisure had filled the map with such names as Nick's Nose Cove, Joe Batt's Arm, Too Good Arm, Come-by-Chance, Run-by-Guess, Blow-me-Down, Right-in-the-Run-Island, Bumble Bee Bight, Ha-Ha Bay, Bleak Joke Cove, Little Hooping Harbour, Famish Gut, Empty Basket, Bareneed, Breakheart Point, Stocking Harbour, Petticoat Island, Ireland's Eye, Nancy-Oh, Heart's Desire, Heart's Delight, Little Heart's Ease, Nameless Cove, Sitdown Pond, Horse Chops, Hare's Ears Point, Cow Head, Dog Fish Point, Fox Roost, Tea Cove and Cape Onion.

Con pointed to an outhouse with seven sides to it, explaining it was one of the old ones where a family of six each had their own personal seat. Then there were houses that had no steps up to the front door which was left stranded four or five feet off the ground. Evidently in Newfoundland they only used the back door and so seldom bothered to construct steps for the front one.

'We're callin' them *mother-in-law doors*,' he chortled and slobbered. 'Out this way, Mother dear. On you go . . .'

The houses were painted in patches of different colours without any attempt to follow lines, leaving a pattern of army camouflage in violent colours. Con knew all the answers. 'Well ye see, this is because paint is quite expensive 'ere, so most folk wait till there's a special offer on. But it sells out so quick they only gets enough for a small job and then have to wait till the next special offer. Unfortunately, that's usually a different colour.'

He let me out in St Johns where the special offers obviously had better stocks as the houses were each completed in one colour, although each owner had bought a different offer from his neighbour. The houses ran in long attached rows, three storeys high, dormer windows sticking out of their concave roofs in uniform style, except for these daring colours which saved each family unit from bashful anonymity. While standing admiring these buildings on a busy street as the evening light began to fade, I noticed many people giving me knowing and suggestive looks. After casually glancing down to make sure my kilt was where it should be, I saw nothing obvious amiss – but still they stared and winked.

'Shouldn't be standin' there, moy dear,' said an elderly man from behind. 'For this 'ere's Water Street, it be. 'tis the first street ever built 'ere an' th'oldest in all America. An' this bein' a seaport, moy dear, 'tis also where th'oldest profession is 'appenin'. So 'tisn't proper to be standin' 'ere where yer standin'.' As an unfortunate victim of circumstance I thanked him and picked up my pack before anyone could do the same to me, and moved out of the gaze of the Water Street clientele. Just in case they thought they had chanced upon some multi-coloured special offer.

Two days later I was sitting with a couple of drunk fishermen on New World Island where the squid-jigging season was in progress. They lowered red lures into the sea and jerked them up and down to attract the squid onto their treble barbs. The squid were then hung on lines to dry in the sun. They had previously been used merely as bait until it became known that they were a prized delicacy in Japan –

much to the locals' amusement as they considered both the squid and the Japanese palate to be astonishing.

' 'tis 'ard to believe but they squid swim arse first, so they do,' said an old seadog. 'an' oy be wonderin' if they Japs be walkin' t'same way?'

'Oy wouldn't be knowin',' said the second, 'but must be a poor country to be eatin' squid.'

'That's a fact,' returned the first, 'an' we'd be all t'poorer if they wasn't, even if squids weren't so scarce at present. Was roight surprised to see ol' Pete's clothes-line wi' clothes on't t'other day. Allus been chock full o'squid – so ee's feelin' t'pinch too.'

A third seadog joined us and gazed blankly at my kilt.

'A'sh' you a–man or's a–woman?' he asked in a slur akin to a dog growling at a hissing kettle.

'Do your women here have beards?' I asked, taking a gamble. His friends erupted in laughter but he slumped back without understanding.

After leaving the squid–jiggers I made my way to a hamlet called Leading Tickles, mainly for the purpose of seeing if there was a signpost to confirm the name on my map. The name was correct but inappropriate in my case and I paid dearly for my curiosity. I tripped on a rabbit hole while walking up a hillock to see the view and wrenched my ankle so badly that it swelled to the size of a big apple and left me writhing on the ground in pain. An hour later the first car passed and found me sitting morosely by the road with my ankle in a ditch of cold water. The driver helped me into his car and drove me to the district nurse. She applied packs of ice and then bandaged it securely, wanting to tell me to rest it for three days but hesitating on hearing that I was on a tight schedule to see the world. She compromised and allowed me to travel on if I did no walking and restricted myself to standing by roadsides and sitting in cars. She offered to lend me crutches but I refused because of the difficulty in returning them, even though the image of a hitch–hiker wearing a kilt in a Newfoundland storm and balancing on crutches seemed an infallible combination for success. She drove me to the main road and on one foot I set up camp in a picnic area. I was angry with myself for my carelessness, and with whoever had given Leading Tickles such an absurd name.

The next day I struck camp and hopped to the main road. The

swelling had gone down but my ankle was still too painful to support my weight. The following two days consisted of a great deal of standing, hopping, sitting and explaining why people who wore kilts couldn't walk like normal people. By the third day my ankle could tolerate a slow limp and I began to feel more mobile as my journey progressed up the western coastline.

There were few trees on the island, just ferns and coarse grass to cover the gentle hillocks that lay between the ponds and the rocky coastline. At the approach to L'Anse-aux-Meadow in the northern tip there were vegetable plots by the deserted roadside guarded by scarecrows dressed in fisherman's oilskins and sou'westers. A Swedish archaeologist excavated some mounds here in 1960 that had previously been thought Indian, and found that they had nothing to do with the Indians. He was searching for Vinland, a land mentioned in an Icelandic saga as having been found in the west. These mounds proved to be the first conclusive evidence of a Viking settlement on the American continent, predating the arrival of Columbus by five hundred years. I wondered if Leif Ericsson had been here on this very spot.

The site displayed enclosures where Vikings had kept their animals, slept, cooked and formed the middens which had provided the scatological clues to their diet and lifestyle. Other revelations about their daily habits came from a psychic woman, claiming to have been here in a previous life, who arrived with a group of visitors and a local guide. She plugged her hands into holes in walls, held out her arms as antennae and closed her eyes while tuning in to each tumulus of déjà-vu Vikings. She said she liked collecting driftwood for its artistic shapes. She said she felt that animals had been slaughtered on the turf where she stood. The guide agreed this was quite possible for the Vikings were not known to have been vegetarians. He was a quiet man. He didn't say so, but I guessed he collected driftwood to burn on the fire.

As I left the village, walking uphill and into a blustering headwind, the very worst combination for a kilt, a schoolboy was talking to his friend over a garden wall. There was silence for a moment, then a muted whisper.

'Gosh! He looks just like a real piper.'

With my heavy limp I followed the road south to the ferry once more, feeling refreshed that the Newfoundlanders had managed to retain a simple and honest outlook on their pleasant island which progress had been late in finding. And that final remark had endeared these people to me forever.

15 · Canadian colonies in a big, bad world

The kilt was my everyday wear except in cities when I usually wore jeans to become inconspicuous for a while, and on those days when my tartan had been washed and was drying. Cape Breton was no place for jeans and welcomed the sight of a kilt; it is a Scotsman's home from home, a small part of Scotland transferred to foreign soil ever since the mass emigrations to this area after the Highland Clearances of 1750–80, and in the first quarter of the nineteenth century. Even the town names have been preserved; Elgin, Inverary, Iona, Skye and Inverness (although finding it as the first town in Aberdeenshire was a geographical surprise), as well as the family names that appear on roadside postboxes; MacKenzies, MacMillans, Farquhars and Chisholms. The telephone directory for Cape Breton lists thirty-seven 'John MacDonalds' living in Sydney alone. Scottish country dancing is taught in the schools, pipe bands compete for honours amongst keen rivalry and each town holds an annual Highland games. These Nova Scotians speak with the same soft voice found in the outer isles of Scotland, and some still have the Gaelic language, but in general the influences left behind by Micmac Indians and French colonists have coalesced with those brought in more recently from the south and west to produce a pleasing accent unique to the Celtic fringe. There were other intruders into the traditions such as the undisguised 'Lick a Chick Fast Food Counter' and its overdisguised neighbour 'The MacPuffin Restaurant'.

The famous giant Angus MacAskill died here in 1863. He stood seven feet nine inches tall, weighed 525 pounds and his chest measured eighty inches – these dimensions were perfectly proportioned and never caused him any discomfort. He once posed alongside Tom Thumb and was presented to Queen Victoria, but he died at the age of thirty-eight, largely as a result of injuries sustained when a stage collapsed under his feet while he was holding an anchor (reputedly weighing one ton) above his head. Cape Breton is also well known for the old French Fortress of Louisbourg, the largest on the continent except for the Inca strongholds; it has now been meticulously reconstructed.

I spent a day wandering around Louisbourg's old buildings where figures in period costume went about the traditional tasks of making bread and candles, blacksmithing and leading animals to pasture, while guards warned me not to speak to any English prisoners and to be off the streets by the eight o'clock curfew. It was a novel presentation, although people frequently approached me as if my costume belonged to the exhibits.

After being evicted along with the other visitors before the curfew, I begged some water from a house nearby and sat by the sea contemplating where to camp. It was dark and the terrain was entirely hillocks or bogs which made the choice harder. A car came to the end of the side-road and stopped some distance away from me. Two figures got out and their torches suddenly played over the area. On an impulse I quickly ducked down out of sight. A beam became fixed on the grass above my head and they must have caught a glimpse of my movement because they began to come nearer, marking my spot with the beam. I gathered my pack and crawled around a few corners and lay still in a depression. Cold water seeped into my clothes. Who were they? What did they want? If they were police then I had nothing to fear, but why didn't they call out that they were police? If they weren't police . . .? They reached the spot where I had been and their torches lit up the surrounding grass as they searched for me. Somehow the beams missed this one spot even though they themselves came so close I could hear their breathing, but then they moved off, searching another area for five minutes before giving up and driving away.

Shaken by this experience I went back to the man who had given me water to ask if it would be possible to camp near his garden. He listened to my story suspiciously and somehow got the impression that I knew who the men were – the longer my explanation became the more his doubts grew until my denials of any involvement only served to convince him that I had committed some crime and was being hunted. He shook his head anxiously and immediately shut the door, bolting it when it had previously been unlocked, and the curtain moved as he watched me walk back up the road. I walked on and on, a fugitive expecting my pursuers to arrive at any moment, until tiredness forced me to camp near a refuse dump. I felt the cruel exasperation of being helpless and trapped like an innocent Kafkan victim in a circumstance where reason and logic simply failed.

Normality returned with a beautiful dawn, smiling to convince me that its absence the previous night had merely been a temporary inattention which would not be repeated. But my world appeared as frail props for the irrational and I viewed the cajoling rays of the early morning sun with mistrust. Not even its warmth could conceal the frost on my tent and with the added burden of feeling hounded by the seasons once again, I left Louisbourg Fortress and its short history of persecution, intent on retracing some of my Alaskan dash route before turning towards the warmer south.

I would spend a little longer in Canada and then I would look for the American cowboy. It was another impulsive idea but it provided a new sense of purpose. My cheerfulness returned and I was able to smile back at the sun.

Hitching on Prince Island proved relatively easy but slow going, this 'garden island' having the greatest concentration of roads in Canada which made a direct route impossible as my lifts were always branching off at the first intersection. Houses scattered sprays of flowers beyond their fences to flank the way with colourful petals, and a patchwork of cultivated fields had been neatly stitched into the ups and downs of the panorama. My seventeenth lift of the day (which had naturally entailed the seventeenth explanation of what this Scotsman was doing here in a kilt and the equally tedious repetition of my life history) was on the mudguard of a tractor. After gazing at the splendid scenery for twenty minutes while bumping noisily along at eight miles per hour, it seemed to me you could have too much of a good thing. My body was still vibrating when I was let off near a man sitting on a fence, who called me over to extract my eighteenth recital. I tried to make it sound as inspired as possible but ran it directly into the question of my main interest, which was the way to a certain bird sanctuary marked on the map.

The instructions were no clearer the second time he gave them, though I did take in his figure of six thousand geese. I thanked him while he chewed on a piece of grass and nodded encouragement, and eventually found the churches, the bridge and, after backtracking, the overgrown path that could not be missed. Approximately 5,980 birds had also missed the way but that evening twenty successful Canada geese declined to share several slices of bread with me but watched, with mild distaste, the transformation of cream of chicken soup into a lumpy macaroni sauce (which was not offered to them). Their raucous protests at either my choice of campsite or my menu lasted all through the night and were not to be quelled by the offer of brose and more bread for breakfast.

A local farmer, Iain MacDonald, took me to see a small graveyard which was filled entirely with MacDonalds and Campbells as if there had been a regional vendetta between these historic rivals, some repeat of the Glencoe Massacre on this very spot. I was not sure whether to offer sympathy, congratulations or to ask who had won, but we drove on before a choice was necessary. MacDonald's farm lay next to that of his brother which was adjacent to his parents' land and opposite the holding of his uncle, as it had apparently been for generations. Doubtless it would remain so as none of the family seemed to move far from home – but with so many Campbells in the area, perhaps they had good reason.

When he let me out I walked past a factory where workers were arriving like columns of ants to start their shift. Apart from beaches and horse-racing, Prince Edward Island is noted for fish and potatoes, and these ants were working in a food-processing plant. A billboard proclaimed the bountifulness of Canada's smallest province with schoolroom humour: 'We eat what we can and can what we can't.' It felt good to be a different sort of ant, they with their routines and I with the expanse of Canada to wander. We exchanged friendly waves as fellow ants because the world needs all sorts of ants. My particular subspecies was clearly less in demand; the flow of cars ceased and the expanse of Canada became an unenviable prospect. At last one did appear. It was being driven by a young girl out with her old mother who sat bolt upright in the passenger seat and, even from a distance, looked very glum. They were kind enough to stop and deliver me to the ferry terminal although it was not on their way to the kennels which lay in a different direction. The elderly mother, on closer inspection, was in fact a spaniel. From here a French Canadian took me to Quebec City.

★   ★   ★

Between the years 1608 and 1760 when the French controlled what is now Quebec, relations between the Indians – 'les sauvages' – and the colonists were for the most part extremely harmonious. By French law all Indians were regarded as illegitimate, being born of unlawful marriages, and the legal consequences of being in one of approximately twelve categories of illegitimacy could be severe. The new 'Canadiens' were opposed to their motherland's policy of discrimination and priests readily baptised and gave full legal status to Indians, colonists and halfbreeds alike. Where Indians had unmanageable names they were given new Christian names and, to get around the legal requirement of a surname on the certificate of legitimacy, this Christian name was merely doubled. The Quebec telephone directory is full of such names as Jacques Jacques, most of them descendants of Indians.

The economic incentives of the fur trade drove an increasing number of young trappers into the woods and into closer contact with Indian communities. Mixed marriages frequently took place but if a white child was born to an unmarried Indian girl, it was customary for the child to be discreetly returned to its father. The expression 'Les sauvages ont passé' – 'the Indians passed by' – was common and accounted for the baby that many a trapper found on his doorstep one morning. These halfbreed children were often sent away to be adopted, sometimes under doubled Christian names, but were fully accepted into Quebec society.

My driver, Jean Jean, was as proud of his mixed blood as he was of his small son who bore the same name and was crawling around on the back seat. It was confusing as there were four Jeans in the family just between the two of them. 'Ee eeze a great leetle boy. I treat eem like a dog,' he said, which was either a slip of the tongue or intended as a high accolade, but Jean Jean Junior certainly looked a healthy enough pet as he sank his teeth into the shoulder strap of my pack.

Jean Jean Sr pointed to one of history's 'leetle' ironies concerning the capture of Quebec City by the English (1759) when General Wolfe and his men 'scaled the Heights of Abraham', the natural rock walls surrounding the city. The French, he claimed, were expecting a convoy of provisions to arrive the same night that Wolfe happened to float his army in for an attack. By chance the current took them to the gentlest incline on this coastline of cliffs, and to the exact place where the sentries were waiting for the supply boats to land. As a result, no alarm was raised and when the sentries asked if they had brought the food, some of Wolfe's men knew enough French to bluff a confirmation. The English walked up the slope (there is now a road following their route and a man was cycling up it) and launched their successful attack. The English wanted it to sound more daring and the French were embarrassed at having been caught napping and so in both languages it was recorded that the British heroically 'scaled' the Heights. Such at least is the understanding of the Québecois, who have seldom shown much affection for Wolfe, or any of their fellow countrymen who speak his language – and not without some just cause.

The French Canadians have been referred to as the 'white niggers of North America', and with regard to the differential treatment that has been levied against them owing to their language, culture and religion, the analogy would appear to fit. Until very recently the top job opportunities went to the twenty per cent of the province's population who speak English and distinct wage levels existed between the two groups for comparative work. Quebec's situation never changed with each new Federal government, which was always based in English-speaking Ontario, and this resulted in the emergence of the Rhinoceros Party, a protest movement set up to mock the national elections.

The movement took off and helped to foment Québecois disquiet into a force that aims for complete separatism from Canada. The rest of this officially bilingual country mumbles abuse at this uppity province, saying, 'We are Canadians but they are the French in Canada. They won't even speak English.' The inhabitants of Quebec, Canada's largest province and containing its largest city, defend their standpoint with countering accusations; 'We are as bilingual as the rest of Canada. They don't speak French, we don't speak English. Our loyalty is first to our province, secondly to our country.' This dissension is merely the continuation of a struggle that reached a peak in 1759, and its solution is as contradictory as a certain hill which may now be cycled up, but whose heights remain unscaled.

Quebec City, capital of the region once known as New France, is divided into an upper and a lower half and the two are connected by narrow, winding streets. It is an imposing city and easily lends itself to the notion that it is worth fighting for, especially when seen from within the 'Upper Town', the only walled city in North America. I found that my native tongue got me cold rebuffs (only five per cent of the city speak English) and even the kilt achieved no practical advantage in its efforts to recall Scotland's 'Auld Alliance' with the inhabitants' ancestors. The magic words were all in French and any attempt at them, even Franglais, immediately won sympathy and attention. '*Non! Non! Non!*' rebuked a citizen, pointing to my feet – this was *not* the way to see the city. And so I found myself on a horse and cart, clattering along the cobblestones, being shown *vieux Québec* by *vieux* means of transport – the capacious Basilica of Notre Dame, Hôtel Château Frontenac which dominates the city as an elegant tower of grey granite set with small windows and a copper-green roof, and the mighty city walls bristling with old cannons whose barrels point hopefully towards Ottawa; clip-clopping alongside pavements obstructed by market stalls and portrait artists, passing below mesdemoiselles who looked out from balconies ponderously garnished with flowers, and through accordion music dancing out from street cafés where idlers sat under parasols with bottomless glasses of wine. The air was heavy with the aroma of tobacco and the atmosphere was distinctly Parisian – leisured, sophisticated and pleasurable – so that one could almost disregard the faint waft of open drains.

Yet the French Canadians become indistinguishable from other Canadians in their love of icehockey which they display with the same prenatal fervour, and also in their ability to produce syrup from their symbolised tree; a delicacy that is enough to sweeten even an English-speaking tongue. The connoisseur of maple syrup distinguishes between four different qualities, as well as taffy (a thick treacle), butter and two types of sugar. They are all produced without additives by boiling the raw sap of the maple tree at different temperatures and for varying durations of time. From one to six holes are bored into a tree, depending on its size, and the sap flows out naturally during the summer daylight hours and is collected in buckets placed underneath. Each bucket holds almost one gallon and it may have to be emptied twice on days when the flow is greatest, particularly when a hot day follows a cold night. The producer, who must have enough trees to yield three thousand buckets of sap annually for the business to be commercially viable, boils the sap until his experienced eye judges the consistency to be correct by noting how the drops fall from a test spoonful. Consistency, colour and the time of the year that the sap has been extracted are the vital factors governing the final quality. At harvest-time maple syrup is often eaten at outdoor parties as a fondue, or else in winter it is poured onto the snow to form a long trail. It is hard on the base but sticky on top, a 'tarbaby' to trap those who use their fingers instead of breaking bits off with a sharp knock of the spoon.

No other tree reacts to autumn in a way to rival the ostentatious display of the maple whose dying leaves turn into a carnival of dashing colours with the first frosts. My road back to the west ran through forests of these three-fingered leaves wilting in orange and vermilion and curling up their ragged edges for the helical fall into deep beds of posthumous gold.

Ontario fell behind me for the last time and the great prairies of Manitoba began. The fields extended for mile after mile as unfenced tracts of yellow stubble, covered in parallel bands where stalks had been flattened under the wheels of seven combine-harvesters which had simultaneously cut the wheat in staggered rows. The level landscape was broken only by the frequent grain elevators standing tall in compact groups, painted in bright uniforms to distinguish the particular association that owned them. They were gathered at railway sidings to disgorge their stores into trains over one mile in length.

The scenery could not make up for the lack of inspiration in the conversation of the car salesman who gave me an eight-hour lift. He talked for the entire journey about cars, engines and how he had once sold twelve new cars in a single day and thirty-six in one month, but that there was only money in second-hand cars.

The driver/hitch-hiker relationship is unique in that two strangers are brought together into a situation of forced intimacy and yet where they are not on an equal footing; the hitcher is under a sense of obligation to take the subservient role to the driver who often feels the privilege of being the master. My experiences showed me that the majority of drivers try to break down those differences and create a genuine friendship, but some revel in their dominant position by preaching or lecturing. Others even reverse the ranks, using this single temporary acquaintance, which will soon end and never be repeated, to ask the hitcher's advice as a confidant, pouring out their problems, fears and inadequacies with a frankness probably denied their wife, doctor or shrink. My reaction was to comply with the driver's lead, offering an opinion, stories, jokes, an argument, a sympathetic ear or merely returning silence for silence in response to his or her lead. In this case I was a silent listener for an insecure man who wanted to open up his heart.

He dismantled all the components of his being and laid them before me as a detailed shatter diagram of his career. Hard work had made him rich. It had broken his marriage, ruined his health and made him suspicious of his friends, but he was a good salesman, the best, addicted to the ambition of remaining the best and craving only more sales. Sales were the quintessence of his existence. Each completed receipt stimulated his metabolism and made him tremble with excitement, and he trembled with fear at the thought of losing the monthly bonus.

There is a flaw in the philosophy of capitalism as it affects the individual; he knows that without money he cannot live, he knows the bottom limit, but he has failed to see that with a lot of money he cannot live either; he does not know the top limit.

Laughter did not oil the machinery of life for this working, sleeping, eating, miserable success, this juggernaut of statistics who could relate the modifications to design and performance for each model over the last decade, talk the rear wheels off a brand-new Lincoln Mercury in a world where donkeys were meaningless and horsepower was worshipped, and who could recognise the annual mutations of each model from a distance of a quarter of a mile. My unnecessary contribution about the mini I had once owned filled a momentary lull but was overlooked and promptly followed by a stop at a beer parlour.

'Dozy drivers rest in pieces,' flashed its signs encouraging long-distance travellers to rest for a while in its own morbid atmosphere. Beer parlours were loathsome dens, always full of doped morons, the lonely steeped in regret and tarted-up whores parading with the smiles of clowns, proffering dry clichés of expired humour and the comfortless touch of sandpaper. They were the places where funerals should start from, where the dead should lie in state, and where most of the regulars did just that. We drank our beers, recapping on a few minor alterations to the 1980 Pontiac below a wall of stuffed animal heads, where a mangy wolf with only one eye gave a flaccid snarl through human dentures towards a mountain goat, wearing curlers in its hair and peering out through glasses at the dingy scene of hanging smoke.

We drove on into the night, leaving the prairies to enter an area of pine forest and lakes. Here the huge herds of caribou had been decimated after the introduction of rifles to the Idthen and other Indians, and largely as a result of the corrupt practices of some traders who exploited the Indians' gullibility. One company outpost offered the Idthen a pittance as a bounty for each caribou tongue delivered to them, merely as an inducement to increase sales of profitable ammunition. The carcases were left to rot where they fell, the tongues were later thrown away. Where the migrating deer swam across the narrows at a certain lake, the antlers of the dead animals were said to be piled up so high in the water that canoes could not pass through. Now the Indians perform quieter pastimes, such as their annual 'flour packing' contest. The winner is the one who can stagger a set distance with the heaviest sack of flour on his back, and this becomes his prize to take home. This year his legs quivered and splayed into bows under a weight of 960 pounds, while the best woman managed 460 pounds.

My driver had not stopped talking all day when I decided to leave him and camp in the woods. He was surprised but let me out, calling to me through his window, 'Thanks a lot – you really were a most interesting person to talk to.' It nicely demonstrated the adage that the art of being a good conversationist is to be a good listener. I came to a derelict cabin in the dark and slept on the decaying floorboards beneath two sets of shrivelled beaver testicles that hung on a line, once used as a strong bait in wolf and lynx traps, as a reminder that I was not the first to have suffered a miserable day.

The biting cold night was followed by a lengthy wait for a car, and breaking the ice on every puddle within a fifty-yard radius of my pack provided some warmth through activity, but scant entertainment. A car with another Scots couple finally came by. They shivered as the cold draught entered the car. The driver hadn't lost his Glaswegian brogue in all the years he had lived here, but then Scottish dialects are notoriously incomprehensible and thus extraordinarily loyal to their original owner. 'When ah first came oot here ah had tae cross Canada by bus. Wis hellish, man, 'cos it stopped at every flamin' lamppost 'tween Winnipeg an' Vancouver.'

Jimmy let me out at one of his many lampposts in Alberta. It stood at a side-road to the Drumheller Badlands, an area of rocks eroded into unusual shapes where a museum displayed parts of the skeletons of over thirty dinosaurs that had been found in the area. There were tape recorders for hire giving a self-guided commentary on the display, but knowing that these things sometimes have a mind of their own, I asked a woman at the ticket counter if these ones were worthwhile.

'Oh heavens, yes!' she replied. 'If you don't have one of these it's like going on honeymoon without your bride.'

When I reached the Indigenous People's Section where there were life-sized models in Indian costumes standing here and there, the recording burst into life at the touch of a button, and my heart sank . . .

'*Zehehetovazemenotto heamoome zehesthoestovetto, hoxeetanotoeneha nivehestoz. Nimaheone – nitaehistanovostoz hienettnoeha. Nszheseto-vaomohetanoxtoz* . . .' Fortunately the voice spoke to me in English once the Lord's Prayer in Cheyenne had finished.

Standing there silent and motionless I was looking at one of the few known photographs of an Indian woman with a split nose, the punishment for an adulteress, when a reflection in the glass case caught my eye. A group of schoolchildren were gathered in a doorway, staring at me.

'He's not real. I've been here before,' said one.

'But he moved a bit . . .'

'No, he didn't. He's not a real man. I know. I've been here before.'

'Yeah. He can't be real. He's not moving.'

Conscious of eight pairs of eyes fixed on me I squinted at the dummy beside me, wondering if my appearance really did resemble that of Lieutenant Young-Man-Afraid-Of-His-Horses of the Oglala Sioux. I walked on to the Fossil Section.

'Look . . . he moved!' Whereupon they turned to their teacher. 'Look, Miss. That's a real man over there.' She at once removed my Indian heritage and feathers by explaining about Scotland in a hushed tone. '. . . and the costume he wears has special colours for his own family and it's called a quilt . . .' which forced my eyes to the ceiling and a deep sigh of resignation from my lungs, while I recalled the simple respect of the Newfoundland schoolboy.

The teacher then instructed her charges to do sketches of all the things that they found interesting and, judging from the prolonged stares they continued to give me, it is possible that I appeared alongside crude copies of Tyrannosaurus Rex's kneebone or Edmontonosaurus's femur, dressed in a quilt and sprouting feathers. When they eventually left, passing me by with smirks and giggles, peace returned once more to Young-Man-Afraid-Of-His-Horses, Scotsman and dinosaur alike. There was only a trail of toffee papers left behind, the customary spoor when little savages *ont passé*.

Not far from the Badlands was a group of identical buildings, freshly painted in white with blue roofs, similar to the colony I had passed on my dash to Newfoundland, and one of the seventy such groups of Hutterites in Alberta. In order to find out more about these curious, close-knit communities, I felt the kilt might help by turning me into a curiosity for them.

The Hutterites are a group of Anabaptists originally from Switzerland who still adhere strictly to a lifestyle and religion almost unchanged since their formation in 1525, inspired by a literal translation of the Bible. Their beliefs have caused them 450 years of persecution, forcing them to move from Moravia, Russia and the United States, and finally to Canada, mainly because of their refusal to bear arms or to comply with compulsory military service. North America is the home of other religious refugees such as the Amish, also originating in Switzerland and similar to the Hutterites in lifestyle (except that the Amish have no church buildings and often shun modern farming equipment), who are mostly found in the United States. Russian Dukhobors live in Canada but they are distinct in that they reject the Bible, and have been known to make nudist marches, commit arson and dynamite their own and neighbours' property as protests against materialism. (Not in any way wishing to jeopardise my kilt, I decided to visit the Hutterites.) The populations of these three groups are similar in size but the Hutterites have particularly large families and their numbers, currently estimated at thirty thousand, double every eighteen years.

Hutterites are farming communities and they have become rich enough to buy up large areas of prime land as well as the most modern agricultural machinery. They drive their own trucks but cars are banned as are television, radio, films, musical instruments, tobacco, women's hats and cosmetics. A special chest for storing clothes and small possessions is given to each child at the age of fifteen and girls, in addition, acquire a rolling pin and a sewing-machine. Otherwise members have no personal assets and all wealth accruing through their efforts is put into a central fund, from which they may draw pocket money for rare visits to the city. Each colony elects a council of six elders who shrewdly manage their business affairs and arrange the colony's growth. They live within the colony except to sell their produce at markets and trips into the city to make bulk purchases at the keenest prices, a practice which makes them unpopular as they contribute nothing to their regional community in the way of participation or business.

The Hutterites appeared to have just stepped off the *Mayflower*. The puritanical air of the men was heightened by their black suits, bowler hats, moustaches and the straggling fringe beard that fol-lowed the outline of their lower jawbone, the compulsory mark of the married man. The women had also stepped out of the past in their drab skirts, blouses and navy headsquares with daring white polkadots. From children to the elderly there was no difference in dress, only in size and shape as they seemed to get fatter with the acquisition of each wrinkle, but all ages wore wire-framed spec-tacles; the men favouring round lenses, the women preferring large tear-shaped ones. They didn't express surprise or inquisitiveness at my own clothes, but stared at me as if I were just another representa-tive of the inexplicable world beyond their fields. They vehemently refused to be photographed so I put my camera away and was shown around by an old man who asked if Scotland was near Germany.

'Yes, very close. Do you know Germany?'

'No, I don't know where it is but I heard the name at the time of the war in 1918. War is a bad thing, you know.' He didn't say if he had heard that there had been a later war.

The men worked in the fields and were helped by the womenfolk when they had finished the domestic chores – all work was consid-ered of equal importance and jobs were rotated to avoid monotony. My guide explained that there were one hundred people in this colony and a shortage of men meant many women had to do a man's work. As we talked, one drove past on a tractor. Some of these girls would have to find husbands in other colonies – marriages were usually arranged and always had to be approved by parents and community. Only married couples had separate rooms in the houses which were shared by three or four families.

We passed the church which they attended for half an hour each day and for two sessions totalling four hours on Sundays, holding services of prayers, lessons and unaccompanied singing. The children were shy, blushing and turning away if I looked at one directly, and chewed gum all the time. I went into their communual dining room and some women gathered around me, exchanging feverish whispers and finding it hard to believe that someone could travel alone and sleep outside in such a wicked world. They had just eaten their midday meal, the men sitting at one table, the women at another and no children allowed because they ate at a different time. Each family took it in turn to cook the community's meals for one week, and the duty cook, a large matronly woman, came striding up to me with such forcefulness that for one ghastly moment I thought she was going to crush me to her bosom. She yelled for some soup to be brought instead.

'And have some bread. This is not like city bread which is garbage and doesn't even last for two days,' she said, with a strong lacing of everyday German dialect.

'We work hard,' added another, 'not like those soft city women.'

'Are you married?' asked the matron. I shook my head. Her breasts heaved ominously.

'You can have her then,' joked one, pointing at her sister or cousin.

It would not have been an easy choice between my Qeqertat Eskimo or this Hutterite as both seemed to involve marrying not just a girl but also her extended family, an isolated region and a way of life. At least these were Dariusleut Hutterites; they still lived within severe monastic regulations but were nevertheless considered degenerate by the extreme Leherleut group for allowing their women to wear dotted headsquares and their men to go into the city bars to drink a beer. Yet it was a very closed society, for the young were brought up to fear the outside world and without experience, money or friends, they were ill-equipped to try to leave the colony. I decided again that the time was not right for settling down with a wife, so set off walking alone down the road that led through a blue gate, and out into the big, bad world.

16 · Guts, guns and God
on the way to New Mexico

South to the border at Sweetgrass.

The grass might have been but once again the American immigration official was not. He had been handpicked for his suspicious nature, stubborn disposition and mean temperament. These attributes, which were even more important than the obligatory predominance of animal instincts and low powers of reasoning, had become honed into the formidable weapon of his despotic pen and rubber stamp. On a whim he could refuse me entry and so he had to be humoured as one would a rabid dog when cornered by it. He took my passport as I sat under my pack in the back seat of a car that was going to give me a long lift, and did not even bother to look for my valid visa. Instead, he lectured the driver on the dangers of hikers and then turned to me with a sardonic sneer.

'I don't see your stamp. You just get your stuff together and get out, 'cos you ain't goin' anywhere.'

When my car had gone he disappeared with my documents and only returned five minutes later when another car arrived, ignoring me to serve them first. After warning them about hikers he eventually found my visa and gave me my entry stamp without a word of apology. I swallowed my anger but couldn't refrain from giving him a friendly wave when the car he had just warned offered me a lift.

We stopped to see an old buffalo jump which was a natural hill with a gentle incline on one side ending in a sudden steep slope. The Indians hunted this essential source of food and skins by stampeding a herd of buffalo and channelling them over the end so that many were killed or injured when they fell.

This was Montana, 'Big Sky Country' as the motto read on car number plates; a slow-moving state of open empty space, politically and industrially stagnant and an artistic incest of the paintings by the great cowboy artist Charles Russell whose works were revived at intervals to make up for the lack of any new output. It was also Big

Foot country, and a retired farmer invited me to stay at his cabin in Wolf Creek, which he claimed was on the migratory route of these elusive apeman primates.

The town sheriff, I was told, had casts of a footprint eighteen inches long and eight inches wide, and the farmer said he had come across footprints in this area on several occasions. His tone was matter-of-fact and he winced as he recalled the horrible stench that always hung in the air around these tracks and whenever Big Foot was sighted. Some local people believed in the creature's existence while others scoffed at the idea but he was firmly convinced that it was only a question of time before conclusive evidence was obtained.

It seemed hard to believe that such large apemen could remain undiscovered in a country whose explorers have already left their own smaller footprints on the moon, but the forests of the north-western states are vast and seldom visited without noisy machinery, so no one can be sure what secrets they hold. Indians too have long been aware of the existence of an apeman, calling it the Sasquatch. Big Foot sounded to me like some dreadful combination of Loch Ness Monster and Moostletoe, but the farmer spoke with such sincerity and conviction that I never doubted for a moment that his words were anything but the truth.

Another strange phenomenon had been reported in this area which was believed to be unrelated to Big Foot and even more sinister, concerning cattle found dead with inexplicable mutilations. The wounds were said to have been perfectly regular serrations that had not been caused by a sharp instrument (implying something similar to a laser) and always to have followed the same pattern, the cutting off of a distinctive feature such as an ear, a milk teat or the genitals of a bull. Most disturbing of all was that apparently the carcases were always completely drained of blood in a way that perplexed the experts, for any known method in use today would result in some blood remaining owing to the collapse of the blood vessels. Not long before, I was told, killed cattle had been found in the snow with no other footprints around them and all the indications suggesting that they had suddenly dropped dead in their tracks without a struggle. These mutilations had become 'almost common' in some areas, but farmers tended just to wait until they stopped and refused to talk about them for fear of ridicule.

The following day I crossed the state to the scene of another slaughter, where General George Custer made his last stand after unwisely attacking the main camp of the Sioux, Hunkapapas and Oglala Indians on 25th June 1876.

Ever since the white man's expansion into the West, particularly after 1860, the government was faced with the increasing problem of the Indians who were defending their lands and way of life against the encroaching newcomers. The government drew up treaties granting the Indians certain reservations to live in, other areas where they could only hunt and others where they were banned. Some tribes accepted while others refused until they were hunted and massacred into surrender. In some instances their leaders were murdered when they finally came to sign their acceptance. In the Black Hills of Dakota a gold rush brought prospectors pouring onto Indian land, thereby breaking the treaty of 1868 which granted this land to the Indians 'forever'. After the government had failed to evict the white men, it tried to buy back the land from the Indians. Some tribes agreed, others refused and in the atmosphere of swindle and mistrust the treaties were considered void and many bloody skirmishes resulted. Fearing the situation might get out of hand the government finally laid down a date by which all Indians had to be inside their reservations . . . or else. Custer was one of those sent out to enforce the 'or else'.

Having won his fame in the Civil War he became the youngest Brigadier-General at the age of twenty-six and the most ardent Indian-hater. He had a moustache and shoulder-length blond hair (the Indians called him 'Long Hair'), and an impulsive nature which often brought him into conflict with his superiors. He had been demoted to Lieutenant-Colonel and was on his way to face a court martial when he came to the Little Bighorn River that fateful day. Custer had expected only five hundred braves when he marched his men hard without sleep for a surprise dawn attack, but found three and a half thousand under the brilliant leadership of Crazy Horse and Sitting Bull. Some of his men escaped but Custer and 220 soldiers were surrounded, fighting on through the night with their dead horses piled up as their only barricade, until they were all killed. Sitting Bull later recalled the final scene when Custer was one of the last to fall. 'His hair was the colour of the grass when the frost comes. Where the Last Stand was made, the Long Hair stood like a sheaf of corn with all the ears fallen around him.'

This victory was the beginning of the end for the Indians. There had been no justification for Custer's attack and had he prevailed he would have killed every Indian there, but Custer's death so outraged the country that public opinion was turned against the 'redskins' forever – within a decade they were all subdued and in closed reservations.

They were moved from one reservation to another before their crops could grow, until winter was upon them and they were left without food or blankets. The promised provisions and welfare were frequently forgotten or plundered and they were under threat of death if they tried to leave. Reservations were often unsuitable to the lifestyles of the tribe, with buffalo-hunters being placed in empty fields and crop-growers sent to areas of desert.

One of the most puzzling aspects of the white man's behaviour to the Indian was his disregard for nature. He felled trees, overgrazed pasture and destroyed the great buffalo herds. Between the years 1872 and 1874 the Indians killed 150,000 buffalo while the white hunters butchered 3,550,000 only for their skins. The plains stank for many years with the rotting carcases which were left behind. On 26th September 1874 thousands of Bluecoats with repeating rifles and artillery came to the Palo Duro Canyon to hunt down a few hundred Kiowas who were only trying to save their buffalo herds. Many of them were shot, over a thousand Indian horses were slaughtered and their village was razed. When those who had escaped later gave themselves up because of cold and starvation, the warriors were locked in cells and each day were thrown a piece of raw meat. Most were dead within a few years.

'Know the power that is peace,' said one chief, but for the Indian there was no peace. Murdered, raped, massacred in cold blood, tricked and cheated in 389 broken promises and treaties, the Indian nations fell – not just killed but also vilely desecrated; the private parts of women were occasionally cut off and used as hatbands, those of the men were stuffed into the mouths of the dead and their scalps were removed. (It is not known for certain that the Spanish brought this custom to the New World but the white colonists certainly encouraged it by offering bounties for the scalps of their enemies. The Indians did the same as a means of retaliation.) General Sheridan reflected the mood of the time when he said, 'The only good Indians I ever saw were dead.'

The great buffalo herds were slaughtered, the powerful Comanches and Kiowas crushed and, all within the space of ten years, the mighty chiefs had disappeared. But here at the Little Bighorn River they won their greatest victory. The warden at the Last Stand Museum told me how the Indians still came to this spot and stiffened with pride as they walked over the battlefield that had become a shrine, the symbol of a successful fight against oppression.

'It's a shameful history,' he said, as we passed the exhibit of a notebook with a hole in it caused by the bullet that had killed the owner. 'Kinda makes you want to go out and shoot an American, doesn't it?'

There was nothing to add to that and I went outside in low spirits, burdened by the cruelty of the past and the guilt of my colour. A new grave was being prepared amongst the rows of white stones for a soldier's relative who had obtained special permission to be interred here. When the gravedigger stood up to throw out his next shovelful of earth I saw that he was an Indian from the Crow tribe who owned the surrounding land. It made me smile to think on the poetic justice of the situation – for here, after one hundred years of humiliation, the Red Indian was still burying the white man beside the Little Bighorn River.

A young Crow Indian, the bass guitar player in a local band, gave me my next lift in his fast car. His tribe was fighting a case against a mining company who claimed that the Indian treaty did not include mineral rights in the river that ran through their land. It was not an isolated incident as more of these old treaties were being contested in courts and legally broken as a result of inadequate wording to cover unforeseen developments in technology.

Today the Indians are generally regarded with contempt by their fellow North Americans. The more charitable offer pity and admit that there are admirable exceptions, but the majority consider them wasters, drunkards and degenerates. They all receive welfare as treaty money and some tribes are wealthy from royalties on mining rights, land leases and sales. A housing inspector in the Yukon told me of Indians having houses built for them free of charge and then wrecking them within two years and having them rebuilt, again free of charge. They tore down walls and cut up the furniture to burn when it became cold rather than go out to cut wood, and they misused their right to free hunting by illegally selling the meat or their ammunition allowances. They received free education, tax concessions, low interest finance and marketing assistance for their businesses but most of these perks were never used. The Indian has fallen victim to the welfare that never came when it was needed but is now offered in excess, to leisure and to his inherent weakness for alcohol. The plight of the Greenlander is the plight of the Red Indian. He has been engulfed by a way of life that is at odds with his ideology.

How can we hope to understand a different culture or to identify with it until we can think as its people? To the Indian, land has a deeper, more spiritual significance than merely its geographical features and the wealth of its produce. The arbitrary boundaries set by the white man have not only restricted the physical movements of the one-time wandering Indian People, but also isolated them from their beliefs, legends and religion. Their social structure is naturally orientated towards communal values. I met a girl who had been a teacher with an Indian community in West Canada. She had found many of the children to be natural athletes and yet poor at sports. They simply lacked the competitive urge and felt no motivation to prove themselves better than their opponents. Once she laboured all day helping a family collect clams, and they arrived home with a sack full of their prize. As was usual, friends drifted in for a visit, but before they left each helped himself uninvited to a bag of clams so that by the end of the evening there were none left for those who had collected them. The family shrugged it off, but the teacher was furious until a week later. By then she had been invited out to clam meals by families from all over the village and she realised that her share of the clams had been returned to her – only their way provided enjoyment for the whole community and a week of hospitality and friendliness as well.

When Chief Sitting Bull went around the country with Buffalo Bill's travelling show he was shocked at how unmindful the white man was of his own poor, and on seeing a beggar he once commented, 'The white man knows how to make everything, but he does not know how to distribute it.'

*　　　*　　　*

The road became bumpy as a car took me through the pine trees and pastureland of South Dakota.

'Hell, this is a rub-ass road,' said my driver.

'SMILE,' read the sign of The Last Resort Motel, which had given up trying to attract custom. It was derelict, its gutters sagged into smiles.

'GOD, GUNS AND GUTS MADE AMERICA FREE, AT ANY PRICE LET'S KEEP ALL THREE,' read the sticker on his dashboard, as a slogan in the campaign to stop the government from banning the use of small arms, and in ominous contrast to 'SMILE'. There was a loaded Colt revolver on the floor at his feet. This American gun mentality always made me afraid, especially after my own Alaskan bear experiences. It was only illegal to conceal a gun in many states, otherwise you could freely wear, carry or keep a loaded firearm with you. It was unnerving to sit beside an armed stranger who could raise his gun at any moment and take everything I owned, or even worse. This man came from an area of West Virginia noted for hillbillies, whose attitudes were like the people's of the south. Everything was either black or white. No room for discussion. Life was good or bad, right or wrong and God was great or had vanished completely. The priceless, pathetic formula – God, guns and guts – was still patriotically heralded as the natural progression towards freedom.

'My father always said, "You can't kill a good man, you can only slow him down for a while," ' he remarked suddenly as he accelerated into the corrugations and swerved around the deeper potholes. Magnum bullets rolled about on the floor where the revolver was slowly pointing its barrel in circles as it slid from side to side, and I hoped I was good and his father was right.

He left me in the rain on the side of a freeway at dusk. The prospects were bleak as cars sped past with their lights on low beams and besides, hitching was illegal on all freeways. A police-car spotted me before I had a chance to disappear and the stern face of the law beckoned me over as he pulled up opposite me and flung the door open. I feigned surprise and pleaded ignorance, but he took out a form and wrote down my particulars.

'Hitching is a state offence, punishable by ten days in jail or a one hundred dollar fine,' he recited by heart, and my own sank in dismay. 'Seeing as you're a foreigner, I'll not bust you this time. But if we find you hitching again . . . Now you cross over to the other side and walk away from here on the grass. OK?' I nodded cordially, and he drove off.

I crossed over, walked along as suggested until he was out of sight, then immediately returned and resumed hitching. There was probably a ten-minute safe period before he could come back, so it was a choice of either risking a spell in jail or a long walk into the void of my map. The safe period passed without any lift and then the poor light made it hopeless so I went off to camp on the far side verge. My tent was no sooner pitched than a car drove off the road and down the bank towards me, dazzling lights throwing their full beam into my face. Only when it had come to a halt could I make out the police beacon on the roof. Damnation! It was the same policeman. Now he was coming to tell me how many days in jail I'd get for camping here.

'Look, I didn't mean to be hard on you back there as you aren't really doing anything wrong . . . it's just that I've got a job to do. But there's a difference between the letter of the law and the spirit of the law – and it sure is a lousy night for camping. How would you like to come and stay the night with my family at our house?'

Scarcely believing my luck I tore down my tent and bundled it into the boot of the police-car, and off we drove. As he had an hour of duty still left, we cruised along the freeway with the instruments that bulged out across the length of the dashboard all glowing and activated. The speed limit was fifty-five m.p.h. but he did not impose a fine for speeds under seventy m.p.h. The revenue from the fines went to a school book fund. A car approached doing sixty-five m.p.h. 'Normally I'd let that guy go but I'll show you what we do.' He immediately braked, crossed the central reservation to the other carriageway and gave chase with beacon flashing, siren wailing. The car drew into the side, he checked the details of the documents by radio computer and fined the man twenty dollars. I tried to sink down out of sight in case this victim on my account would one day be my only hope for a ride.

The next morning he drove me to the end of his beat and left me on a good (but still illegal) spot on the road to Mount Rushmore. The sculptor Gutzon Borglum carved the famous faces of four presidents here, high up at the top of the cliffs. By 1941 he had finished six and a half years' work and removed 450,000 tons of rock to create the faces of Lincoln, Washington, Jefferson and Roosevelt. Each has a head in proportion to a giant 465 feet tall, with a nose twenty feet long and eyes eleven feet wide. After walking around the area for an hour I began to see faces in the rocks everywhere and to feel the hard gaze of their scrutiny. Eventually a car took me on to Crazy Horse where other sculptors were at work.

A Polish American called Korszak Ziolkowski spent the last thirty-four years of his life using bulldozers, drills and explosives to carve a half-length bust of the great Indian chief, the symbol of undying Indian tradition. Unimpressed by Mount Rushmore, Ziolkowski set out to create the world's largest work of art and if his ten children complete the project, an entire mountain will have been sculptured into a figure 563 feet tall.

The cold winds of the new winter ruffled my kilt and blew me back west into Wyoming where the towns became generously spaced out and shrank in size to no more than a single building with an official roadsign on either side: 'HILAND: Altitude 5,998. Population 5.' I wondered if they altered the sign each time a baby was born. Through the town of Cody where William Cody, better known as Buffalo Bill, ran a dude ranch for easterners who came for holidays to see how cowboys and the wild westerners worked. He died in 1916 after a varied career which saw him as an army tracker and scout, buffalo hunter for a meat company (but later he became a conservationist when he saw the herds of buffalo vanishing), a friend of the Indians and host of a huge travelling circus. 'The World Congress of Rough Riders', with horsemanship as its theme, included Indian chiefs, Cossack dancers, a Mexican lasso expert, women sharpshooters and many other preternatural entertainers who travelled as far afield as Europe. This spectacle ended with the death of its remarkable host but the fascination for the Wild West and the skills of the cowboy which Buffalo Bill did much to make popular, is a cult that shows no sign of diminishing.

That night I camped in Yellowstone National Park with its magnificent canyon (sculptured by no one in particular as far as can be ascertained), whose walls were covered in nature's graffiti, geological hieroglyphics in gentle pigments. Here too were many geysers which reminded me of the ones I had seen in Iceland. A caretaker of the thermal area at Selfoss explained how one of their geysers could be activated by pouring detergent into its crusted nozzle, and this trick was performed on special occasions. One year an Icelandic detergent was used instead of the usual imported brand when the Queen of Denmark came for an official visit. The geyser was the highlight of the tour but became an embarrassing incident because, for once, there was no eruption. Her Majesty, Dronning Margrethe, and the royal entourage stood looking at the hole in the ground and nothing happened save one dissatisfied burp of steam.

But other geysers needed no detergent and 'Old Faithful' erupted every ninety minutes for paupers and queens alike without any inducement, sending seven thousand gallons of boiling water up into the air to form a fountain 130 feet high. Buffalo, elk and moose grazed around the stunning colours of steaming mineral pools and rudely bubbling mudpots, on grass that thrived with underground heating.

After dark, with the cold creeping up from the ground where grass was not thriving and in a steady drizzle, I went down to one of the hot springs close to my tent. Hot and cold seemed able to exist here as very close but distinct neighbours. Steam made the atmosphere eerie, drifting around like mist concealing the horrors of a swamp, and providing clammy expectations of a scream from *The Hound of the Baskervilles*. It was an odd sensation to swim in a river of natural bath water at night and in the rain, to relax behind a waterfall and within a dome of water while individual cascades lightly pummelled my body in a sensuous massage. But it was far from wonderful having to get dried in the rain and return to a damp and dismal tent.

That night it snowed and snowed and snowed, and my tent was reduced to a slight bump on the landscape. I woke up inside an igloo with walls three inches thick, feeling cosy in my sleeping bag but finding the dull light and silence mystifying. I got dressed, putting on socks that were wet from the previous evening. (I think wet socks were the part of this lifestyle that I hated the most. Sometimes I would go to sleep wearing them for then they would be dry by morning, but either way they made me suffer.) I guessed what had happened and carefully poked a hole through the crust over the doorway but snow still fell down my neck and slid down my spine, causing a cloud of suddenly exhaled breath to greet the icy morning air. I looked about the scene that was unrecognisable from the previous day in its winter coating. With childhood joy I hurled a few snowballs at a tree stump, without my childhood accuracy, before coming to the awareness that being snowed in was going to be a problem for a camping foot-traveller. A buffalo was finding the conditions troublesome too, standing with ice frozen to its hair and pushing the snow away with its forehead to expose a few mouthfuls of grass.

In a maintenance hut belonging to the park wardens I met a charming girl who told me the roads were temporarily blocked but snowploughs were trying to clear them. She continued to be charming until I finally ran out of questions and reluctantly had to leave and face the cold once again. The next two days were spent with wet feet but happily tramping through snow and forest, encountering more wildlife and my old friends the moose, still enjoying that intriguing joke, and the porcupine, still as grumpy as ever. These blatant attributes, which seem such essential parts of being either moose or porcupine, led to my thinking up Pooh-rhymes.

> Oh what a ruse
> To be a moose
> And to smile from my nose to my toes
> My puzz'ling mirth
> Stems not from birth
> But from a youthful grin that just froze

★

> T'choice ain't mine
> T'be born a swine
> An' just look at t'mess that oi'm makin'
> Oi'd like t'be slim
> An' dain'y an' prim
> But seems oi'm cut out fer bein' bacon

★

What's my line?
A porcupine
An' I'm 'urtin' like 'ell as of late
For me quills are long
Pointed and strong
And they come between me and me mate

They passed the time on a lonely walk in the falling snow, until a thaw let me carry on south to Utah.

Car stickers are a useful source of information. 'Eat, drink and be merry,' said one, 'for tomorrow you may be in Utah.' It referred to the killjoy attitude of the Church of Jesus Christ and Latter Day Saints, the Mormons, who dominate this state. Their founder, Joseph Smith, was shown in a vision where to find some ancient gold plates engraved with the doctrine of their faith, supposedly recorded by an early prophet called Moroni. Smith translated their message (with divine help) in 1830 to produce the *Book of Mormon* – parts of which are now believed to have been plagiarised from an unpublished novel of 1816. To escape persecution the sect moved west under the guidance of Smith's successor, Brigham Young, until they reached the present site of Salt Lake City where Young decided that this was the place to set up house for his nineteen wives. He kept them in individual cells and each evening he would put a cross on the door of his choice for the night to remind him which one he had decided on when he returned later, but it was rumoured a jealous wife would erase the cross on a rival's door and chalk another on her own. He was a talented leader, and the scatter-brained father of fifty new Mormons.

The community was saved from a famine at the end of their first year in Utah when flocks of seagulls auspiciously arrived in time to devour a plague of Rocky Mountain crickets which threatened to destroy their crops, and now they are the fastest growing religion in the world. Mormons are encouraged to donate ten per cent of their annual income to the Church which has invested its wealth into mining concerns, property and such monumental buildings as their Tabernacle. Its pindrop acoustics are world-famous, and enough spotlights crowd the ceiling to make even the most lowly preacher shine like a deacon. Polygamy, although renounced, is not uncommon. Tobacco and alcohol are forbidden, as are blacks from entering

the church until recently, having been regarded as descendants of the
murderer Cain.

Salt Lake City made me feel unclean. The streets appeared to have
just been swept, statues dusted, fences painted, lawns trimmed and
windows washed. I felt like a blemish on the pavement as I looked
for a certain street which was supposed to have an illusive incline,
where cars appeared to freewheel uphill, but I never found it. I crept
self-consciously past people dressed in their Sunday best, for every
day was Sunday to them. (Girls were particularly striking. I was told
they spent hours each day over their appearance for their ambition
was to be married with two children by the age of twenty.) I came to
a building which offered tours through Mormon memorabilia but
lost my group when I lingered behind to photograph a sculpture of
Christ. I was moved by the serenity of the figure and its setting
against a mural of the Earth in a nebulous purple space but before I
could try to reconcile guns and guts with the imagery, a cleaner with
a mop moved me on. My tripod's three feet were marking her floor.
The doorman wouldn't let me into the most revered Temple but he
directed me along manicured flower-beds to the six-spired Tabernacle where the Tabernacle Choir was trampling out the grapes of
wrath in the most beautiful harmonies, and spotlessly radiant costumes. My lasting impression was one of cleanliness, as if both
people and city were regularly purged by the Church that owned
them. But I couldn't be sure that only one illusion existed on the
slanting streets of Salt Lake City.

My first lift was with a renegade Mormon who owned a bar.

'Utah surely can't be a very profitable place to run a bar?' I
commented.

'Hell,' he replied, perhaps aptly, 'them Mormons are the best
customers – as long as you've a back door, of course.'

When he let me out I was amongst some of the most bizarre rock
formations on this planet – vast areas of natural arches, some
half-formed and needing only another million years or so of rain,
wind and ice before they stood supreme like the others already
complete in bows of sandstone, spanning ravines as bridges or
supporting cliffs as flying buttresses. So impressed were the first
settlers that they named one area 'Zion' (the City of God). Brigham
Young then came to see it and solemnly declared, 'It is *not* Zion'. It
was called 'Not Zion' for some time as a result of this observation

but now the name has reverted and the deep canyon is called Zion National Park. But if it was not God's City then Utah was possibly His Quarry for experimental masonry, where He dabbled in all sorts of styles (predominantly Gothic) with stones coloured in the reds, yellows, pale purples, oranges and whites of ores and minerals. At Bryce Canyon He filled a valley with the most bewildering array of stone chimneys in every conceivable combination of colours; stone stalks of a Dutch (or Scottish) tulip field, ranks of petrified pre-Cambrian soldiers, thousands of prehistoric heads, castle turrets, colossal pieces congested into stale-mate in a chessboard which fills the gorge – it is nature's cake icing, a wonderland gasping with abstract shapes, where even the least imaginative might see something more than the omnipresent Mormon shadow.

17 · U/∩

Nine months had now passed since my flight from Reykjavik to New York. Nine climacteric months in my development as a grass-roots traveller. They had hardened me to life on the road, sharpened my instincts for survival and had been forgiving when my judgment proved unsound. But there were times, such as the present, when little things irritated me out of all proportion (I still had a week's backlog of diary to write up) and the constant moving left me jaded. My luck was holding. Hitch-hiking still worked. My route had criss-crossed the map from the Big Apple to Anchorage and from L.A. to Newfoundland. Excluding short trips within cities, land transport had cost me one fare of six dollars – a bus out of snowbound Yellowstone. Six dollars happened to be a result, it was not a goal. I was content with little, but I was not travelling in order to live off the land. I had never been denied my destination for lack of a lift, but on occasions my patience was tested by the exceptional wait of over two hours. Photography continued to provide a strong motive for travelling, camping was still enjoyable and the cup of kindness was constantly offered to me. Only in three cities had I needed to take paid accommodation during my stay in North America and they accounted for a total of five nights. Although I camped often, the degree of hospitality I received was overwhelming. My growing sense of gratitude remained staunch and upright, but there were still those niggling little things, buttons to be sewn on . . .

After hitching 17,300 miles in nine weeks my journey had completed a loop. I was back in New Mexico, jaded, hoping to work for a few months to earn some money, build up my strength and prepare for the next stage of the trek which would take me into the lower half of the continent. The money I had earned in the Arctic would be enough to last a further eighteen months on this level of travelling, but the third world countries would be unpredictable quantities. I didn't feel confident that my funds would cover one year in places where work was scarce, hitching hard or impossible, camping inadvisable and there was a high risk of illness. My health was robust and not a single day's travelling had been lost through illness in almost two years of rough living, porridge and stodgy soup. Many miles with a heavy pack had kept me fit and my muscles firm. I wanted to work more for the inner satisfaction of knowing I was still capable of earning a wage, to feel productive and to see a physical result from my sweat and energy such as a hole dug, stones lifted or a wall built. There are times when a traveller yearns to plot his progress by means other than diary pages written, rolls of film exposed and milestones passed. (In my case there were respectively 910 sides of A4, 5,184 photographs and a little over 50,000 miles.)

The area I was passing through was where William Bonney was born around 1860, shortly before the Civil War broke out and as the conflicts between the Indians and the settlers in the west were gaining momentum. Neither of these events affected the short life of this ranchhand but the murder of his employer, Tunstall, sparked off his infamous career as Billy the Kid. Tunstall's men, including the Kid, swore revenge against the rival group of businessmen, Murphy and Dolan, who had arranged the murder, and this started the Lincoln County war which ended in a five-day shoot-out. By then the Kid was wanted for shooting a sheriff and also as a witness in another murder trial. A deal was struck whereby he was to give himself up and testify as a witness, and his own crime would be absolved. Shortly before the trial the Kid felt he had been tricked and walked away from the jail to become an outlaw. The new Lincoln sheriff, Pat Garrett, captured the Kid and locked him up in the courthouse where he was chained to two wardens while awaiting his own trial on all offences. When one warden went off to the nearby hotel, the Kid found a gun, shot the remaining warden (the two holes are still visible in the wall), hopped to the window and shot the other as he came running from the hotel. He then removed his chains and leapt from the roof to freedom. Several months later Billy the Kid, aged twenty-one, was shot dead by Garrett. Although some of the murders accredited to him are under doubt, it is said he shot a . man for every year of his life.

An old man with an asthmatic cough took me from Lincoln County through the Capitan Mountains to the desert plains that led to Socorro, New Mexico where I had worked as a Scottish wetback five months earlier. Black clouds gathered above us but the horizon remained clear.

'The weather looks a little brighter up ahead,' I said, trying to make conversation. 'Maybe it'll clear soon.'

'Well, wouldn't hold ma breath waitin' fer it,' the old man wheezed in a rasping voice so dry that it made me want a glass of water. Then he dissolved into spasms of airless gasps, struggling even to catch that very breath.

'Shouldn't you perhaps see a doctor about your cough?' I suggested.

'Don't want me no doctors. Them quacks jes' find summat wrong. What ah need is to find me an optimist', and his grin managed to stifle the affliction for the rest of the way to his house.

It was a ramshackle old ranch with rambling corridors full of mementoes, cobwebs and holes in the plaster. Old muskets, Colt revolvers, an Edison phonograph and portraits of Confederate soldiers took me back almost exactly one century, and then I stumbled over a leg sticking out from an armchair, where an apparently disjointed pile of arms and legs lay in a chaotic heap. I was introduced to Tom and a hand emerged from the jigsaw of limbs to present a void handshake, and I discerned a head somewhere. The hand recoiled back into the human relic, the face resumed its glazed stare at the television set placed a few feet away, and the only comment Tom made the whole evening was an out-of-the-blue, indignant 'Why hasn't that clock chimed?' It was addressed to nobody and referred to an antique clock whose hands had read, I was told, two minutes to seven for the last ten years. So I passed on not knowing who Tom was or, more to the point, who Tom had been, and my kind host led me to the next curiosity.

I paused by an early George Eastman box camera. (Eastman was the founder of Kodak. He liked the hard, unyielding quality of the letter *K* and thought up a name for his company that was easy to spell, pronounce and remember, the same in any language and distinctive enough to protect its copyright.)

'So, you're a photographer, are you?' he scoffed. ' 'tain't easy. Takes fifteen, maybe twen'y years 'fore ye'll be an overnight success.' He was overcome by another fit of coughing before finding something of that optimist to palliate his suffering. 'But ya stick at it, son, an' remember; luck is jes' what's left over from good plannin'.'

Then he brought out a desperately thick family album. This was the most tedious part of claiming to be a photographer; I was doomed to suffer gazing at people's snapshots . . . but there was a picture of a less scrambled Tom in his younger days. He appeared to have been a rodeo champion and there were pictures of him on bucking broncos, and newspaper cuttings which recorded the achievements of Tom Bonney. It was an unusual surname but the possible connection only occurred to me when it was too late to confirm. The fates of these two cowboys nevertheless posed a stark contrast; young William Bonney had died instantly while old Tom Bonney was lingering on, having been gradually rattled to pieces.

A week later I was wearing a safety helmet and my arms and trousers were caked in mud as I worked for a small family business drilling water wells for private houses and irrigation projects on farms. We used an old cable drilling rig; the drill bit was the size of a telegraph post with a sharp point, suspended from a mobile derrick by a steel cable. The hole was formed by an engine tugging on the cable, raising the heavy bit and letting it fall to punch the ground and gradually chisel its way down. When the hole reached a certain depth we would pour in driller's 'mud' – a barite gel which helped to lubricate the bit and acted as a binding agent to prevent the collapse of the sides. It was a noisy process involving a lot of water and much mud, but it was effective and they had drilled down as deep as nine hundred feet by this method.

'When you get used to the idea of being plastered in mud, there's something quite pleasant about it,' I said to the taller, broader and yet equally muddy figure of my boss, Joe Jackson.

'Yeah? I wouldn't know anything else, Alan,' he said, for no one could ever remember my real name and any word over four letters in length was automatically whittled down into an abbreviation or a vaguely similar corruption. It was a notable exception to the American 'think big' philosophy. Joe continued, 'Fact is, I don't think my wife would recognise me if I came home clean.' He rested his hand on the cable, reading the bit's progress by the vibrations and knowing instantly whether the ground eighty feet below his boots was sand, clay, gravel or rock. Then he thrust a finger down a hole in the engine to test the level of the oil. 'You have to furnish your own dipstick in this outfit,' he explained with a grin. It came up to the fist joint which was evidently normal, then he wiped the dipstick on his trousers.

Generosity filled the brawny frame of this man who would lend the shirt off his back to help a friend – as long as the friend didn't mind a muddy one. His family took me under their wing and I stayed at their house, bringing my own mud back to Ma Jackson's washing machine. Each day it discharged the grime from four sets of clothes, as the two Jackson sons were also drillers, returning it to the land so that we could dig it up and recover it another day. It got everywhere but it could never conceal the many smiles that spread out as cracks in our plastered faces.

'It hasn't been easy,' Joe meditated over a can of beer at the end of one day, watching a completed well gush water into the irrigation canal of a chilli farm. 'I've had bills that I don't think even Jesus Christ himself could've afforded. An' sometimes I've lost my religion two or three times just on one well. We're only a small outfit here, not like those oil companies. D'you know, Alan, some of them have got people in their offices that have been asleep for the last ten years? An' most of them have their heads so full of education I guess it just pushed their brains out.' He watched each gallon of water flow out with a satisfaction that had not been dulled by the years. He had started his career in the construction business, serving his time as an apprentice in the use of explosives. 'Dynamite – that's a different game from this. You have to think it all out real careful. Too big a charge and you blow the place to smithereens. Not enough, then the rock doesn't move and you don't know how weak it is for your next one. Got to judge it spot on so the rock just lifts up and no more. You think about it every hour you're awake, and a good few that you're asleep too. I was taught by this old boy, crazy as a bedbug he was. My first day he let me push down the handle to detonate the charge he'd set but he'd put in too much. There was this almighty bang that removed half the mountain. I was just a kid then but he turned to me and said, "Goddamnit, Joe, you pressed too darn hard." '

My days that had once been measured in gallons of paint, yards of fishing hooks, sacks of saltfish, boxes of prawns and piles of chilli peppers now passed pleasantly as depths and diameters of muddy wells. One of these belonged to a neighbour who rang up to say that her well was blocked, adding, 'An' Joe, you gave me a lifelong guarantee there'd be no problems with it.'

243

'That's right, Lena,' replied Joe, 'an' I apologise. I just never figured you'd live this long.' We fired a high velocity rifle down into Lena's well and the shock waves were sufficient to clear the blocked slits in the casing.

And each evening Ma Jackson would take in the dirty, hand out the clean and spread an assortment of steaming bowls across the supper table.

'I hope you haven't been hard on our Scotsman,' she said to Joe one evening.

'I'm havin' to watch that new roughneck 'cos he's comin' along fast. Now he knows enough to do some damage.'

Ma gave me an extra helping of pinto beans because I was smaller than the others.

'You're always pickin' on our Scotsman,' she said possessively. 'Well, I still remember that first letter you wrote me, Joe Jackson, when you were working up north. It said, "I'm sitting here in front of two fried eggs which remind me of you . . ." Made me madder than hell, that did.'

Joe smiled in embarrassment, then he looked hurt. 'No, I never said that. It ended, ". . . and I'm thinking of you . . ." '

The months slipped inconspicuously by and would have continued to do so had I not decided to shake myself out of my comfortable routine. My diary was up to date, my clothes were repaired and water wells had returned my enthusiasm for travel by showing me life from a different perspective. One tires of comfort just as one tires of the lack of it and suddenly I longed for the open road once more to break the regularity of the day's events, and to seek a bit of hardship by roughing it again. Where there is hardship, there is adventure – and that is what I was beginning to miss.

We had once drilled a well on a remote ranch and the cowboys who worked there had invited me over any time I was 'passing by'. It was not easy to pass by a place that was sixty miles from anywhere but there was a local bus which would take me close, and leave me the last eighteen miles to walk. I decided to end my stay in the United States by visiting the American cowboy. There was a manifest speechlessness on the day of my departure and even Joe's stories and jokes seemed to have worn thin as he ran me to the bus station.

'Now you take good care of my Scotsman, won't you?' Joe demanded of the ticket office, and then he was gone. With him went my feelings of comfort and security and I sat there with the chilling awareness that I would have to fend for myself again, become hard and suspicious, defensive and careful once more, and I drew my pack in closer to me and looked about my new hostile world.

An aged man sat with a tiny radio clamped to his ear with shaking hands as if his life would go out with the volume; a baby-faced adolescent minced past in skin-tight, pre-shrunk, stone-washed jeans trying to conceal the agony of their revenge; a thin, stooped black man in a stetson sat smoking a pipe with an expression of resentment that asked just why a black man shouldn't smoke a pipe and shouldn't wear a stetson; a white idiot crouched on top of a radiator, grunting, his mouth agape. Why was there such an ego problem here?

The bus mercifully removed one restless inmate from this madhouse.

There was a magazine lying on the seat next to mine and I read it during the journey. The articles concerned New Mexico, 'Land of Enchantment', and one related an incident that took place at the time when Carnation Milk first appeared in the shops. The manufacturers were keen to promote the new product and ran a competition to find a good advertising slogan, providing the first line of an unfinished rhyme. A farmer's wife could only think of one line to add and wrote,

> 'Carnation Milk, best in the lan'
> Comes to the table in a little red can.'

She gave the postcard to the cowhand to post. A few weeks later she was surprised to receive a letter from the sponsors saying how much they had enjoyed her effort, but for obvious reasons they could not use it. Puzzled by their reaction, she went off to find the cowhand . . . There was no time to finish the article as the bus stopped to let me out. In my haste to get my belongings together, I left the magazine behind.

The ranch lay near one of the great herding trails of the past, a trail two hundred miles long, over five miles wide and with water wells drilled every ten miles. In the peak year of 1919 drovers moved

150,000 sheep and 21,670 cattle along its length, the sheep averaging
five miles per day, including grazing, while cattle managed ten
miles. I covered my eighteen miles on the dirt track through the
unsociable vegetation of semi-desert, prickly cacti and the yuca
plant's sphere of spikes. These were inhabited by the equally unsociable gila monster (a lizard with a poisonous bite), scorpions, the
relatively common black widow spider with its red hourglass marking on its abdomen, and the ubiquitous rattlesnake. The smaller
snakes tended to be more dangerous than the older, larger ones and
could strike from a distance equal to their own length. Cattle were
occasionally killed by snakes if bitten on the head as the swelling
quickly causes asphyxiation.

There were three cowboys on the ranch looking after three
thousand head of cattle on 45,000 acres. They earned a mere fifteen
dollars per day plus their keep for a full day in the saddle. These were
the real cowboys, working the land for the love of it and gripped by
the lifestyle as feverishly as their celluloid counterparts.

'Well, daggone,' said Gary, 'if it ain't the Scotchman. Alastair,
isn't it?' I was amazed he could remember my name after our last
brief encounter, especially when no one else could. 'Well, we don't
get too many Alastairs in these parts. C'mon over and meet the rest
of the team.'

RC, who was always just called RC, was teaching the young
newcomer, Will, how to lasso a dummy plastic cow head that was
embedded in a bale of straw.

'Keep that loop turnin' . . . lower . . . drop it to yer shoulders . . .
keep yer eye on that steer . . . okay . . . oh Pilgrim, y'gotta lot to
learn.'

Gary was the most experienced of the three, a lean man whose
patient and gentle manner had made him a genius at breaking in
horses. RC was tall and broad, the gap of a missing eye-tooth adding
mischief to his handsome smile. He seemed to have done everything
under the sun and spun endless yarns about it all. Will was a stocky,
barrel-chested youngster, an apprentice to these buckaroos, and
already wearing what seemed to be the standard moustache. Their
choice of clothes was largely dictated by their work; boots with
raised heels to prevent a foot slipping through the stirrup and
becoming trapped, leather chaps to minimise the abrasive action of
riding, and cowboy hats for protection against the sun. Gary said

you could tell a real cowboy standing on the horizon if you could see the sun set between his bow-legs. And then he added that the sun was setting for all real cowboys – they were a vanishing breed of men, being rapidly replaced by radio-linked pick-ups.

Will gave me a quick lesson on how to lasso. The rope was surprisingly stiff and kept its coils if dropped. Even standing firmly on the ground at close range, it was not easy but I gave the plastic cow a few frights until Gary decided I would be able to help round up all the heads that were dead or asleep. A crash course in horsemanship followed but they decided the horse was a bit too lively for me and old 'Hollywood' was brought out of retirement. They said she knew all the ropes, when to cut, turn and where to go. 'Jes' like ridin' a milk horse, she is. Knows every place to stop an' how many pints to unload,' Gary said, as I limped across to this second choice, adding, 'Yeah, we'll soon make a cowpuncher of you.'

'What's a cowpuncher?' I asked, looking down from the dizzy heights of Hollywood's many hands.

'They're just the general labourers who had to push an' punch the cattle in the ol' days to load 'em into the railroad wagons.'

There was more to this job than simply riding around herding cattle. They had to keep a separate tally of the numbers of heifers, steers, bulls, wets (cows in milk), dries and doggies (motherless calves) they came across in each area, as well as branding, gelding, treating for parasites, rotating their grazing, segregating groups for market, maintaining fences and the windpumps that brought up water from artesian bores for the drinking troughs. Their days had no fixed length and no special names, for the work had to be done as and when it arose. They lent me a hat as the sun burned fiercely. 'You'd better put on the suicide strap too or else you'll be losin' it when the action starts,' said Will, indicating the chin loop on the hat. Hoping that there wouldn't be much action I asked why it was called that.

'If you gallop under a few trees I reckon you'll see why,' he laughed. So off we went and I sat in leather chaps fringed with tassels, behind two brown ears that occasionally went upright on catching a strange sound in one of RC's stories, in blissful elation as my cowboy shadow flickered with each bump and hollow, moving over the desert sand amongst a posse of other shadows.

'Ah used to work the rodeo circuits for a time,' said RC in a relaxed offhand tone, frequently punctuating each comment with a period of silence to delay the climax, 'but ah got tired of starvin' to death so ah moved back into this line of work. Goddamn life workin' the rodeos; in ma best years ah rode 218 saddle broncs an' 108 steers, earned $23,000 an' still starved to death. That's not countin' four or five hours practice daily where ah could, drivin' thousands of miles and sleepin' in horseboxes – hell, it's hard on a man. Broke so many ribs ah reckoned ah'd never see thirty. But ah'm doin' all right now for an old young man.' And there was the car he had once owned, 'fastest on the road she was, sure thing, but ah sold her 'cos she was a gashoggin' sonofagun.' He told of how his horse once slipped on a steep mountain, breaking its leg, and he lay under it pinned against a stump with a broken back for five hours before someone came and dragged him out. And how he had stood-in for a star in a cowboy film to do the horse stunts and they had shot the sequence for twelve days but only thirty seconds' worth ever appeared in the final version . . .

A group of cattle moved off slowly as we approached, being channelled along a boundary fence to a new area. RC rode up behind them. 'Come along, gals . . .' he sang out sweetly in a high-pitched voice, dropping down an octave a moment later when a cow made a break and he gave chase, 'Goddamn ol' whore, git back in there.'

The stories and the miles fell away until we reached a back-country hut to camp for the night. It was only then that my back began to ache and my legs felt rubbed raw, forcing me to walk by swinging my legs out in small semi-circles as I had once seen an old Greenlander do many months earlier. Gary soon had some steaks sizzling over an open fire.

'Well ah hate to tell you this, boys,' he said after a while, 'but it's ready.'

'Ah declare!' exclaimed Will, looking at the huge plateful, 'am ah supposed to try an' eat this, or climb it?' He handed it over to me. 'Here, you'd better take this one, Al. Poor ol' Hollywood'll be saggin' in the middle tomorrow after you gotten through that lot.'

Before going to bed Gary withdrew from the fire to sit by an old wagon where he lit a candle and took out his Bible. He was a simple, honest man and he had his faith. I watched my real cowboy with his round glasses intently reading the Scriptures, his forehead lined with concentration, occasionally looking up and gazing into the night to ponder a point and nodding thoughtfully as he returned to the much-fingered pages. My deep respect for him deepened still further.

The next day we made our way back to the ranch, only RC went off on his own to check another area. When he was out of sight, Will said he could hardly keep a straight face when RC told a story now.

'Aren't his stories true, then?' I asked, disappointed.

'Hell no. Most are a load of bullshit.'

'Yea, bullcorn,' added Gary, 'but you kin never be sure what's true an' what's not 'cos RC has certainly been around. But ah guess he's heard many stories an' jes' sort of fabricated them into his own life. But ah like RC an' we gets along fine.'

'Yeah, he kin sure tell 'em good,' agreed Will, 'an' it's all harmless.'

'We've all got our shortcomin's,' said Gary philosophically, 'in fact ah've got so many ah think someone else must 'ave given me theirs as well. Ah figure there's someone goin' around all good 'n' happy an' ah've got all his shortcomin's.' Then he began to tell of one of the ranches he had worked on in Colorado during winter when it had been brutally cold. The wind had cut right through any clothing and snow was blown hard into the eyes and down the neck, ' 'til you could feel it collectin' in yer boots.' Gary's stories were always less dramatic, less exciting than RC's and usually uncertain about figures – but every word sounded sincere.

For two days my camera was hardly out of my hands, and my horse was continually being pulled to a halt between all her usual stopping places to allow a 'click', which made her ears go up. When we reached the ranch the cowboys patiently posed for more photographs, somewhat bemused by being subjected to such a variety of shots. I dismounted and was looking through a 200 mm. lens while trying to coax them into 'mean' expressions. I stepped back one pace with the camera still to my eye, tripped over a low trough, fell over backwards and ended up lying in a puddle. The mean expressions vanished. RC and Gary collapsed against each other in uncontrollable mirth, and Will slumped forward on his horse in hysterics. For two days the snaphappy Scotchman with the unusual name had not once fallen off a horse called Hollywood but the moment he stood on solid ground with his big lens . . . and gradually the laughter affected me too until I lay there in the puddle until my stomach hurt and tears formed in my eyes – for it suddenly occurred to me that I had just furnished RC with another story to add to his repertoire.

In the ranch I chanced upon a copy of the same magazine I had left behind on the bus and was able to finish reading the article about the farmer's wife. It explained that when she found the cowhand, he confessed that he had added a couple of lines himself because her slogan seemed to lack an ending. The postcard had finally read:

> Carnation Milk, best in the lan'
> Comes to the table in a little red can
> No teats to pull, no hay to pitch
> Jes' punch a hole in the sonofabitch.

It made me smile, then it made me think. This little red can seemed a part of the cowboy's sunset. The modern cowpuncher opened cans, and next came radio-linked pick-ups to end a piece of reality. Buffalo Bill's cult would become confined to the spectator's corral, the video screen and the truck driver's vanity.

That evening Gary invited me back to his home. He lived on the ranch with the other cowboys during the week but at weekends, if work permitted, he returned to his family forty miles away in Carrizozo. He was a cowboy through and through and everything in his house showed that it was his work, his interest, his life; books, ornaments, photographs, horseshoes and souvenir reins were all associated with the world of buckaroos. It had been a hard week and he collapsed into a chair and was soon dozing peacefully below a painting of a cowboy leading his horse into the hills. It was entitled *Lonesome but Free*. His spurs were still on his boots and dug into a frayed patch in the carpet.

'I've tried everything to stop him wearing them in the house,' his wife said, eyeing the inert figure with a tenderness that had apparently not waned since the day they had married, both aged nineteen. 'Even put up signs saying 'NO SPURS', but I just never could break him of the habit. Still, I wouldn't trade him for anything, but I sure wouldn't want a duplicate of him either.' She took a branding iron off the wall and showed me the sign U/∩. 'This is his special one for the horses he breeds as they've got to have a brandmark. It was his idea; sometimes U're up and sometimes U're down.' She smiled. The figure in the chair slept. One foot moved, pivoting on the spur, digging the points deeper into the carpet as it rolled over to lean against a milking-stool.

'Most cowboys won't milk cows as they reckon it's woman's work, but it's really only because they can't do it from the saddle! But Gary likes milking. It's his time for meditation and reflection.'

It was my time for reflection as well. Two years had now passed since my old kilt-maker had counted the number of stitches in that work of art, now stained, patched and faded. I had travelled from the backstreets of Edinburgh to the North Arctic, from Alaska to the cowboys of Carrizozo. The reasons for my journey had become more diverse than those at the start, although quite why anyone travels into the unfamiliar has long been a poser, made popular by chicken and road-crossing riddles. The answer is as personal as the lure of mountains and sea, and changes with each spontaneous prompting. If travel must have a purpose, if that purpose must be defined simply, then for me it was this: those places where time was meaningless and the others where every second was accounted for brought me the raw and subtle sentiments of discovery.

Had I found the real American to match the real Greenlander? Yes indeed, but they had all been 'real', not just those exceptions who matched the preconceptions of my mind. Travelling meant having to accept the world as you found it and not as you wanted to see it. Yet some illusions must remain, for that is also why you travel; illusions are hopes which you travel to realise and fears which you travel to dash – and therein lies the pleasure when you succeed, and the disappointment when you fail.

North America had proved to be so big and so varied that it was impossible to put in a nutshell. Perhaps Orly the chef had come close when he said it contained the biggest, the most beautiful and the worst – only he had used different words. Or perhaps more simply, it could be branded *U/∩*.

All along my journey I had met with great kindness and hospitality from people who offered not just a hot meal and a comfortable bed, but who gave the traveller a sense of belonging in a foreign land. Each time I moved on and became an instant stranger once more, that sense of belonging was my most cherished memory.

'Why don't you stay on with us?' asked Gary. 'Why not settle down here and become one of us?'

Why not indeed? . . .

But no. Whenever I stayed in one place I was merely a shadow, an outline of myself with no substance. That urge drove me on, searching, ever searching for my body and a place to keep it. That urge was a constant but unstable force, sometimes gentle and lax, sometimes raging like a fever. At times its rewards seemed meagre. Travelling appeared to be little more than a succession of easy hellos and oh-so-hard goodbyes. The more you saw, the more you realised how much you were missing. Life was a series of compromises. Yet travel was compulsive and its grip grew cumulatively tighter, so much so that periodically you stopped to wonder why you continued – but the good times of the past kept pushing and reasons for the future were unnecessary; they were self-germinating along the way.

So, rush on, lad. The world is yours, and all for the price of your sweat. Go and trample on another few thousand miles to become a short-term lodger under a pot-pourri of nameless roofs. Don't slow down, keep the globe turning while your boots are still held together by string, for the way ahead is long and the grains of sand in that hourglass of the great five-year plan just keep on tumbling down.

Yes, and why not? The rewards were always there, usually in excess. Sometimes I had to look a little harder to find them but for the most part, they found me. I often thought afterwards: I'm glad I did it. My string was strong. I was my own master. I too was Lonesome but Free . . .

'Well, I'd like to Gary, honestly, but – '

'Ah know, Al.'

U/∩. I had been up, now I was going down. I turned my back on North America and set off to face the big unknown once more, the twenty-three pleats of my kilt swinging to and fro as they are wont to do under an eager stride, south, down the desert road to Mexico. And beyond.